SOLUTIONING

SOLUTIONING

Solution-Focused Interventions for Counselors

Willyn Webb, M.A., L.P.C., N.C.C.

Solutioning Counseling and Consulting
Delta, Colorado

Adams State College
Alamosa, Colorado

ACCELERATED DEVELOPMENT
Taylor & Francis Group

USA	Publishing Office:	ACCELERATED DEVELOPMENT
		A member of the Taylor & Francis Group
		325 Chestnut Street
		Philadelphia, PA 19106
		Tel: (215) 625-8900
		Fax: (215) 625-2940
	Distribution Center:	ACCELERATED DEVELOPMENT
		A member of the Taylor & Francis Group
		47 Runway Road, Suite G
		Levittown, PA 19057-4700
		Tel: (215) 269-0400
		Fax: (215) 269-0363
UK		ACCELERATED DEVELOPMENT
		A member of the Taylor & Francis Group
		1 Gunpowder Square
		London EC4A 3DE
		Tel: +44 171 583 0490
		Fax: +44 171 583 0581

SOLUTIONING: Solution-Focused Interventions for Counselors

1 2 3 4 5 6 7 8 9 0

Printed by George H. Buchanan Company, Philadelphia, PA, 1998.

A CIP catalog record for this book is available from the British Library.

⊛The paper in this publication meets the requirements of the ANSI Standard Z39.48-1984 (Permanence of Paper).

Library of Congress Cataloging-in-Publication Data
Webb, Willyn H.
     Solutioning : solution-focused interventions for counselors.
    Willyn Webb.
       p. cm.
    Includes bibliographical references and index.
     ISBN 1-56032-744-8 (pbk.: alk. paper)
      1. Short-term counseling. 2. Solution-focused brief therapy.
   3. Problem solving. I. Title.
   BF697.C6W385   1998
   15B'.3 dc21

                                                      98-41205
                                                       CIP

ISBN: 1-56032-744-8

CONTENTS

Chapter 5
FORGET ME NOT: THE FINAL P—PROGRESS

Chapter 6
SOLUTIONING REALITY

Acknowledgments

My solution team consists of my family, and I want to thank each of them for their unique contributions to this book.

Thank you Skylyn for your patience. No one else has made the sacrifices you have or know the dedication it has taken to create *Solutioning*.

Thank you Jim for taking over the housework, putting up with my frustrations, and adjusting your life for mine. I hope the habit is formed.

Thank you Daddy for being my lawyer, accountant, sounding board, and hero. Our discussions are invaluable, and ranching with you is my greatest solution.

Thank you Meme for being an on-call 24-hour-a-day counselor, baby-sitter, errand runner, taxi driver, and inspiration. Your support gets me through.

Thank you Mom for being the wisest, sweetest, most solution-focused person I have ever known. You have modeled what I have put in this book, without even knowing it.

Thank you Huntley for being impressed with me once in awhile. It means so much.

Thank you Lyndall J. and Jerry for baby-sitting, getting books, sending faxes, and so much more, whenever asked.

Thank you Mary for counting hundreds of words, getting books, and giving advice. You are a real trooper.

I would also like to acknowledge John Mason, LPC, and Tim Fay, almost LPC, for their valuable reviews. A special thanks to all of my adult students, whose enthusiasm for *Solutioning* pushed me to go one step further, and to my clients, whose efforts at making their lives the way they want them have given me so much motivation, inspiration, and hope. I hope that therapists reading this book will experience *Solutioning* as we have—that it will bring them happiness.

When you see this book, you might ask me the typical solutioning question, "How did you do that?" I won't have an answer except for these people, running, and God, who gave me *Solutioning*.

INTRODUCTION

In my development as a therapist, I have discovered something that works, something true to the solution-focused philosophy that says, "Once you know what works, *do more of it*" (Carpenter, 1997, p. 117). I am doing more by sharing it in this book. Seeing the growth, empowerment, healing, and responsibility *solutioning* has brought to my life and to my clients inspired me to write about it.

When I first experienced *Solution-Focused Brief Therapy (SFBT)* as a school counselor, I was sold. By adapting a couple of the questions into my daily interactions with middle-school adolescents, I ended my path toward burnout and jumped on the solution-focused bandwagon.

Leaving the school system to earn my Professional Counseling License and enter the world of private practice, I thought I had all the tools I needed for success. I soon found, however, that dealing with clients in the mental health world was very different from handling adolescent spats. I found that SFBT was not a one-size-fits-all cure. My clients came in many varieties from many different walks of life, and they required a more intense relationship than I was able to develop by jumping right into SFBT. Some wanted insight, some looked for causes, others needed time. I found myself returning to my original training, getting new training, blending and adapting. By altering slightly the ideas of SFBT and blending in what worked for me, I could meet the needs of my clients, stay true to my philosophy of counseling, and live in the real world of managed care.

The result of that process of altering and blending is the *4-P process of solutioning*. Solutioning is not designed to be a cure-all; it is just one option in treatment planning, with interventions that can be blended into whatever else you are doing that works. If you've ever wanted to check out SFBT, but you are not ready to give up all the things you do that are effective, replace your basic beliefs, or learn an all-encompassing new treatment, solutioning is for you. It offers time-saving methods designed to enhance, not replace, what you are already using.

Think about the work you do with clients, all the ways you help them. Now think about having a quick, easy, practical intervention to help clients get past blaming and excuses and take responsibility for making their lives the way they want them. Adding solutioning to your practice will enhance whatever you are doing. The questions and language of solutioning may someday be as familiar as the old favorite, "How does that make you feel?" Now we can add, "When *isn't* the problem happening?" "How do you *want* things to be?" And, "How did you do that?"

Solutioning has its roots in Solution-Focused Brief Therapy. A comprehensive model, full of valuable practices and philosophical assumptions, SFBT has been criticized by some as a "band-aid approach," dealing only with surface issues. According to the critics, the "real problems" get left untreated, to arise again later (Todd, 1992, p. 172). Nylund and Corsiglia (1994, p. 6) had this to say: "In his or her enthusiasm (or impatience) to identify exceptions and facilitate change, the [solution-focused] therapist may minimize and even trivialize the client's experience of the problem."

Even at its best, SFBT is not for every client, issue, or situation. It is just not enough for some clients. For example, much of the healing process for survivors of sexual abuse involves the past and takes time. But you can bring closure to your sessions with solutioning, discussing how the survivor wants the next week to be (back in the present), what the ideal would look like, and how she can make it that way. Even clients who have painful issues in their pasts—issues that cannot be ignored—must continue living in the present while healing the old pain. Solutioning takes care of the present and the future in a practical, motivating manner without detracting from the healing process.

Solutioning can be used in conjunction with any other therapy. In play therapy, for example, a therapist chooses an experiential approach, allowing the children time and freedom to direct the play and work through their issues. Then, he or she can use solutioning to play out how things *could be* from now on, tell stories with positive outcomes, and cocreate new dramas. A parenting educator might use solutioning to help adolescents and their parents realize their existing skills and relational positives, which opens the door for communication education.

Rather than adopting an all-encompassing model of treatment and working exclusively in the future, solutioning allows the practitioner to blend in interventions where they fit. Subscribing to a solutioning mindset does not mean making radical changes in your philosophical basis; solutioning is simply a technique to supplement and an attitude upon which to build. It is a process of working away from blaming, excuses, and the past (even if you spend time in therapy on the past) and working toward responsibility, ability, and the future. Solutioning can be part of each client's therapy at some point. A quick look at the evolution of the solution focus, first as a model and now as an intervention, will illustrate the need and value of Solutioning.

THE SOLUTION FOCUS

Originally, counseling focused primarily on the past. Therapists and clients sometimes spent years searching out the roots of problems. But many felt that finding those roots did not necessarily make the present different, so a here-and-now emphasis developed in the 1960s. However, being in the present did not create change for all clients either. The trend of the 1990s is to look more to the future with a "then-and-there" focus, attempting to bring about change and help clients live satisfactory lives (Huber & Backlund, 1996, p. 15). Conjunctively, the view of problem treatment has moved from finding causes to finding solutions.

The pioneers of the solution-focused brief therapy philosophy are de Shazer and Lipchik, of the Brief Family Therapy Center in Milwaukee (de Shazer, 1985, 1988; de Shazer et al., 1986; Lipchik & de Shazer, 1988); the Brief Therapy Center of the Mental Research Institute in Palo Alto, California (Weakland, Fisch, Watzlawik, & Bodin, 1974); O'Hanlon, who developed *Possibility Therapy* (O'Hanlon, 1996; O'Hanlon & Weiner-Davis, 1989); and White and Epston (1990), who developed *Narrative Therapy*. Others who have used solution-focused thinking therapeutically are Dolan (1991), with sexual abuse survivors; Weiner-Davis (1992), *the Divorce Buster*, with couples; Friedman and Fanger (1991); Furman and Ahola (1992); Walter and Peller (1992); Andrews and Andrews (1995); Huber and Backlund (1996); and Juhnke and Osborne (1997).

The premise and language of the philosophy have also spread into pediatrics (Klar & Coleman, 1995), nursing (Mason, Breen, & Whipple 1994; Shires & Tappan, 1992; Tuyn, 1992), employee assistance programs (Czyzewski, 1996), parenting education (Metcalf, 1997), home preservation programs (Washburn, 1994), and schools (Bonnington, 1993; Downing & Harrison, 1992; Kral & Kowalski, 1989; Metcalf, 1995; Murphy, 1994; Paull & McGrevin, 1996; Rhodes, 1993). The time now seems ripe to blend the valuable contributions of the various approaches in a way that can fit with any therapist, with all clients.

Like solutioning itself, this book is intended to be usable, blendable, and adaptable. I encourage you to try a section, skip to another, pull out worksheets, add your own, whatever works best for you.

- *Practices*—activities designed to facilitate your learning, either as session cheat sheets, supervision supplements, or personal exercises—are included at the end of each section.

- *Skill Highlights* focus on preexisting skills that can be given a solutioning slant.

- *Solution Applications* illustrate how particular solutioning interventions apply to common issues in mental health.

- *Case Studies* are clinical descriptions based on actual interactions. The names have been changed to protect confidentiality. These are not intended as the right or perfect way to treat a certain scenario, but as illustrative examples of ways to use solutioning.

The idea is to mix and match, pick and choose, and use what works for you. In order to be truly effective, therapy must be creatively approached each time, with each client, in each situation.

Chapter 1

Building Blocks

TIMING IS EVERYTHING

"We must use time as a tool, not as a couch."
—*John Fitzgerald Kennedy*
(Webster, 1992, p. 281)

In this era of managed care and sound-bite attention spans, *time* has become a big issue in counseling. The age of brief therapy—whether 10 one-hour sessions (Weakland, Fisch, Watzlawick, & Bodin, 1974, p. 142) or one 20-minute session (Huber & Backlund, 1996)—definitely has arrived. The relevance for solutioning is not time, but *timing*. Regardless of the number or length of sessions, solutioning has a place in any individual's therapy—it's only a matter of timing.

The way we practice psychotherapy and interact with our clients expresses our basic beliefs about human nature, problems, and change. Determining your *philosophy of counseling* was probably a major part of your graduate training. Perhaps looking at some beliefs of solution-focused brief therapy (SFBT) will help you reexamine your own basis while considering where solutioning fits in. As Walter and Peller (1992, pp. 2–5) illustrated, there are three distinct models of therapy, each formed from a different basic question: "What is the cause of the problem? or What maintains the problem? or How do we construct solutions?" They went on to explain, "Solution-focused brief therapy is not a collection of techniques or an elaboration of a technique; rather, it reflects fundamental notions about change, about interaction, and about reaching goals" (Walter & Peller, 1992, p. 28).

Based on my own experiences and those of my adult students, I pose the following questions: Does believing in the fundamental notions of SFBT rule out believing in the relevant and helpful ideas of the other models? Can they be used in conjunction? Are the fundamental notions of SFBT enough? Does talking about the problem undo the benefit of talking about the solution? Are there times when problem talk, insight, understanding, and input are required?

Looking at the needs of clients gives us the answers. Some clients come into therapy heavily burdened with symptoms, which solutioning will readily relieve. This clears the way for them to clearly define their therapeutic purpose, which may require additional use of the 4-P solutioning process or some other model. But some clients need to find the cause of their problems, gain some understanding and insight, or form a relationship with their therapist before they can begin solutioning. Because solutioning is an intervention, it can be used varyingly. This is not an either/or situation. If you can see how the building blocks of humanism, constructivism, causality, systems, and change apply, you can insert solutioning *when the time is right.*

BUILDING BLOCKS OF BELIEF

Humanism

"Treat people as if they were what they should
be, and you help them become what they are
capable of becoming."
—Johann Wolfgang von Goethe
(Peter, 1977, p. 393)

Solutioning, like SFBT, sees clients, families, and all individuals as having the abilities and resources they need to flourish, grow, develop, and live satisfying lives; in other words, people can solve their own problems. Additionally, solutioning acknowledges that other models of therapy (or even medication) may be necessary to get the client to the point that he or she can access those abilities and resources. This description of solution-orientated therapy illustrates its nature:

> It is a method that focuses on people's competence rather
> than their deficits, their strengths rather than their weaknesses,
> their possibilities rather than their limitations. (O'Hanlon &
> Weiner-Davis, 1989, p. 1)

At the core of solution-focused therapy is the claim that, wherever a problem is said to exist, there are almost always exceptions—times when the problem occurs less frequently or not at all. Problems do not occur 100% of the time (Metcalf, 1995). *No behavior happens all the time.* Yet clients often ignore these exceptions or consider them flukes (de Shazer, 1985, 1988). Solutioning aims to help clients focus on and learn from the exceptions.

We all encounter problems in life, yet we all have within us the strengths to face these difficulties and cope with or overcome them. "Counseling is a means of facilitating the time and effort it takes to do so" (Huber & Backlund, 1996, p. 16). Operating from this belief, the therapist can help clients identify the resources they have to resolve their complaints, see their exceptional times, turn those into potential solutions, and act on the information with a plan. In the following case study, a client came into therapy feeling incapable and left knowing she had the abilities required to be the parent she wanted to be.

I *Am* a Good Parent! The Case of Rhonda

Rhonda brought her 15-year-old daughter, Mary, in for counseling. Mary reported that she was fine with her life, that everything was okay, except when her mother tried to enforce restrictions. Then Mary would become upset, hate her mother, and generally cause an uproar.

Joint sessions illustrated Rhonda's inconsistencies and lack of confidence as a parent. I requested a session alone with her. She came in feeling like a failure as a parent, aware of her inconsistencies and loss of self-control, and continually expressing her shortcomings. She was on the verge of giving up and sending Mary to live with her father. Believing that every individual has the necessary abilities to cope with life, I set out to *codiscover* them with Rhonda, using solutioning language as a tool. Rhonda had already established as her purpose of counseling becoming a more effective parent.

Willyn: You've told me about all the shortcomings you feel you have as a parent, and I know you are frustrated. What I'd like to talk about now are the times when are you a good parent.

Rhonda: When I say what I'm going to do and stick to it. I just don't stick to it very often. I get upset or tired and go back on what I've said.

Willyn: You've told me you are a middle-school special education teacher. Are you a good one? Do you have classroom discipline? Do you stick to what you say as a teacher?

Rhonda: Oh, yeah. I post the rules and the consequences and stick by them. If I didn't, my classroom would be in chaos and I'd be a real mess. I really make my students toe the line.

Willyn: How do you do that, make your students toe the line?

Rhonda: Well, when there's a problem and they disobey or break a rule, I know exactly what to do because the consequences have already been determined. I don't get so emotional because I have a plan and follow it.

At school I'm really good at keeping my cool and being consistent.

Willyn: Wow! That is really impressive, how well-managed your classroom is and how you keep your cool at school! It sounds like having rules and consequences, which everyone understands in advance, is the key.

Rhonda: Yeah, those are a lifesaver. I even have them on the walls so we can look at them and be reminded when we need it.

Willyn: Having clear rules and consequences that everyone understands really works for you at school, and you are skilled at classroom management. Sounds to me like you have all the capabilities of being a great parent.

Rhonda: You know, I never compared the two. I am very capable at school, and most of those kids are a lot worse than my own. I've just never done anything at home like rules or consequences. At home, I usually just fly by the seat of my pants and try to ground them or yell or something.

Willyn: How about trying at home some of what works at school—rules and consequences—and see what happens?

Rhonda: Yeah, I'll sit down with my girls, just like I do with my students during the first week of school. We'll talk about what we need for rules and what would be appropriate consequences. I'll even post them on the refrigerator. You know another thing I do at school when I feel I'm starting to blow is a chill-out. I have the student go to the hall for a minute. Then I go talk to them when I've had time to cool off a little. I can't really send my girls to their room, they're too big, but I could go to my room for a minute for a chill-out, to remind myself of the rules—like school.

Willyn: Great idea. That sounds like it will really work. I can't wait until next week to hear about all the great changes you make using your school skills at home.

A couple days after that session, I got a call from Rhonda, reporting that she *did* have the skills she needed to be a good parent, she just hadn't used them before.

Reminding herself of her teaching skills whenever she felt incapable as a parent worked for Rhonda. I hadn't told her she had the skills, but my language assumed it. Rhonda realized it for herself as she answered some solutioning questions. This proved more successful than if I had implied that Rhonda needed a lot of instruction on parenting, which would have fed her self-perception of being incapable.

Simply believing that clients are capable and have resources and abilities affects how we approach, communicate, and assist them in leading satisfactory lives. A humanistic attitude, supported by the language of solutioning, makes all the difference.

Frequently, clients overwhelmed by life's difficulties lose sight of their problem-solving strengths. They may simply need to be reminded of the tools with which they are equipped to develop long-lasting solutions. At other times, they may have some capabilities that can be added to or honed in order to help them sort out their situations. (O'Hanlon & Weiner-Davis, 1989, p. 34)

Experiences like Rhonda's are hopeful and motivating for therapists and clients alike. The 4-P process of solutioning is a burnout prevention method for therapists as much as an intervention for clients.

"I always prefer to believe the best of everybody—it saves so much trouble."
—*Rudyard Kipling, (Webster, 1992, p. 93)*

Constructivism

Constructivism maintains that the observer can never mirror a reality; instead, the observer *constructs* a reality that fits with his or her experiences. Duckworth (1987, p. 112) defined constructivism this way: "Meaning is not given to us in our encounters, but it is given by us, constructed by us, each in our own way, according to how our understanding is currently organized." In other words, *our perception is our reality*. Rhonda's initial perception of herself was as an incapable parent. Through solutioning, she constructed a new reality in which she could see herself as a skilled individual who could be an effective parent. She went on to make that perception a reality by using at home the skills she already was using in her job.

"There is nothing either good or bad, but thinking makes it so."
—*William Shakespeare,* Hamlet, *Act II, scene 2*

Counselor-client interactions are perception-altering events, which can facilitate positive change. Solutioning as a constructivist is energizing for counselors and motivating for clients.

Constructivists believe that our awareness of the world is a direct result of our active interaction with it. We never see the world directly, only through the lens of our own perceptions. Reality, so to speak, is in the eye of the beholder. (Kiser & Piercy, 1993, p. 234)

Solutioning interactions produce hope from which solutions emerge—or are made unnecessary as the perception of the problem itself is altered.

Troublemaker: The Case of Charlie

Charlie's parents brought him in for therapy because he had been diagnosed with ADD, had been kicked off the school bus, and was disrespectful to his mother. Their label for him was *troublemaker*. After two sessions with the delightful 1st-grader, I was amazed at his vocabulary and creativity. I met with his parents and shared my observations of Charlie as an energetic and gifted little boy. They thought about it and agreed. They had been worried about what others (teachers, the bus driver, people at the mall) thought. With their newly constructed view, they decided therapy was not necessary. Instead, they decided to look into a gifted and talented program for their son.

The way we view problems is a key element and crucial starting point. With a constructivist attitude, problems become putty in our hands, and we can manipulate their power and their solvability—shaping them into a more normal, temporary, controllable form. Constructivism makes problems elastic and negotiable, and a perception-creating process can begin (O'Hanlon & Weiner-Davis, 1989).

Solutioning works in part by *creating reality through language*. The therapist helps channel a client's thinking away from negative labels (i.e., Charlie the troublemaker) and toward solutions (i.e., enhanced education for the energetically gifted). After sharing, empathizing, and connecting, we can shift clients' talk from labels—which close possibilities for change—to solutions—which assume positive change will happen. This can alter the person's view of reality and jump start the change process immediately.

For example, an adolescent client may say, "I'll never pass math!" The counselor could respond with, "So far you haven't passed math." This puts the problem squarely in the past and opens the possibility of a different future. Another example would be a wife who described her husband as "introverted and lazy." The counselor could help her construct a more workable perception, describing him as "self-confident and relaxed." This change in how the woman perceived her husband's behavior would affect her attempts at communication, eventually allowing her to have meaningful dialogue with him. Just knowing that clients come to us with the resources they need to solve their problems is a start. Then we must remember to meet them where they are, in their reality, and begin construction.

Most traditional counseling philosophies advocate this kind of beginning, yet counselors and clients spend vast amounts of time discussing their problems and their feelings and behaviors surrounding those problems. Solution-focused counselors, on the other hand, maintain that you don't need to know a great deal about the problem. Instead, they spend their time discussing possibilities, exceptions, and solutions. Both can create a one-sided world view.

Solutioning, as a middle ground, does not set standards for how much or how little we need to know about the problem. Regardless of the amount of information, when the time seems right, construction toward solutions can begin.

I'm told that successful potters work *with* the clay to create a desired object. In solutioning you work *with* clients to create or recreate the problem or purpose before it can be solved or achieved. For example, a depressed client can become depressed *some of the time*. A solution might be participating in more hobbies (recreating the nondepressed times). The thief can be viewed as one who "forgets to pay." The therapeutic goal is remembering. Participating in hobbies and remembering to pay are more attainable solutions than curing depression or kleptomania.

Causality

"Let us not go over the old ground, let us
rather prepare for what is to come."
—*Marcus Tullius Cicero*
(Peter, 1977, p. 373)

Managed care programs, families, schools, therapy sessions, and society in general are all practice fields for what Susan Stewart called "the blame game" (1996, p. 3). Remember Rhonda? How different might Rhonda's subsequent parenting experiences have been if I had assumed she had some underlying issues with her own parents that had to be treated before she could become the parent she wanted to be? Well, she would have had an excuse (and someone to blame) for her girls not turning out the way she wanted them to be. A delay of months or even years would have been a likely result. With teenagers, however, time is fleeting. Using skills she already had enabled Rhonda to bypass causality and begin positive change immediately. If she needed to, Rhonda could examine her past after she began making changes, but she could no longer blame it.

> Victimhood is definitely in. The blame game has all but replaced baseball as America's #1 sport. Legal excuses run rampant. If you steal money from work and blow it in Las Vegas, you're a victim of impulsive gambling syndrome. If your boss fires you for showing up late every day for a month, you're being discriminated against for chronic lateness syndrome. The goal of the blame game is to avoid any responsibility for your actions. (Stewart, 1996, p. 3)

Addicts are all-star players in the blame game. "My girlfriend dumped me, so I had to get wasted." "If my parents had provided for me as a kid, I wouldn't have to get high." "It's hard growing up poor. Speed gives me the push I need to make it."

In an interesting turn on the game, victims of domestic violence often blame themselves, finding excuses for causing and taking the abuse. Some creative excuses result from learned helplessness. "Well, if I hadn't burned his dinner, he probably wouldn't have hit me." "If I didn't push his buttons, he'd be able to control his temper."

Avoiding responsibility is not the only drawback of the blame game:

> By blaming others, we spend our lives as victims—blaming parents, race, gender, or economic situation for our inadequacies. Victims define themselves by their problems. And if their problem is something they hate, they come to hate themselves for identifying with it. (Stewart, 1996, p. 4)

This kind of thinking gets in the way of solutions. In our search for a place to put the blame and so avoid responsibility, we focus on why *we are not* achieving success instead of on *how we can* achieve it. We use blame as a license to give up or to justify our failure. At other times, we may be sincerely attempting relief, thinking the first step is to determine *why* the problem is occurring. But this simply feeds the victim stance and cheers on the blame game.

"Why not spend some time in determining what
is worthwhile for us, and then go after that?"
—*William Ross (Peter, 1977, p. 9)*

SFBT does not typically look at causes, which may stop some blaming, save time, and facilitate solutions. The entire philosophy discourages insight as simply not necessary and as possibly limiting (Walter & Peller, 1992). In fact, in SFBT even the most valid reasons for problems do not automatically offer clues about how clients can change (O'Hanlon & Weiner-Davis, 1989).

Sometimes, however, insight and understanding can be valuable tools for healing and can act as motivation for finding inner resources, *if we can avoid the risk of encouraging the blame game.* This is where solutioning comes in. Stewart acknowledges, "Terrible things do happen. Real victims have experienced real tragedies. But, that experience doesn't have to define who you are for the rest of your life" (1996, p. 4). Solutioning can be blended into

a practice in which causes are explored. Once exploration has begun, when the time is right, solutioning can help clients get past
the victim definition, make choices, take responsibility, and regain
control of their lives. "Making a choice and accepting responsibility for that choice, regardless of past hurts or future risks, is what
true freedom is all about" (Stewart, 1996, p. 4). *Solutioning is
empowerment.*

"I like the dreams of the future better
than the history of the past."
—*Thomas Jefferson (Peter, 1977, p. 168)*

Systems

Our own unique experiences and perceptions of the world are
largely created by our interactions with others. Solutioning sees
individuals as reacting to and interacting in their environment systemically. This is the basis of family counseling, in which SFBT
has its roots. Classrooms, businesses, neighborhoods, and other
organizations often operate like families—groups of people functioning and interacting together. Clients do not operate indepen-
dently. Peers, parents, parole officers, friends, and others may all
be seen as the system within which a client operates. Solutioning
does not depend on having everyone involved in therapy, but makes
the most out of clients' relationships.

A therapist may use solutioning with an individual or with an
entire system. The only difference is how many people are asked
the questions. Often clients feel others should change first. Because it is an intervention of empowerment, responsibility, and
action, an important question of the 4-P process is this: What can
you do to achieve the purpose? This does not mean, however, that
solutioning is not systemic. The interactional nature acknowledges
that a change in the thinking, feeling, or behavior of one individual
affects the entire system and that the system can be used to facilitate and support individual plans. In addressing problems,
solutioning, like SFBT, sees no one individual or system as the
problem—only the problem itself is the problem (Walter & Peller,
1992).

Focus on Fighting: The Case of the Whipples

The Whipples came in all fired up. The mother, father, 13-year-old daughter, and 7-year-old daughter each took a turn telling me why the family had come in for counseling. The father wanted the mother and the 13-year-old daughter to stop fighting. He said they were both too stubborn. The mother wanted the 13-year-old to change by following rules and being more respectful. The 13-year-old wanted the mother to stop nagging and trying to control her. The 7-year-old said she was tired of all the yelling.

In one brief sentence, I named and externalized the problem, and every member of the family teamed up against it: "So," I said, "it sounds like you all have a purpose of overcoming *fighting* and getting along in the family." The problem was no longer the mother, the 13-year-old, or their personality traits; it was fighting. "Could each one of you tell me about when fighting isn't winning and things are better?"

This approach does not rule out looking at the coalitions within the family, the balance of power, the marital relationship, and so on. It does move clients away from a mindset of changing someone else and into a mindset of battling a problem (instead of one another). The 4-P process is applicable whether you are working with one person or a dozen, thinking systemically or individually, or are somewhere in between.

Change

> "There is nothing permanent except change."
> —*Heraclitus (Peter, 1977, p. 99)*

Whenever we work with clients, change is a purpose, even when unexpressed. Seeing change as ongoing facilitates this purpose. Even clients who seem stuck probably are changing in an attempt to remain the same. Keeney (1983) maintained there is a dualism between stability and change. The more a person tries to keep things stable, the more change is required. For example, a skier must be constantly moving and adjusting as he or she moves down the hill to account for the bumps, ice, powder, and moguls. If we view clients as always changing, we will interact with them in a manner in which progress is always being examined.

The type of change desired is a basic issue in therapy. Is it a change in interactional patterns, communication, thinking, feeling, or behaving? Once again, this is often determined by the therapist's theoretical orientation. A basic premise of SFBT is that "sessions should be conducted in such a manner as to assist families in leading more satisfied and fulfilling lifestyles, not to meet the therapist's theoretical and clinical needs." (Todd, 1992, p. 174). Some therapies value shared feelings and relating in a close relationship; others value insight. These types of changes are worthwhile and can be accentuated or cemented through the addition of solutioning. An added emphasis of solutioning is the empowerment of clients. The 4-P process is designed to achieve positive change, whether it be in thinking, feeling, behaving, or some other realm.

A question regarding the type of change issue is this: What is changeable (the personality, the symptoms, or something else)? This is an area of difference between solution-focused therapists and traditional therapists.

> As change-oriented therapists, we want to focus our attention on the changing and the changeable aspects of our clients' experiences. We do not, therefore, focus on entities or aspects of the client or the client's situation that are not amenable to change. ... Long-term therapists often contract, wittingly or unwittingly, to try to change people's relatively fixed characteristics, like their personalities and their complexes. (O'Hanlon & Weiner-Davis, 1989, p. 49)

Solutioning is the marriage between traditional and solution-focused therapies. For example, a counselor who does long-term therapy can use the 4-P process to relieve symptoms that may be getting in the way. The solution-focused viewpoint acknowledges this potential: O'Hanlon and Weiner-Davis advised counselors to "focus on those aspects of the person's situation that seem most changeable, knowing that to start positive changes and to help the person realize small goals may have wider and unexpected effects in other areas (perhaps even in his personality)" (1989, p. 50).

A final element of the change issue is the idea that small changes can have a ripple effect. Solutioning can be incorporated into a practice that is built on achieving larger, more permanent changes. Despite your orientation, and even if you are going for the big change, using the 4-P process can get the ball rolling with small changes. With some clients this takes just a couple of questions at the beginning or end of the session on a weekly basis. The momentum of therapy is ongoing, while the big picture is being addressed during the remainder of the session. In fact, Walter and Peller point out,

> Saying that small change is generative also means that we hold to the belief that a client who has experienced some success at achieving something manageable is, therefore, in a more resourceful state to find solutions to other, more difficult problems. (1992, p. 19)

Clients who have had some success making small changes are in a better position to find solutions to other or more difficult problems. This is common in learning theory, which maintains that success builds success. In training a horse, the first step is getting the animal to do something—anything, in fact—right, so you can praise or reward. After the animal feels that sense of accomplishment, the rest becomes specific and goal-oriented. Until they get a taste of positive change, many clients are not in a position to make great achievements or to work on a large goal.

Even the most complicated client may seem simpler "if one recognizes that people usually use the same attempted solution for all problems. By making a small change in the attempted solution to the problem(s), clients can change in several situations simultaneously" (Walter & Peller, 1992, p. 18). When working with anorexics, borderlines, alcoholics, or just about anyone else, it never hurts to encourage different behavior in some small area while using a standard treatment for diagnosis. It may be that the client uses the same type of solution for all problems, and the change will ripple, generalize, and expand. Metcalf suggested asking clients to "do something different the next time something doesn't work" (1995, p. 22). This may produce changes in interactions with others, changes in thinking, feeling, or even behaving, which may alleviate some symptoms or help in healing the disorder.

In conjunction with the constructivist attitude, solutioning works in changing the way clients view problems. The ideas clients have about their problems encourage or discourage the likelihood of solutions. Problems are only as powerful as our perceptions of them. Helping clients view their problems differently is often the first or only needed change. Seeing the problem as outside of oneself, as controllable, as temporary, as more normal, or as solvable can be the change that leads to a larger, rapid change and eventually to the desired solution.

Moody: The Case of Adam

Adam came to therapy after being released from the psychiatric ward of a local hospital, where he had stayed briefly, following a suicide attempt. He arrived with a diagnosis of bipolar disorder and some medication. After a couple sessions in which Adam talked about his life and experiences, problems and frustrations, feelings and moods, I suggested that perhaps he was extremely moody. His demeanor changed considerably. His whole life, Adam had been told—and had believed—that something was very wrong with him, that he was abnormal and needed to be fixed. When we began to talk about normal moodiness that he controlled through a combination of diet, exercise, and music, Adam began to change the view he had of himself and his "problem."

This change in thinking was all it took. Adam stopped taking medication, learned to manage his moodiness, and graduated valedictorian of his class.

Clients are never hopeless. They are not locked into negative behaviors that happen all the time. By seeing people in constant change, we can look for the exceptions that are bound to happen sometime. By believing that small change grows, we are in a position to begin helping clients make their desired movie, videotaping each day as it comes.

"The hopeful man sees success where
others see failure, sunshine where
others see shadows and storm."
—*O. S. Marden (Peter, 1977, p. 22)*

To begin assimilating some of the background beliefs of solutioning and considering how it will fit for you and your clients, stop reading now and do Practice 1.1.

PRACTICE 1.1

Building Blocks of Belief

Instructions: Answer the following questions. There are no right or wrong answers. The questions are designed simply to get the wheels rolling.

Is there a basic question that governs your work with clients? What is it?_____

_____

What does that question say about your beliefs about people and therapy? Does it leave room for incorporating an intervention evolved from the beliefs in this chapter?

_____

_____

Think about a client with whom you are currently working. Do you feel he or she has the skills and abilities to actualize solutions? What might those skills be?_____

_____

_____

Is this client's perception his or her reality? Would a perception-changing process be motivating? How might the problem be constructed in a more hopeful and solvable form?

_____

_____

Are you focusing on the system as the problem, or is the problem the problem? Could a change in the client affect a change in the system? Are those invested in the purpose of therapy involved in some way?_____

_____

_____

Are the causes of the problem relevant to the solution? Could the client go one step beyond causes? Has there been (or do you foresee) a point in the treatment plan where there is a need to get past blaming and excuses? Explain.

_____

_____

_____

Do you see this client as constantly changing? Would a small change lead to bigger changes? What small change would be realistic? Explain._____

_____

_____

Does this line of thinking create any new ideas or illustrate the need for an intervention such as solutioning? Ready to read on?

BUILDING BLOCKS OF LANGUAGE

"Notice the difference between what
happens when a man says to himself, 'I have
failed three times' and what happens
when he says, 'I am a failure.'"
—*S. I. Hayakawa (Webster, 1992, p. 92)*

Which comes first: the chicken or the egg? This classic mind
teaser has some application when we discuss the power of language in our lives. Which comes first: the words or the meaning?
We use words to describe our situations, ourselves, and our relationships with others. Do the meanings of these words give meaning to our lives, or do we choose words to communicate our meaning? A problem to one client may not be a problem to another. A
problem for the first client may be a source of joy to the next,
because of the meaning each attaches to the situation and the words
chosen to describe it.

"How can I know what I think
till I see what I say?"
—*Graham Wallace (Oxford, 1979, p. 562)*

In our constructivist view, words play a central role in expressing and sometimes creating our perceptions and realities. It follows that we should pay attention to the words we use with clients.
In helping clients change, our language may lead to different perceptions, feelings, and behaviors. Encouraging a description of the
situation that is normal, solvable, and hopeful will help clients see
themselves as having the ability to overcome their concerns.

It seems our society has become focused on problems rather
than on their opposite—times when life is working. In fact, we
don't even have a word for the opposite of problems. What does it
say about our focus that such a word is missing from our vocabulary? Solution could be said to be the opposite of problem, but
what about the times that are not problematic, yet are not a solution to something either; they are just working. It is these

nonproblem times our society has forgotten. These are the times on which the language of solutioning encourages clients to focus. Let's look at a typical solutioning session and note the importance of the language used.

Straight Home: The Case of Joe

Joe had been in counseling with his wife for three months. They had worked on a genogram, communication, and control. Finally, they decided to discontinue therapy because things were going the right way. Two weeks later, Joe called and asked for a private session.

Willyn: What would you like to talk about? *(This does not presuppose a problem. Had I asked, "What problem can I help you with?" I would have implied there is a problem that needs help from the outside.)*

Joe: I'm always cheating and I hate myself for it. Even though I love my wife and everything is better than ever, I go out and get myself in trouble.

Willyn: What is different about the times when you overcome cheating and stay home? *(The language assumes there are times without the problem when Joe stays home—presupposing that he can control the urge to cheat. The problem is externalized, named, and personified as something that can be overcome.)*

Joe: Well … *(He pauses. The question seems to throw him. My sense is that he had some excuses for why he cheats.)* When I pass the bar and go straight home from work the kids usually get me playing or watching TV with them. She fixes dinner, and after all that I'm usually too tired to leave again, so I just go to bed.

Willyn: Sounds like you control cheating by going straight home from work. *(I restate the exception—the potential solution—using his language.)*

Joe: You know, I never thought of it before, but it works every time. If I will just go home from work, I won't have all the trouble.

Willyn: So next week, after you have had a week going straight home, you can tell me how it works. Okay?

Joe: Sounds great. I really like what my wife and I have going. I think going straight home from work will keep me out of trouble and we can have the good marriage we have been having most of the time lately.

Joe called two weeks later to say that he had been going straight home, things were fine with his wife, and he didn't think he'd need therapy anymore.

"Words are one of our chief means of adjusting
to all the situations of life. The better control
we have over words, the more successful
our adjustment is likely to be."
        —*Bergen Evans (Peter, 1977, p. 503)*

Words are tools for incorporating solutioning into our interactions with clients. You've heard the old saying, actions speak louder than words. Think of the implications for therapists, whose actions are primarily done with words. Changing problem talk to solution talk is one of the basic tenets of SFBT. As O'Hanlon and Weiner-Davis noted, "the creative and mindful use of language is perhaps the single most influential indirect method for creating contexts in which change is perceived to be inevitable" (1989, p. 60). As you read this book, you will be learning a new language—a language of empowerment to use with your clients.

As therapists, we continually give our clients clues, both subtle and obvious, as to our view of them and their prospects for change. We think ... that it is imperative to be aware of these communications in therapy and to use them to facilitate the change process. (O'Hanlon & Weiner-Davis, 1989, p. 61)

In preparation for learning this new language, let's survey all the effective phrases you are already using. Look through Practice 1.2. What would you *probably* say in the situations there? What message does your language give your clients? Fill in the chart. Later, come back and incorporate what you might say using solutioning as an intervention.

"Words are, of course, the most
powerful drug used by mankind."
—Rudyard Kipling (Peter, 1977, p. 503)

PRACTICE 1.2

Building Blocks of Language

When this happens	You would probably say	If you are solutioning, you might say
A 17-year-old rape victim shares that she was sexually molested when she was 8.		
A woman tells you she is depressed all the time.		
A man makes a rude comment to his wife during the session.		
An adolescent boy says his parents can't make him do anything he doesn't want to.		
An alcoholic client fails her weekly urine analysis twice in one month.		

An older woman in for
  depression shares that she
  has been hearing voices.

A young man says he is
  frustrated that he cannot
  choose a career and that he
  obsesses about it all the time.

Source: Idea adapted from Shenkle (1989, p. 33).

Your Own Personal Script

We all have phrases or questions we use repeatedly because they seem to feel right, express our basic beliefs, and are effective with clients. This is not to say we go into sessions and play like broken records. Of course we are there to connect with our clients, to get into their world views, and to respond sincerely and spontaneously. However, one cannot deny that our responses come out of our working vocabulary and often sound similar, regardless of the situation. Being aware of the things you say to clients is just as important as being aware of your beliefs. What we say is how our meaning is communicated. Do your beliefs and your language match?

"Words are the best medium of exchange of
thoughts and ideas between people."
—*William Ross (Peter, 1977, p. 504)*

Friedman and Fanger (1991, p. 8) neatly summed up the importance of language in solutioning:

> The language of the therapist is most effective when it is the language of change, of optimism, of positive expectations, and of normal growth. By participating in a conversation that amplifies options and positive outcomes, the therapist provides a context for the client to both see and act on new possibilities. The therapist, by using the language of possibilities rather than that of limitations, of strengths rather than deficits, of successes rather than failures, provides a positive foundation for successful solutions. The questions we ask and the

words we use to talk about clients' situations influence the responses we get.

As you continue reading through this book, you will find practice exercises that deal with language. These will provide you with a wealth of language options for use in solutioning. These practices may be copied and used as cheat sheets to review before sessions.

Take a few minutes now and begin documenting your script. During your next few sessions, try to be aware of what you are saying and of what you repeat in more than one session or more than once during a single session. Write down what works for you in the top half of Practice 1.3. The bottom half provides space you can add to as you continue in your own solutioning process. Throughout the book, as we discuss the language tools of solutioning, think about how you might blend them into your own personal script.

PRACTICE 1.3

My Own Personal Script

Things I say that work for me: _____

_____

_____

_____

Solutioning questions and phrases to try:_____

_____

_____

_____

How I might blend in or adapt solutioning language with my own:

_____

_____

_____

BUILDING BLOCKS FROM WITHIN

Solutioning adheres to the philosophy that says, "If it works, don't fix it—if not, do something different" (Metcalf, 1995, p. 24). Part of doing what works for every professional is growth. You have already expressed your desire to grow, expand your effectiveness, and learn by choosing this book and reading this far. As you learn and use solutioning, you will be doing what works.

In your quest for improvement, don't forget your best tool: *you*. We have already established some of your effective language tools. Now let's look at your other talents, strengths, and resources. This may seem like an activity you would use with a client who is working on self-esteem, which you are not. It is included because it is reflective of the mindset of solutioning and will set the stage for confidence in trying some awkward (at first) language and new processes with clients. Creating a context of competence begins within. You can only ask of your clients what you have first asked of yourself.

In Practice 1.4, you will examine your competencies as a first step toward incorporating solutioning in your work. Practice 1.5 takes you through a line of questioning derived from the 4-P process: purpose, potentials, plan, and progress. This will give you an initial feel for the process and some confidence for trying a new intervention. Solutioning will only be as strong as the blocks of your current strengths and abilities you build upon.

PRACTICE 1.4

Building Blocks from Within

According to past evaluations from clients, supervisors, teachers, and so on ...

My highest ratings are:_____

My useful skills are:_____

One of my greatest qualities is:_____

The area I do the best in is:_____

According to my personal evaluations ...

My most effective talent is:_____

My most effective procedur s:_____

My greatest quality is:____   _____

My best activity is:_____

My exceptionalities and potentials are:

_____

_____

_____

Note: Use extra sheets of paper as needed.

PRACTICE 1.5

The 4-P Solutioning Process

Instructions: This is a simulation of some of the questions of solutioning. Later, we will use the same process with a problem— it may be helpful to suspend judgment until then. For now, have fun answering the following questions:

What is your *purpose* for learning a new intervention?

_____

_____

What are some potentials you have from the past that have helped you learn and incorporate new ideas into your practice before? How did you do it then? _____

_____

_____

Are you presently using some solution-focused thinking or talking in your practice? What potentials do you have for incorporating solutioning?_____

_____

_____

Visualize yourself successfully achieving your purpose of using solutioning (what you know about it so far). What are you doing?_____

_____

_____

_____

What suggestions or examples would other people have for achieving your purpose? How do they do it?_____

_____

_____

_____

The *plan* is to choose and try at least one potential solution from above this week._____

_____

_____

- If it is from the *past*, do it again.
- If it is from the *present*, do more of it.
- If it is *pretend*, do a small piece of it.
- If it is from other *people*, try out some of their ways.

Observe what is effective, then celebrate what worked as you consider your *progress* the following week. We're on our way!

AN OVERVIEW OF THE 4-P SOLUTIONING PROCESS

The 4-P solutioning process is a conversation, an intervention, a problem-solving process in which the therapist uses key questions to cripple blaming and excuses, encourage responsibility, and allow clients to solve their problems. This conversation can happen as a whole or in parts, in order or randomly. Each part of the process and the language used will be elaborated in the following chapters (see Figure 3.1).

The Purpose. Cocreating a clear, detailed description of the externalized problem encourages an achievable purpose and begins clients on the path toward solutions. After building a teaming relationship, very specific language is used to reconstruct the problem, take care of negative labels, make it solvable, and create a motivating purpose.

The Potentials.　Finding and describing potentials is a process of looking at times without, before, or beyond the problem. Potentials offer keys to solutions. *Past* exceptions to the problem are times when things were better. *Present* potentials are current times when things are satisfactory. Next there are *pretend* or visualized representations of the purpose. These are movie-like explanations that answer the question, "How do you want things to be?" Finally, there are *people* potentials, which can be either examples of how others solve the problem or resources and support. Questions asked in assuming, motivating language enable the client to realize all of the potentials that are available as solutions to the problem. Finding potentials may take one or several questions. Once a potential solution is found, you may go directly to the plan.

The Plan.　Three types of plans—positive, pretend, or perform—encourage working up to the doing of the solution, empowering clients with choice. Based on the potentials, select a thought or behavior to do again (from the past), to do more of (present), or to try (pretend, people) as the first step or maybe even the solution itself. The plan is precise, in the present, personal, process-oriented, and worded positively. Rehearsal of the solution is visualized, emotions are added, people are incorporated, and possible roadblocks or setbacks are accounted for as an empowering, proactive component of the plan. A positive change *will* begin with the plan.

The Progress.　During the progress, you will follow *through* (not up) and monitor the solution process with questions designed to discover the positive changes being made, to determine what is going right, to see when the problem is smaller, and to find what is better. Careful attention to progress will encourage responsibility, build further potentials and self-esteem, and ensure continued success in solutioning.

Chapters 2 through 5 present detailed explanations of the intervention tools for each step of the 4-P process. Chapter 6 discusses using solutioning in the mental health field. We will look at issues such as managed care, reimbursements, reports, and assessments from a solutioning perspective. Chapter 7 gives specific uses of solutioning for families, couples, children, and groups, complete with a *Solutioning Group Program.* Chapter 8 gives lesson plans for teaching the 4-P process to clients, parents, couples, and groups.

SOME SOLUTIONING QUESTIONS FOR YOU

These days, we are asked to do more with more clients in less time. Are you ready to save time while creating a hopeful atmosphere and encouraging decision-making, self-esteem, and life-long problem-solving abilities? Are you ready to focus on what works?

On a scale of 1 to 10, where are you now in accomplishing how you want to be as a therapist?

_____

1   2   3   4   5   6   7   8   9   10

Where would you like to be by the end of the year?

_____

1   2   3   4   5   6   7   8   9   10

Based on your potential, how might you do this?_____

_____

_____

_____

Are you ready for another intervention option? Are you ready for solutioning?

Chapter 2

Ready, Set, Go:
The First P—Purpose

The first step of solutioning is called *purpose* rather than problem or goal because there is so much variation in clients' motivation for therapy. Clients come to therapy for specific reasons: a
problem, a desire, a need, or some other form of motivation (for
example, a court order). We must start with clients.

In fact, solutioning may or may not be the method of choice at
the onset of therapy. You have a choice: Solutioning can begin
immediately, with the first word out of your mouth, as it fits in
treating the presenting problem, or you can use it as additional
issues, problems, or symptoms arise. Whenever you use solutioning,
you can begin with the first P and follow the entire 4-P process
sequentially or you can use whichever intervention fits the client
and the situation in the moment.

For practice, jump in and try the language with current clients
at various applicable points in their therapy. You may integrate
into your repertoire some of the steps, some of the questions, or
some of the interventions and not others. Most likely you will find
that elements of the language are already part of your vocabulary.

No matter when or how you choose to use some form of solutioning, lessening the power of the problem and forming a purpose will be helpful. The philosophical orientation from which you operate probably has a lot of influence over the way you define problems and the emphasis therapy takes from there. Whether you choose to define problems systemically, behaviorally, or emotionally, being on the same team and working together against the problem will enhance your efforts and motivate your clients.

Mental health is primarily a consumer business. We may sometimes take our relationship with clients for granted, devoting fewer efforts to cultivating them. Managed care is forcing therapists to spend less time with clients and thus to put less emphasis on relationships, yet the value of relationships cannot be denied. Even the brief therapy texts—which claim relationships are not necessary for solutions—devote some time to establishing them. Solutioning, however, provides language tools and the idea of *teaming* to build onto and into your counseling relationships.

Solutioning builds relationships and works on problems by *externalizing* and *reconstructing*, both of which empower clients to form an achievable purpose. Rather than avoiding discussion of the problem (which is often the case in SFBT), solutioning *manipulates* problems, motivating clients, giving them responsibility, and relieving you of some unnecessary stress. Solutioning holds as much benefit for the therapist as it does for the client. Rather than wallowing in self-pity, endlessly searching for a cause, and blaming, solutioning takes away the power of the problem and puts it in its proper place, so to speak, while enhancing relationships with clients.

> By the end of the initial interview both client and therapist need to be clear and in agreement about what the client wants, specifically, and how the client will know when he or she gets it, described in behavioral terms. (Friedman & Fanger, 1991, p. 79)

Again, this is where solutioning differs from SFBT. Some clients come to therapy to find out what it is they want. Some need to sort through issues, gain some self-esteem or insight, experiment with some symptom relief, and so on *before* they can develop clarity on what they need. Clients may feel unheard and rushed if the therapist forces them to decide right away exactly what it is they want from therapy. Most like to become familiar with the therapist, form a relationship, test the waters, and get some things out first.

On the flip side, some clients leave therapy frustrated—never becoming focused, never working on anything specific, never reaching a goal beyond closeness with the therapist. When the time is right, you can use solutioning as a direction for therapy or in addition to ongoing treatment. By referring to the purpose for therapy, you are not immediately hooking clients into a goal before they are ready—you're not belittling or bypassing their problems—you are simply acknowledging where they are and using solutioning to bring in teamwork, hope, and responsibility.

> "Do what you can, with what you have,
> where you are."
> —*Theodore Roosevelt (Peter, 1977, p. 37)*

TEAMING

Most likely, rapport and the various skills to build it were an integral part of your training as a counselor. A caring and trusting relationship with the client is considered valuable in virtually all counseling approaches. Depending on your philosophy of counseling, you may see rapport as *the* therapeutic tool and spend all your time on it. You may feel, like Carl Rogers, that unconditional positive regard, empathy, and understanding alone can facilitate clients' changing (Rogers, 1951).

On the other end of the continuum, brief therapists assume "rapport from the moment of contact," spend little to no time on it, and move right into solution construction through careful questioning techniques (Walter & Peller, 1992, p. 42). If you're like most of us, you are somewhere in between. One thing everyone seems to agree on is that rapport is beneficial. Various skills have been linked to rapport—from the basics of attending, listening, and reflecting to more sophisticated ones like joining (Haley, 1973), empathizing (Rogers, 1951, pp. 348–349), channeling (O'Hanlon & Weiner-Davis, 1989, pp. 66–67), and sensory matching (Bandler & Grinder, 1979). The skills seem to run hand in hand with various schools of thought.

Solutioning uses the idea of *teaming*. The therapist may use any of the standard skills—whatever fits their practice and their clients—and the language of solutioning to build rapport and a feeling of togetherness against a problem. Teaming is a term used in education and business to describe the integration of various individuals' talents and disciplines. Teaming up involves using the best resources and abilities of all involved. As Buhler and McCann (1989, p. 14) noted, "The greatest coaches have always known that creating winning teams requires the assembling of a variety of talent and getting them to work towards a common goal."

Teaming springs from the old adage that says, "two heads are better than one." It is one step beyond the initial understanding and communicating of rapport; it moves on to integrating, collaborating, and connecting. Each player has a specific role or job to do. Although interconnected, team members must take full responsibility for carrying out their part of the play. The therapist is the team leader: "For a team to be truly effective, it needs leaders who can communicate and coordinate action in a coherent way" (Flores, 1992, p. 8). One suggestion from the business world that applies to our relationship with clients is Horton's (1992, p. 60): "You need to know where things stand, and your people need to know where they stand. They need to tell you what you are doing or not doing to help them. And you need to listen in a nondefensive mood."

The therapist-client team is bonded, so to speak, through competition: In solutioning, this competition is manipulation of the opponent—the problem. Through teaming, clients feel part of something bigger than themselves—togetherness, support, and power—yet have full responsibility for their part. Teaming is a dimension of therapy that is not new—yet is rarely named, discussed, or taught—and that enhances the traditional stances of, "I am here to help you," or "I will help you help yourself." Teaming says, "We will work together."

While SFBT has been described by some therapists as too directive to mesh with their methods, solutioning is blendable; it is more facilitative than directive in design, but it can be as directive as you want it to be. Teaming is carried throughout the 4-P process: establishing a *joint* purpose, *sharing* potentials by both members, *collaborating* throughout the session, and *cocreating* a plan (not a task designed and given by the therapist to the client).

Resistance is rarely a factor in teaming. As Friedman and Fanger (1991) pointed out, labeling clients as resistant does not fit within a partnership or team relationship. Teaming enhances the close relationships we all know to be so therapeutic with clients. It is practical, useful, and, above all, respectful to clients.

> All therapy takes place within a collaborative interpersonal context, without which treatment will fail. … The neglected aspects of the collaborative relationship may be the elements which differentiate exceptional therapists from adequate or poor therapists. (Budman & Gurman, 1988, p. 50)

Skill Highlight: Team Relationships

The elements of a team that can be incorporated into your relationships with clients are

1. mutual respect and acknowledgment of individual strengths, abilities, and talents;

2. different but collaborative positions; and

3. working together.

Establishing mutual respect and acknowledging strengths, abilities, and talents comes with letting go of the "expert" role and involving clients in the decision making of therapy. As you continue reading this book and the language practices, you'll see how much respect is given to client input. *It is client input—not the therapist—that discovers or creates the solution.* The positions are those of teammates and the roles may switch at any point in the game: The therapist may lead, both therapist and client may be players, or the client may take some leadership. This differs from the one-upmanship of many traditional models. Yes, the therapist is the trained, educated, paid professional. However, no one knows the client, his life circumstances, his current situation, or his relationships better than the client. Equality is brought to therapy with teaming by realizing differences and how they can be complimentary. We have all seen talented teams go astray because individual players had their own separate agendas—not unlike some therapeutic relationships you may recall. The skills of teamwork—assisting, practicing, communicating, motivating, and encouraging—will enhance any therapeutic relationship.

EXTERNALIZING THE OPPONENT

Our game plan is to get to know the opponent (the problem) by *externalizing* it. Teaming highlights O'Hanlon's idea that "The person is never the problem; the problem is the problem" (1996, p. 76). Through the externalization process, the team is solidified and the client gains hope, motivation, and power. Externalizing the problem makes it more livable, more solvable, and more workable—useful attributes, whichever method you use from here on out.

Taking Sides

Remember the playground fights of elementary school? A frequent question of onlookers was, "Whose side are you on?" Being on the "right" side was important. Choosing teams in PE was another stressful situation, wondering which *side* you would be on. As adults, we sometimes hear of marriage and family therapists accused of taking sides. Or you may have worked with children of divorce who were pressured to take sides. Taking sides may even be at the heart of our nation's gang problem.

Despite all of these negative connotations of taking sides, once you are on a side, there is a certain comfort in being sided. Being together with someone else equals teaming. It is an empowering and powerful feeling. It is that powerful feeling we want to invoke in our clients as we side with them against their problems. The first step in doing this is what White and Epston (1990, p. 38) called "externalizing of the problem":

> Externalizing is an approach to therapy that encourages persons to objectify and, at times, to personify the problems that they experience as oppressive. In this process, the problem becomes a separate entity and thus external to the person or relationship that was ascribed as the problem. Those problems that are considered to be inherent, as well as those relatively fixed qualities that are attributed to persons and to relationships are rendered less fixed and less restricting.

I have found three benefits from externalizing problems: it discourages blaming, it empowers the client, and it gets the problem *out there* where the team can *fight it,* which is very motivating. Few sport players would be successful against an unknown opponent, against themselves, or against a system within which they operate. Yet we sometimes spend time on these in therapy. White and Epston listed the following ways in which externalizing is "helpful to persons in their struggle with problems" (1990, p. 39):

1. Decreases unproductive conflict between persons, including those disputes over who is responsible for the problem [lessens blame];

2. Undermines the sense of failure that has developed for many persons in response to the continuing existence of the problem despite their attempts to resolve it [empowers];

3. Paves the way for persons to cooperate with each other, to unite in a struggle against the problem, and to escape its influence in their lives and relationships [teaming];

4. Opens up new possibilities for persons to take actions to retrieve their lives and relationships from the problem and its influence [empowers];

5. Frees persons to take a lighter, more effective, and less stressed approach to "deadly serious" problems [motivates]. (White & Epston, 1990, pp. 39-40)

If you gain nothing else from solutioning, talking about problems as separate from the person will be a big benefit. People who feel as if *they* are problems do not have the greatest self-esteem, which often impedes change. Notice how the client in the following case study comes to life as her problem is externalized, separated from her and from the disappointment she feels when she blames someone she loves (her mother). Feeling intruded upon by the problem rather than *being* the problem, she readily joins the team—motivated, empowered, and hopeful.

Fighting Against Fighting: The Case of Telly

Fourteen-year-old Telly had a long history of moving back and forth between parents, changing schools, and failing grades. Telly's mother brought her to therapy because Telly did not want to leave the house, was depressed, and had mentioned suicide. Telly's mother was too busy to come to sessions; she popped in just long enough to sign the disclosure statement as she dropped Telly off at the first session. The following is a condensation of the session, highlighting the process of externalizing the problem. The conversation took place after Telly had listed a number of areas in her life with which she was not happy. I listened with empathy, reflected her feelings, and felt we were ready to move ahead.

Willyn: Telly, you've told me about a lot of sources of pain in your life. What would you say is most important for us to work on first?

Telly: Well, the thing that brings me down the most is my mom and I always fighting. She says I just push her buttons. It's awful. I don't mean to. I guess I make her really mad a lot.

Willyn: So fighting is the problem we will be battling.

Telly: Yeah, let's try to stop fighting! I hate it. It makes me not want to go home.

Willyn: What other characteristics does fighting have?

Telly: Fighting makes me yell things at my mother that I don't mean. It makes me think bad thoughts about her, and then I feel mad at myself. I feel disappointed in her sometimes too. She acts really wild sometimes.

Willyn: Sounds like fighting brings out the worst in both of you. When do you control fighting and not let it make you say things you don't mean?

Telly: *(thinking for a few seconds)* Sometimes I change the subject when I feel fighting is about to happen. I pick something safe to talk about. One time I just left the room and went and listened to music. We didn't fight that time.

Willyn: Cool! I'm impressed that you already have some ways of beating fighting.

Notice that Telly used language that personified fighting. She is a good example of what happens when a client immediately picks up on the externalization process. As a result, she no longer had to defend herself or her mother. No one was to blame—except fighting.

In order to externalize you must first identify the problem (symptom, difficulty, or complaint). O'Hanlon illustrated some creative ways to do this, one of which was "naming/personifying" the problem (1996, p. 76). A word of caution here: You must make sure clients have the most input regarding what the problem is. *We are not in the business of giving people problems.* As Budman and Gurman noted, "the therapist and patient must first define the problem collaboratively and consensually" (1988, p. 14). Diagnosis sometimes challenges the team concept, but it is a necessary reality that can be incorporated into solutioning (see chapter 6).

Next, you want to help the client get to know the opponent as something truly separate from him, discussing the power of the client over the problem, "mapping the influence of the person" (White & Epston, 1990, p. 45). This further separates the problem, motivates, and leads directly into the potential questions of the next chapter. A natural flow will result in an obvious purpose that is workable and achievable. Clients are relieved of the burden of *being* the problem and are one step closer to overpowering it with a solution.

Practice 2.1 gives some examples of how you might externalize a problem with individuals, couples, families, or groups. Often the answers to these questions lead right into potential solutions (chapter 3) by creating a wide array of areas for investigation. In your own practice, choose a client who is feeling like she is the problem or who is blaming someone else as the problem. Help her externalize the problem, and take a look at what interactions are happening between the problem and the person as a motivating intervention. Guiding clients in solutioning can begin as early as the intake paperwork if you add a couple of the questions from Practice 2.1 or use the Problem Resume in Practice 2.3. You'll be impressed with the responses and the difference they make when approaching problems.

PRACTICE 2.1

Externalizing

Identify the Problem

- Sounds like the name of the problem is *anger*.

- So, you are battling *fear*.

- *Depression* is your enemy.

- So, it is no longer your mom you are wanting to work on, but *fighting*.

- If you were going to name your problem, what would you call it?

- What name could you give to what we are talking about here?

- Is there a symbol, color, or sign that fits what we are working on (the problem)?

- When *anger* is in your home, what happens?

- At work, when *fear* comes over to your desk, what do you do?

- Who else notices when *depression* comes to visit?

- What does *fighting* do to interfere with your relationship with your mom?

- If you were to draw the problem, what would it look like?

- What are some of the characteristics/traits of your problem?

Disempower the Problem

- Tell me about times when you have beat *anger* and kept your cool.

- How have you stood up to *fear*?

- What happens on days when you win over *depression*?

- Tell me exactly what you did to keep *fighting* from interfering.

- What influence do you have over the problem (name)?

Empower the Person

- Wow! That is so impressive. How do you keep your cool?

- What kind of person are you to stand up to *fear* like that?

- What skills do you have that you use to win over *depression*?

- Tell me about your qualities that make it hard for *fighting* to interfere.

- How do you do that?

- What power do you have over the problem (name)?

Note: It is sometimes hard for clients who have had (or been) a problem for a long time to express times when they have had an impact on the problem.

> Ordinarily, it is very difficult for persons to locate examples of their own influence in the life of the problem. This is particularly so when they have suffered under long-standing and apparently intractable problems that they have experienced as eclipsing their lives and relationships. (White & Epston, 1990, p. 45)

Sometimes clients see their situations in black-and-white terms: "If someone calls me a name, I beat him up." Or, "If I am around my friends, I drink." Simply by asking about times when the person has had a positive effect on the problem, you broaden her perspective, preparing the way for potential solutions to arise. Persistence in questioning relays your belief that there are times when the client does win, which shows your faith in him, whether or not he actually comes up with an example. The value in asking these questions is to take away some of the problem's power and give it back to the client, while opening up areas where solution possibilities can emerge. When a client can separate herself from the problem and relate even one instance when she overcame it, you are well on your way toward creating a purpose that she is motivated to achieve. Usually, a couple of potential questions (chapter 3) and the plan (chapter 4) will be obvious.

PURPOSEFUL THINKING

Never Say Never: The Case of Mike

Willyn: When have you resisted anger and not gotten in a fight after someone called you a name on the playground?

Mike: Never. If someone calls me a name, I beat him up.

Willyn: There has never been a time you did not let anger have control? I bet there is someone you haven't beaten up.

Mike: Well, Leroy called me a not-too-bad name one time. I was supposed to spend the night at his house that night, and I knew if I beat him up I probably wouldn't get to go. That time I let it slide. He was just teasing anyway.

Willyn: So you can control anger when you think about what might happen if you don't. Like not getting to go to a friend's house or something.

Mike: Yeah, I guess so.

This short excerpt illustrates the value of considering the results of the problem once it is externalized. Many clients know all to well what happens as a consequence of the problem, how it makes them feel, the trouble it causes, and so on. However, few consider the possible results of *not* having the problem and what will be different then. Often, this is the final step in forming an achievable purpose: knowing what you *do* want.

Once again, using specific solutioning language will help you guide clients away from a problem-oriented view to a purposeful, solution-oriented view of their situations. As Tomm pointed out, this is especially helpful because "Families with problems are sometimes so preoccupied with present difficulties or past injustices that, in effect, they live as if they 'have no future'" (1987, p. 173). Living without a future gives the problem a lot of power. Having a purpose and working toward a better future gives power to the person.

Solution Application: Addictions

An idea of a better future alone may not be motivating enough for some addicts. In conjunction with solution-focused methods, looking at the dark side of maintaining the problem may be more helpful in treating addictions (Reuss, 1997, p. 173). For this, Reuss developed the "nightmare question" as an antithesis to the "miracle question" of SFBT (see Practice 2.2). The following case study shows how solutioning—especially the skills of manipulating the problem in creating a purpose—can be used in addictions counseling.

But What About the Guys? The Case of Tom

Tom was middle-aged, drank too much, and had not responded to prior treatment in a local hospital or Alcoholics Anonymous. He came to me after losing his job; he was on the verge of losing his wife as well. He arrived in my office full of excuses.

Tom: You know, it's not that I don't want to stop drinking ... and I've really tried. It's just that every time I try, when I get around my friends, I go back. It's my friends. They are really important to me, but they all drink. It's not like they force me or anything, but it's what we do together, and I like spending time with them. I have to stop, everything is counting on it. But I'm not giving up my friends.

Willyn: It sounds like you are having a hard time picturing a future without drinking. Maybe we should create two possible futures—one where you stop drinking and one where you don't.

Would you be willing to fill in the details? Which do you want to do first—with drinking or without?

Tom: Let's start without. That's the one I keep trying and screwing up.

Willyn: Okay, pretend you wake up tomorrow and drinking is no longer part of your life. Walk me through the day. What are you doing, saying, feeling? What is different?

Tom: Well, I'm not hung over and I feel pretty good. I wake up with my wife and eat breakfast with my kids. I go to work, because I can keep a job when I'm not drinking. After work is hard. I usually go hang out with my friends, but if I'm not drinking, I guess I should just go home.

Willyn: What do you do when you get home?

Tom: I'm usually a little toasted when I get home, so I go straight to bed. If I went home earlier and was sober, I'm not sure what it would be like.

Willyn: Okay, ready to paint the with-drinking picture of the future? Walk me through a day when you wake up after a few more weeks of continued drinking.

Tom: Yuck. I feel pretty bad and don't get up until really late in the day. I am all alone because my wife and kids are gone. I don't go to work, but I don't have any money to hang out with the guys, either. I guess I just get a beer and go back to bed. I don't know how long this could last. I'd probably lose my house if I wasn't working.

Willyn: After looking at these two pictures, how are you feeling?

Tom: I think drinking has got to go, even if it means no friends. I just can't lose everything else. I'll do what I have to do to quit. I've just got to.

Facilitating a purpose can be done using the questions in Practice 2.2. Remember, we don't call a purpose a goal because the client may not be ready for a goal yet; he may only be capable of a problem statement until a look at potential solutions expands his horizons and he can create a plan (i.e., a goal).

The next step is to solidify the team concept, disempower the problem, and motivate the client's purpose for therapy. You may want to begin using the questions in Practice 2.2 on a new client, a client who seems a little resistant, or one who needs more motivation.

PRACTICE 2.2

Purposeful Thinking

- What will be different/better when the problem is solved?

- What will happen if you choose to maintain the problem?

- If the problem (anger, depression, anorexia, etc.) continues to win, what will happen at work? At home? In your relationships?

- When you overcome the problem (control anger, feel better, are healthier), what will be different/better at work? At home? In your relationships?

- What benefits will you experience when you solve this problem, when therapy is over?

- How will you feel when you solve (no longer have) the problem?

- What reasons might someone else (me, parents, friends, coworkers, etc.) give?

- Tell me about your plans for the future—your dreams, your ambitions. Is there room for the problem (fighting, stealing, pills, etc.)?

- What are you worried might happen if you continue this way (with the problem)?

- When *(not if)* you do find a way to overcome the problem, what will you do to reward yourself?

- Who will be the first to notice when *(not if)* you no longer have the problem?

- How will your work, relationships, etc. improve when you no longer have the problem?

> For example, one might ask an adolescent daughter who is underachieving at school, "What plans do you have for a career? What else have you considered? How much formal education do you think you would need? ... What kinds of experience would be useful in getting that sort of job? ... How will you go about getting it?" (Tomm, 1987, p. 173)

The Miracle Question

> Suppose that one night, while you were asleep, there was a miracle and this problem was solved. How would you know? What would be different? How will your husband know without your saying a word to him about it? (de Shazer, 1988, p. 5)

The Nightmare Question

> Suppose you go about the rest of today just doing what you usually do. You go home, go to bed, and fall asleep, and some-

time in the middle of the night ... oh some kind of a disaster happens ... and all of the fears, all of the worries, all of the concerns, all of the problems that brought you here today ... they come true. This would be a nightmare, I suppose. But because this nightmare happens in the middle of the night, you can't really know it has happened. What would you notice when you woke up tomorrow morning? What would be the first thing you would notice that would let you know your life had become unmanageable? That you were living a nightmare? (Reuss, 1997, p. 72)

The motivational aspects of the language in Practice 2.2 cannot be denied. Tomm maintained that questions can be used to, "instill hope and to trigger optimism" (1987, p. 174). Notice the use of *when* not *if* in reference to the solving of the problem. The questions are *future-oriented,* the problem is already partially in the past, which is part of the next set of tools to use in manipulating the power of the problem and establishing a purpose.

"Clients frequently describe their situations in such a way as to make change seem impossible. Therefore, how we guide the initial conversation about what the client *wants,* serves to introduce the possibility of achieving that goal" (Friedman & Fanger, 1991, p. 74). The Purpose Resume in Practice 2.3 should be helpful. It puts externalizing and purposeful thinking together in worksheet form. Try it before, after, or during a session with clients who are working on developing a purpose. Notice this does not perpetuate problem talk, but focuses on and moves toward solutions.

PRACTICE 2.3

Purpose Resume

What is the identification (name) of the problem?_____

_____

What are the characteristics of the problem?_____

_____

_____

What influence do you have over the externalized problem?
When do you beat it, control it, manage it?_____

_____

_____

What skills, abilities, talents, and resources help you win over
your problem (even a little bit or for a little while)?

_____

_____

What reasons do you have for solving or overcoming the problem?_____

_____

_____

If you were to draw your problem, what would it look like?

_____

_____

What will the results be of solving or overcoming the exter
nalized problem?_____

_____

_____

Who will notice or benefit when the problem no longer exists
or is controlled?_____

_____

_____

RECONSTRUCTING THE PROBLEM

The tools of describing, time traveling, normalizing, and scaling are quite valuable in helping clients who feel dominated by a problem. Some clients are not able to see around the problem. By creating a new, more solvable view, you help the therapeutic process gain momentum. Use these tools for team problem reconstruction. Reconstructing the problem is not a huge, time-consuming process. It is simply using language that displays an attitude of hope, wellness, change, control, and the assumption that solutioning will work. By altering the words we use when referring to clients and their problems, we can paint motivational yet realistic pictures of their situations.

Describing

The power of labeling can be dramatic. When naming the problem, labeling the complaint, or discussing the person or situation, we can focus either on the negative or on the positive. We can create a positive expectation or a limited one; we can describe actions or fixed labels. In reconstructing, describing casts the problem in a changeable light. Action descriptions are less fixed than static labels (or relabels). Huber and Backlund gave this example of describing:

> To the client claiming to be an "overeater," the counselor might
> channel communications in the direction of action descrip-
> tions: "It appears that there are many times when you find
> yourself eating too much." Action descriptions ... depict so-
> lutions being employed by clients. "Eating too much" is a
> solution that can be more easily altered than a static descrip-
> tion such as "overeater." (1996, p. 27)

The intent is not to change a diagnosis, deny the reality of the
situation, or undermine the value of what you are working on, but
to describe the problem in a way that acknowledges that it can be
solved.

> An orientation that "talks pathology" and uses linguistic la-
> bels that emphasize "pathologic" language and terminology
> fosters a negative and pessimistic view of human capacity
> for change. We believe that you can be more effective by
> avoiding "pathological" and "static" diagnostic language ...
> by defining the original request for service, not as reflecting
> "illness" (with the need for "cure") but simply as a request
> for change. (Friedman & Fanger, 1991, p. 115)

Often, the client feels that it is she, and not the problem, who
is labeled. This is frightening, because labels can easily become
self-fulfilling prophecies. Descriptions, on the other hand, are more
problem-specific, can aid in the externalizing process, and establish a practice that will be beneficial for solution construction
throughout the 4-P process.

Additional evidence of the benefits of descriptions over labels
was shown in a study by Rosenhan, which asked, "If sanity and
insanity exist, how shall we know them?" (1973, p. 250). Normal
"confederates" were asked to portray themselves as "mentally ill"
in order to gain admission to several psychiatric inpatient units.
Once these confederates were admitted, they were instructed to
return to behaving "normally." However, "The notes kept by
pseudopatients are full of patient behaviors that were misinterpreted
by well-intentioned staff" (Rosenhan, 1973, p. 253). In other words,
the staff continued to interpret the confederates (now normal) behavior as reflective of mental illness and kept them hospitalized

for extended periods of time. The labels stuck with the "patients" and influenced the perceptions of the staff. As Rosenhan noted, "A psychiatric label has a life and an influence of its own" (1973, p. 273).

Rosenhan's study illustrated that you often see what you are looking for. If we label clients (positively or negatively, accurately or inaccurately), we will find facts to back up our labels. Whereas labels often carry connotations, descriptions are specific enough to speak for themselves. *Descriptions are more clear, more adaptable, and more changeable.* This is why the first step of solutioning is called the purpose, not the problem. Clients have reasons, purposes, and desires for therapy, not necessarily all of which are accurately labeled problems. The word *problem* itself could turn a complaint into something larger and harder to change. If we describe a client as having a lot of energy (as opposed to being ADD), he may have a better picture of what he is trying to control. If a "depressed" client is described as "sad at times," she can focus on the times when she is not sad rather than be stuck in a state of "being."

In fact, often the opening words of a session initiate the describing process. Paying careful attention is important so labels that perpetuate a client's *stuck* state are not created or continued. Think for a moment how you open most sessions. Is there a focus on problems, solutions, feelings, behaviors, or change? Is there a focus on what is better, worse, the same? Does your opening statement ask for a problem, refer to trouble, or mention the solution? As Friedman and Fanger, noted,

> The way we talk about a situation affects how we think and feel about that situation. If we focus on describing people in static, diagnostic terms, we may be taking part in a process of creating ("reifying") the very "pathology" we seek to transform. (1991, p. 115)

Let's look at some opening statements of SFBT therapists and see what messages, labels, or descriptions they give or request. A case study by Budman and Gurman showed the counselor asking, "How can I help you?" (1988, p. 54). Not very empowering, responsibility-producing, or self-esteem-building, is it? Although valid, that statement is not going to create teaming. Michelle Weiner-Davis used, "So, what brings you in?" in one of her case studies (O'Hanlon & Weiner-Davis, 1989, p. 69). This avoided labeling, but it could be seen as giving the problem the power to "bring" someone to the point of needing therapy. That may be a reality, but presupposing the problem's power from the onset is not suggested. Friedman and Fanger (1991) suggested using, "What would you like to have happen here today?"

> Examining the presuppositions in this relatively simple question, you can see that the treatment goals are embodied in it: increased choice (some change can occur here today); expanded autonomy (the client activates the process); and improved morale (which tends to follow). (p. 99)

The message given to the client in this opener is useful and helpful. However, some clients—especially those heavily burdened with emotion—do not have a clue about what they want to happen. If they knew, they'd already have done it, be doing it, or not require therapy. Asking too much of clients can be a problem. When the client seems unsure about what he wants to happen, a little time spent sorting things out as a team can be useful. It's important to remember that solutioning should happen only when the time is right. We don't want clients to feel "solution-forced" when "the therapist may minimize and even trivialize the client's experience of the problem" (Nylund & Corsiglia, 1994, p. 6).

Giving credit to the client and involving her in the process is an important part of teaming. However, we must remember that clients come to therapy for help; they are paying for our assistance. Good teammates realize when they must take control of the ball and lead the way to victory. "[I]t is ethically incumbent on counselors to take responsibility for guiding the counseling process, and it is to clients' detriment if counselors abdicate this responsibility" (Huber & Backlund, 1996, p. 26). The teammate role requires constantly adjusting to the needs, skills, and abilities of the unique clients (teammates). Walter and Peller suggested the following statement as a first session opener:

> We would like to talk with you for about 40 minutes about
> what you want and about your situation. At the end of that
> time, I would like to take a break for a few minutes, go be-
> hind this viewing mirror, consult with my team, and then come
> back and share with you our combined feedback or advice if
> we have any. We work as a team because we believe that two
> heads are better than one and that this way you will have the
> benefit of different points of view. (1992, p. 41)

The initial statement about "what you want and about your situation" gives the message that clients' desires are important. The counselors do not give any labels to unknowns and acknowledge clients' desires. However, they also imply that clients' "heads" are not a viable resource. The therapist has to talk with other hidden "heads" to come up with advice, completely eliminating the valuable input of the client. Also, the 40-minute time limit may give the message to some clients that their situations are worth only 40 minutes. Many therapists spend extended periods of time getting into their clients' situations.

In subsequent sessions, Walter and Peller used this positive opener: "We start each session after the first with the question, 'So, tell us what is different or better?' This question presupposes that change is happening and that something better or, at least different, is happening" (1992, p. 145).

An effective opener may be as simple as, "Where should we start?" or "What happened?" This focuses the session without any labels or presuppositions and asks for a *description* from the start. Clients are free to relate whichever experiences they feel are valid or need to be expressed. Empowering clients (teaming) begins from the first moment of contact. It is important to open the dialog in a positive way that avoids negative labeling, empowers, and sets up a context for relationship, change, growth, and responsibility, yet still fits your style and the focus of your therapy. This may vary with each client and each situation. Being aware that the messages we give through our language show genuine care for clients. As Metcalf noted, "descriptions do not change the problem, they change the meaning ascribed to the problem (1995, p. 39).

As you work with your current clients, notice what labels you are using. Can you substitute an action description? Is the picture you (and your client) want portrayed the one you are getting? Can you create a more hopeful connotation? Is there a context in which the problem, behavior, or situation would be seen favorably? Can that become part of a description? Does the label give power to the client or to the problem? Can a description start to transfer the power? Is there a more solvable way of describing the person, problem, or situation? Can you and your client describe things differently together?

If you avoid labeling and make good use of action descriptions, your clients will soon be using the hopeful descriptions as well—or will be thinking about them, or feeling better about things, or acting differently.

The Episodes: The Case of Nora

Nora was a 14-year-old who had lots of friends, liked school, and earned good grades. During her first two sessions, her purpose had been getting along with her mother better so she could have boys from school call the house. We had teamed up and were making progress. Then, during the third session, Nora really unloaded. Evidently I had passed her test, so to speak, and she felt enough trust to open up. Nora told me that two times during the previous three months she had "gone insane," and that she was scared she was "crazy."

Solutioning her relationship with her mother no longer took precedence, so I switched gears. Being there in the moment with Nora and letting her share, while gaining more information for a diagnosis, was my only effort. Nora described two episodes of depersonalization with auditory hallucinations—one at home and one at school. She said, "I went insane" a couple of times and "I'm crazy" a number of times. Nora's fear for her mental state was obvious.

I wanted to use a solutioning intervention, just to relieve her anxiety about being insane or crazy, while I talked to her about getting a full psychological evaluation. I said, "Nora, I don't think you are insane or crazy. I think you had two very frightening episodes where you didn't really know what was happening to you. When we talk about those times, let's call them episodes. Do you know what I mean by episodes?"

Nora's nonverbals showed intense concentration on what I was saying; she nodded and then seemed to relax. Feeling relief that she was not crazy and that we could team up and work on preventing further episodes, Nora started to refer to "when she went crazy," but then she stopped herself and instead described the externalized problem—"the first episode."

Nora had started out that day telling me she was insane, crazy, and hopeless. Her view of "crazy" was that it was a permanent mental state; that she was incurable. When I said I told her I not think she was crazy, and instead labeled the events as *episodes*, Nora's attitude changed tremendously and visibly. She began seeing herself as a person who had problems that could be solved. I did not ignore the reality of the problems, and together we planned to address them fully, but without the self-imposed, frightening label of "insane." Nora's new view of herself, as sane but with problems, opened the door for change, for healing, and for hope. She even expressed motivation for a future without the episodes.

PRACTICE 2.4

Describing

Train your ears to catch negative labels and your brain to reconstruct them before your mouth verbalizes them.

Label	Reconstructed Description
depressed	sad sometimes
oppositional	likes to debate
anger problem	has a lot of feeling
dysfunctional family	a family, like all, that has fights
victim	has overcome abuse, survivor
codependent	people are important
stressed out	is coping with a lot
ADHD	energetic sometimes
highly emotional	expressive
low functioning	coping as best he can

For Practice: Have a partner make up a problem and tell you about it. Practice eliciting and using action descriptions that are solvable rather than the label that initially comes to mind. Practice noticing and using the descriptions your partner brings, reflecting back changeable action descriptions rather than labels.

Add Your Own:

_____

_____

_____

_____

There is a risk when you create new descriptions that clients will perceive that you are not hearing what they are saying, you are not truly understanding them, or you are discounting their feelings. Under the umbrellas of teaming and reconstructing, describing is done *with* clients, in the context of a close, trusting, and caring therapeutic relationship, and not until the client is ready.

> [L]ook for the positive intention behind the request, but also put the responsibility for the change back in the lap of the only person who can effect the change, the client. This both restates the request in positive language and also implies that a change can be initiated and maintained by the client. (Friedman & Fanger, 1991, p. 103)

Note that at this point we are talking about descriptions, not diagnosis. In chapter 6, we will look at everyday, hopeful, workable, solvable words to use in diagnosis in conjunction with the *DSM-IV*.

Regardless of the descriptions you use, many clients persist in self-destructive, negative labels for themselves and their problems. We've heard them all: "I'm a loser." "I'm a stoner." "I'm fat." "I'm depressed." Self-inflicted labels often are the most powerful. They show clients' expectations of themselves and of the problem. These labels may come from past therapeutic experiences, from significant others, or from within. No matter where they come from, they influence how the client views and approaches life. Questioning labels and working toward descriptions can begin a reconstruction in thinking. The most useful new descriptions are those created by clients themselves.

The "Slow Learner": The Case of Mark

Mark had battled drugs and alcohol abuse during his teen years, gotten in some trouble with the law, and now was coming to therapy as a last-ditch effort to "get his life together." During the initial sessions, I noted that Mark often referred to himself as a "slow learner." However, he also told me how he had taught himself to build computers and how he really enjoyed the challenge. I thought a new self-description would be a helpful intervention for this young man with low self-esteem.

As he told me about his ability to build computers, I stopped him and said, "Wait a minute. I thought you told me you were a slow learner. This does not sound like slow learning to me. Very few people can teach themselves."

Mark looked perplexed for a moment and then beamed. "You know, you're right! I guess I can learn."

Later in the session, as he alluded to his current use of drugs and alcohol, he noted, "Now that I know I can learn from my mistakes, I shouldn't be making them anymore, huh?"

I agreed, "That makes sense."

A useful intervention empowers clients with the means, the confidence, and the desire to change the ways they refer to themselves both now and in the future.

Skill Highlight: Assisted Reconstruction

Ask your clients to share some of the words they use to describe themselves, their relationships, and their problems. Then work on the list together.

- What is a more positive description?

- What situations are there where (the new description) might be useful?

- Does (the problem) happen all the time, some of the time, rarely?

- In what ways could the problem be seen as more solvable, okay, acceptable, or useful?

- Is there a nicer, less serious way to describe things?

- Can you think of a more positive description?

> You can begin to teach them how to do it for themselves. When they say something self-critical or are "stuck," you ask "What's another way you could describe that?" (Friedman & Fanger, 1991, p. 133)

Time Traveling

The tool of time traveling involves various manipulations of the problem, which will make it seem a part of the past, more temporary, and will remove it from the future. For clients who cannot see out from under a problem, it helps to use language that refers to it as a part of the past, opening up present and future possibilities. Some clients come in believing they have always had the problem and always will, which is not very conducive for change. This is where problem manipulation is most needed and effective. Your awareness of the client's views of the problem's permanence and subtle use of language can help create a new view in which the problem is not all-powerful, but solvable.

Simply using the past tense whenever you refer to the problem encourages change. By using *was, were,* and *have been* rather than *are* and *is*, the problem time-travels to the client's past. For example, you might say, "You *have been* struggling at work" instead of "You *are* failing." Or, "You *haven't been* sleeping" instead of "You *have* insomnia."

In addition, as Walter and Peller noted, "The use of verbs like *show, become, seem,* and *act as if* promote a view that behaviors are temporary and changeable" (1992, p. 17). Describing a client as *showing anger* has a different connotation than saying a client *is angry,* which seems more like an all-the-time occurrence. *Showing* is something done at times, occasionally, or in the past (*showed* anger). This makes the problem less permanent. These verbs do not discount the problem, but approach it in a way that shows light at the end of the tunnel. "The presupposition is that she or he is acting that way now, but could be acting in other ways at other times" (Walter & Peller, 1992, p. 17).

By attaching the word *sometimes* to problem descriptions, the doorway of opportunities is opened. This makes the problem more temporary. Additionally, *sometimes* reflects that nothing occurs 100% of the time (Metcalf, 1995). Most of us, therapists and clients alike, feel more prepared or motivated to deal with *energetic sometimes* than with *hyperactive,* or *sad sometimes* rather than *depressed.* The inferences are subtle yet powerful, leading directly to the potential solution explorations of the next chapter.

Another small but powerful word is *yet.* By adding this word to the end of a purpose statement, you express the idea that the problem is in the past and the solution will happen in the future. For example, you might say that a client is *not coping yet* rather than labeling him as *failing,* or a family is *not getting along yet* as opposed to being *dysfunctional.* The time travel has been accomplished, putting the solution into the view of the future.

Where *sometimes* and *yet* make the problem temporary, *when* affects the picture of the future. It creates expectancy for the solution. By stating the purpose for therapy in a sentence starting with *when*, you show your faith that the solution *will happen.* This may create a self-fulfilling prophecy, an expectation that clients can live up to. *When you are communicating* and *When you are sober* are two examples. Clients can see your assumption that therapy will be effective and the solution will happen, putting them in the mindset of achievement rather than failure.

This attention to detail may seem to jeopardize your genuineness with clients; but it is likely you already use many of these reconstructions without even realizing it. Being aware of every word that comes out of your mouth is asking too much. Helping clients build views of their problems that motivate and invoke a sense of relief, of hope, and of power is crucial. With a little practice, you will be doing it naturally and still be as real, genuine, and in the moment as ever. Take a look at a couple of client files; prepare one purpose statement per client that uses some of the reconstructing tools we've discussed. You would never go into session with a prepared line, but is the new purpose statement something you might say in a session? Don't say anything yet; just think about how you might say it, if you did. Practice 2.5 summarizes the reconstruction tool of time traveling in an easy-to-use worksheet.

PRACTICE 2.5

Time Traveling

Use the following checklist first when writing case notes and then spontaneously with clients. It will soon become a habit to switch to past tense, add on *sometimes*, and so on. Only one or two of the following suggestions may be applicable to any one client.

Use the past tense of the verb in the problem description.

___ was   ___ were   ___ have/had   ___ been

- *When you were* bingeing and purging.

- You *have been* fighting a lot.

Use verbs like *show, become, seem,* and *act as if* (Walter & Peller, 1992).

___ show   ___ become   ___ seem   ___ act as if

- You *seem* sad.

- So you act *as if* you are manic.

Attach the word *sometimes* to the problem description.

___ sometimes

- You say mean things *sometimes*.

- You think about killing your parents *sometimes*.

When speaking of the purpose, could you use *when*?

___ when

• *When* you are having more positive thoughts ...

• *When* you are getting along better ...

Do the words *yet* or *not yet* fit into the description?

___ yet   ___ not yet

• You are not *yet* controlling your temper.

• You aren't staying out of trouble *yet*.

New Problem Description

_____

_____

_____

Normalizing

"Those who have no problems are not living life."
—*Willyn Webb*

All of us—therapists and clients, normal and nonnormal—have problems sometimes. However, most clients feel isolated, singled out, victimized, or mistreated. Many feel as if they are the only ones who have ever experienced a certain event, felt a certain way, or had a family or situation like theirs. That feeling of, "I am the only one who has ever had it this bad" is not typically conducive to change. It can be motivating if efforts are made at correcting a situation, but this type of thinking usually leads more directly to feeling sick, incurable, and hopeless. This is an area where change can begin.

When clients can see their problems as normal, common, and curable, the problems actually are more likely to become so. When clients feel that others, including even their therapist, have dealt with their particular problems successfully, they find comfort and hope, which are much more motivating. Problems become acceptable, even *okay,* when everyone else has them, too. Peer pressure is an undoubtable factor in everyone's life, not just for children and teenagers but in offices, families, and country clubs, as well. Peer pressure has a negative connotation, although it is potentially positive—as in normalizing.

The first step in making a problem seem more normal, common, and surmountable is using the right words to describe it. You may call it a problem, concern, difficulty, reason, purpose, or obstacle. Look through this list of words; some have more serious connotations than others. Note that I haven't even included the pathological labels from the *DMS-IV* or lay terms clients often use in therapy (e.g., crazy, insane, sick). As therapists, we must be careful not to prematurely refer to our clients' reasons for therapy as *problems*; clients may not see them as that bad. Using a word like *concern* or *difficulty* does not take away from empathizing. Whenever possible, try to normalize with common, less serious, less final words.

Another useful skill in normalizing is *responding*. We probably all have practiced responding with empathy and care: For example, "That's tough," "That must be painful," or "How hard that must be." However, there comes a time when these responses do nothing more than perpetuate problems, self-pity, and excuses. At that time, responses like, "That's understandable," "That sounds typical," "Of course," "I've heard that before," or "That's more common than you think" may help clients feel less burdened and more hopeful, not only because they are not the only ones with the problem, but also because you have experience in dealing with it as a therapist.

Think for a moment how comforting it is when a medical doctor tell you, "It's just the common cold," "Sounds like the virus that's going around," "I'm a specialist," or "I've successfully treated several cases like yours." These statements normalize an illness and promote confidence in the patient. We can do the same thing for our clients. The teaming approach lends itself to the therapist sharing similar difficulties and how they were overcome or are being worked on. Many programs and support groups (such as Alcoholics Anonymous, Weight Watchers, women's shelters, and hotlines) build on the idea that the leader has experienced similar circumstances. A normalizing, not a preaching manner is important to the team approach of solutioning. Just sharing that you have experienced similar situations, experiences, or thoughts and feelings may bring a sense of normalcy and health to perceptions of problems.

The Freshman: The Case of Linda and Her Daughter

Linda called me about getting her 14-year-old daughter into counseling. Linda described many typical adolescent behaviors: limit testing, experimenting with clothing styles, questioning the family chore divisions, and so on. She had concluded that her daughter was headed for a worst-case scenario (rebellion, pregnancy, maybe even jail). She was nearly hopeless and said she was a failure as a parent. Linda was sure her daughter's behavior indicated hatred for her.

I told Linda that I worked primarily with young people this age, and that testing limits, questioning chores, and trying some trendy styles are common behaviors, especially for freshmen. The time when kids enter high school and try to grow up fast is typically a stressful one for families, but most live through it and come out okay.

Linda said, "Really? You mean these things are normal for some freshmen? Other families you know go through this?"

I replied that many kids go through this stage. The mother's relief was amazing: "If this is a stage, then she probably doesn't hate me. You know, I think she does love me. And if this is a stage, then she's not going crazy or anything. We can handle this, we've been through stages before."

I said I was sure they could handle it, and that I would be glad to help them in any way I could. The daughter came in a couple times alone and a few more times with her mother. We negotiated some workable limits, boundaries, and chores while we worked on improving their communication. As far as I know, the daughter hasn't ended up in prison or pregnant yet (which is where Linda thought she must surely be headed). The healing process for that family began with normalizing the problem.

Practice 2.6 summarizes the language tools that are available to use in normalizing a problem. These tools may be used at any point during the therapy process, but I find they are most effective when you have developed a close, teaming relationship with the client.

PRACTICE 2.6

Normalizing

Instead of *problem*:

- concern
- difficulty
- reason
- purpose
- obstacle

Instead of *patient*:

- client
- individual
- young man
- young woman

Therapist responses that are normalizing:

- Of course
- Naturally
- Sure
- Understandably

- Like most (children, adolescents, adults, wives, husbands, bosses, etc.)

- That sounds typical of ... (adolescence, middle age, carpenters, businessmen, nurses, whatever).

- "'Well, that's pretty understandable' and then putting the situation they might have presented as psychological or pathological in an everyday frame of reference." (O'Hanlon & Weiner-Davis, 1989, p. 94)

Relate your own experience of the problem:

- Oh, I remember that ...

- Been there, done that.

- Just like you, I have felt/thought ... at times.

- Not unlike you, I have ...

- Me too

Relate experiences from your interactions with others:

- I know what you're going to say ...

- Like many people ...

- Like many situations ...

- Many of my clients find that ... or have experienced ...

- "Don't tell me—the more you try to get it out of your mind, the harder it gets not to think about it" (O'Hanlon & Weiner-Davis, 1989, p. 96).

Add your own here:_____

_____

_____

_____

_____

Scaling

When discussing problems, it is helpful to find out just how serious clients view them with a scale. The scale is a tool from SFBT (Lipchik & de Shazer, 1988) that can be used throughout the 4-P process. It involves asking one question: "With 10 being the best things could be, and 1 being the absolute worst they could be, where are things (the externalized problem) right now?"

The problem is really out there, complete with a number representation. You can determine a number showing where the client wants to be (next week, at the end of therapy, whenever) and discuss the details of what that would look like (see chapter 4). This moves right out of the problem—which is, for example, at 4—to the solution, which is maybe at 8. The discussion becomes centered on what 8 would be. Additionally, you establish a means for monitoring progress.

Various scales can be used, with language that fits the situation. At 1, the problem is in total control, and at 10 *you* are in total control of the problem (Lipchik & de Shazer, 1988). The scale aids in specific descriptions, which lead directly into purpose statements. Scales help clients get out of the past and into the future while putting the team on the same page, ready to construct solutions. Because different clients have different learning styles, you may want to construct your scale visually or verbally. The scale can be used with any age group and can be shown on paper, on fingers, spoken, or otherwise.

PRACTICE 2.7

Scaling

- On a scale of 1 to 10, with 10 being the best things could be, and 1 being the worst they could be, where are things right now? Where do you want them to be next week? At the end of therapy? What will that look like?

1	2	3	4	5	6	7	8	9	10

Worst   Best

- On a scale of 1 to 10, with 1 being no effect and 10 being total saturation, how much of an effect is (the externalized problem) having on your life right now? How do you want things to be? What number would that be? What would it take to move up 1 or 2 places? Where could you be by next week? How?

1	2	3	4	5	6	7	8	9	10

No effect   Saturation

Now, put all your reconstruction tools together with the Purpose Checklist in Practice 2.8. Begin change immediately while establishing an achievable purpose.

> [T]he specific words the therapist uses to talk to the client significantly shape not only the definition of the desired change, but also how the client views it, which is an initial step toward creating that change. (Friedman & Fanger, 1991, p. 9)

PRACTICE 2.8

Purpose Checklist

Teaming

Are you and your client teammates?

____ 1. Show mutual respect, acknowledging individual strengths, talents, and abilities

____ 2. Have different but collaborative positions

____ 3. Work together

Externalizing

____ 4. Does the problem have an identification (a name, traits)?

____ 5. Has the power been shifted from the problem to the person?

____ 6. Have you considered the consequences of maintaining or solving the problem?

Reconstructing

___   7.   Are you using descriptions rather than labels?

___   8.   Are you using the past tense of verbs?

___   9.   Have you tried using *sometimes, yet,* and *when*?

___   10.   What are some normalizing responses you could use?

Scaling

___   11.   Would a scale be helpful?

PURPOSE: IN SUMMARY

Most clients come to therapy because of problems. Many have a goal in mind, but do not have the self-confidence to even express it, can't express it for fear of failure, or won't express it for fear of actually acknowledging how far away they are from it. The first step of the 4-P solutioning process is flexible and sensitive to the readiness of clients and the various processes, talents, and models of treatment used by therapists. You can use the tools of teaming, externalizing, and reconstructing for a clear purpose with a single statement or question, or work on them for entire sessions. Typically, once a solutioning conversation is begun, the rest just follows logically and very few questions are required.

For now, you can get started with an intake such as the one in Practice 2.9. No matter when you choose to incorporate these ideas in forming a purpose, the discussion should propel you right into the potentials, the heart of solutioning, in the next chapter.

"A problem well stated is a problem half solved."
—*Charles F. Kettering (Peter, 1977, p. 408)*

PRACTICE 2.9

Ready, Set, Go!

Client name:_____ Beginning date:_____

Parents' names (if under 15): _____

Address:_____

City:_____ State:_____ Zip code:_____

Birthdate:_____ Phone:_____

Please describe your purpose for coming today._____

_____

_____

_____

If you were to give what you have just described a name, what would it be?_____

What characteristics does it have?_____

_____

_____

_____

What influence do you have over it?_____

_____

_____

_____

Describe what will be different when you no longer need to come here._____

_____

_____

_____

_____

With 10 being the best things could be, and 1 being the worst they could be, where are things right now? Where do you want them to be next week? At the end of therapy?

1	2	3	4	5	6	7	8	9	10

Worst   Best

What are your greatest skills, abilities, and talents? Which of these will help you with solutions?_____

_____

_____

_____

_____

Is there anything else you want to share?_____

_____

_____

_____

_____

Chapter 3

Getting There Is Half the Fun: The Second P—Potentials

The potentials are solution options you codiscover with clients. You begin with skills and abilities the client already has and proceed, if necessary, to skills and abilities that are desired, visualized, or borrowed. The solutioning map shows the potentials as the center of the process, one step many traditional counseling approaches do not use (see Figure 3.1). Virtually all methods discuss problems and purposes, most use plans or tasks, and all follow up in some way—but only the solution-focused and brief therapies have attempted to access nonproblem times. "Because all of us are bombarded by so many stimuli all of the time, the mind usually becomes trained to focus on certain aspects of our environments while ignoring or limiting that which is consciously attended to" (Budman & Gurman, 1988, p. 51).

POTENTIAL QUESTIONS

Most therapies will benefit by considering the exceptional, problem-free, or low-problem times. Because the tools for explor-

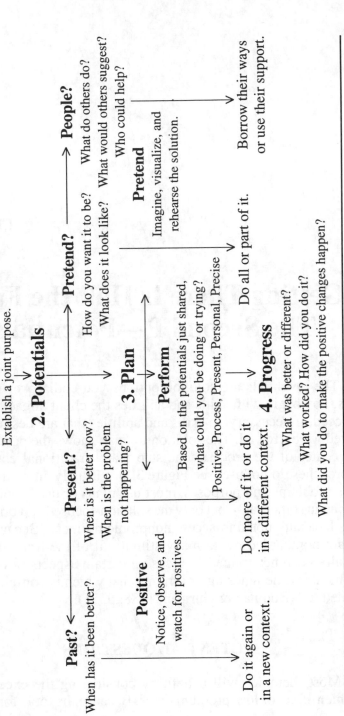

Figure 3.1. The Solutioning Map

ing the potentials are likely more foreign to your counseling vocabulary than any other step of solutioning, let me again stress their blendability. You will positively affect clients just by asking a few potential questions here and there, regardless of whether you are using the entire 4-P process. "Engaging [clients] regarding their strengths and the healthier sides of their personalities may be *the* most useful strategy for rapidly establishing a collaborative context" (Budman & Gurman, 1988, p. 54).

Not only do the potential questions enhance relationships, they actually start a change in the thinking process. This change may be the only one needed, it may have a ripple effect, or it may broaden a client's perspective toward solutions. In other words, the potential questions constitute an intervention in their own right and can create the most motivating interactions you have ever had with clients.

Prior to using the potential questions, however, you must establish a caring, trusting, empathetic relationship. Clients may feel unheard or pushed if you use the nonproblem questions too soon. That is why your awareness of timing is so important; the potential questions are so helpful in moving clients toward solutions, toward a more hopeful perspective, toward faith in themselves, that you might be tempted to use them right away.

In order to assess and acknowledge a client's readiness to move beyond the problem and into the exceptional times, you can simply say something like, "Now that we have fully discussed the problem, let's talk about times without the problem—times when it is less present or when things are different. These times may give us great ideas that we can use for solutions."

You may get a variety of responses, ranging from "Yeah, let's move on," to "No I really need to let some more stuff out," or "What do you mean?" Clients' needs for expression, understanding, and empathy vary. Some want to jump immediately into solutions and have little need to discuss the problem, others require more sharing, and still others want insight and answers as to why the problem exists.

O'Hanlon and Weiner-Davis asked this question of clients who need to understand *why*: "'Would it be enough if the problem were to disappear and you never understood why you had it?' Generally, clients agree that alleviation of the complaint is what they are really after" (1989, p. 41). If this is the response, you have a green light to begin exploring exceptions and potential solutions. However, some clients will hold on to their need for understanding the causes of the problem. In this case, you should address that need before returning to solutioning.

But, Why? The Case of Lisa and Alice

Lisa, a 17-year-old, had run away seven times in six months. The following excerpt is from a session with Lisa, her mother, Alice, and a caseworker from social services.

Alice: I can't understand why she runs away. She says she doesn't even know why she does it. *(To Lisa)* Why do you leave? Are things that bad at home?

Lisa: I don't know. Things are okay at home. I just go.

Willyn: Would it be enough if Lisa never runs away again, without your ever understanding why she did in the past?

Alice: No, I want to know why she did it. I am frustrated that she won't tell me or doesn't seem to know. Even if she does it again, I just want to know why.

From that point on we worked primarily in the past, looking for the causes of Lisa's behavior. None of the causes illustrated potential solutions, but the search seemed to facilitate Alice's willingness to work on the present. Our relationship was enhanced by spending time on areas Alice felt were important. Once that was accomplished, we could move on together as a team.

Clients become ready for solutioning at different points in their therapy. The advantages of solutioning are so great that there is a real risk you will be tempted to push it on clients before they are ready. Part of being on the same team, however, is developing together, which the questions in Practice 3.1 will allow you to do. They will ensure that you and your clients are on the same page, so that the process of exploring for potentials can be used to its full ability.

PRACTICE 3.1

Are You Ready?

- Do you feel ready to move on to an exploration of potential solutions by looking at times before or without the problem?

- My sense is that we have discussed the problem times enough and are now ready to talk about times *without* the problem.

- It seems that you have shared enough of the problem times for now. Let's talk about the *nonproblem* times.

- Is there a reason we should consider the causes of the problem, or are you ready to work on possible solutions?

- Now that we know each other, and have shared and built a relationship, let's move on to discuss the better times in your life, the way you want things to be, and find solutions.

- Do you feel I understand your problem enough to start talking about potential solutions?

- Because you have coped with this problem, I know there are many skills and abilities you can use for solutions. Let's talk about those.

A MINDSET FOR SOLUTIONS

"Allow for possibilities!"
—*Bumper sticker*

Accentuating the problem-free, nonproblem, and low-problem times shows clients they are capable of feeling happy, of having moments of success, and of behaving positively. This builds self-esteem and hope, necessary ingredients of any successful solution. Whether or not any specific solutions are discovered, the exploration is an intervention itself. Most clients can recall some instances of success and are eager to share them. This sets a hopeful tone and leads into solutions and plans.

For example, we can all think of clients whose troubled marriages have pleasurable moments (or at least pleasant memories and happy desires), depressed clients who are energetic or feel happy at times, or rebellious adolescents who follow the rules occasionally. SFBT therapists refer to these times as *exceptions*. Examining them sets a tone conducive to change, leads to potential solutions, and motivates clients to form achievable plans.

> [T]he exceptions to the problem offer a tremendous amount of information about what is needed to solve the problem. Solutions can be unearthed by examining the differences between times when the problem has occurred and times when it has not. (O'Hanlon & Weiner-Davis, 1989, p. 82)

Traveling across the solutioning map (see Figure 3.1) and asking the potential questions facilitates the process of finding and examining solution ideas. Be forewarned, however: Clients sometimes are taken aback when they are asked about times other than the problem times. Most clients find the reminiscent quality refreshing and are eager to share. But some are so immersed in their problems that they have a hard time coming up with any exceptions. Through persistence in questioning and assumptive language, you show faith; and you'll see clients brighten with the realization that their problems, negative behaviors, and poor skills are not there 100% of the time.

Through the visualization of a desired future, clients see some light at the end of the tunnel. Solutioning enables therapists and clients to consider times when the problem is less intense, different, or coped with, and then go on to visualizing times when the problem is solved and to borrowing ideas or help from others. Through the four avenues of *past*, *present*, *pretend*, and *people*, potential solution options are bound to emerge.

HUNTING FOR LOST TREASURE: PAST POTENTIAL

The questions of solutioning will help clients remember times when things were better or different, when they were successful in the past, which illuminates something that could be tried as a solution in the present. If nothing else is accomplished by exploring positive aspects of the past, at least clients can remove themselves temporarily from their current situations and think of happier times—which can hold clues to current solutions. Thinking of times before or without the problem is much more productive than blaming, finding excuses, or wallowing in self-pity. As Metcalf (1995, p. 9) noted, "Most of all, it changes our focus from one of problem saturation to that of a time when problems seemed less dominant."

For clients stuck in a victim stance, complaining mode, or learned helplessness, you may have to be fairly persistent in your search for exceptions. These clients tend to cling to what is comfortable and "normal." They may be afraid of losing their need for attention, their need for help, and maybe even their need for you. Being aware and open during these times will facilitate solutioning or any direction you choose to take.

Asking for the same thing in a variety of different ways is a valuable skill, because a certain wording may help a client access a potential from the past. When nothing comes up with one question, try asking it a different way, allowing the memory time to work, and reminiscing a bit. Solution ideas will come. Through careful language, give the message that you are sure the client has had great times in life, has overcome the problem before, and is good at coping. Once you have a positive, encourage the client to elaborate on it and get as many details as possible, for these are your solution potentials.

Remember, you are hunting for lost treasure from the past, and you need as many clues as possible in your search. Use the questions in Practice 3.2 to get you started in your treasure hunt. From there, be creative and the past may illuminate a positive future for your clients.

PRACTICE 3.2

Past Potential

- Tell me about times when … (you control your anger, you get along, you feel happy, you sleep well, etc.).

- What is different about those times?

- When have you been able to talk to your (husband, wife, boss, etc.) in a calm way? How did you do it? How would he or she say you did it?

- In the past when you have (positive description), what were you *doing* differently? What were you thinking, saying, or feeling differently?

- When was the last time you were happy, successful, and comfortable? What were you doing then that was different/better/worked? How?

- How have you overcome or controlled the problem before? What did you do that was different/better?

- How have you (avoided problems, eaten right, made friends) in the past?

- What has worked before?

- What are some of the things you do that help when (you are bored, depressed, confused, mad)?

- You've coped/lived with this problem this long. How have you done it?

- (School, family, work, anger, anorexia, abuse) has been in your life for ___ years now, and you've survived! How?

- Tell me about times when things were better, more of what you want.

- How did you get (the fight to stop, the kids off your back, to sleep all night, etc.)?

- Have you had this problem in the past? How did you deal with it, fix it, or resolve it then? What would you need to do to get that to happen again?

Past Perspective

> "Life is a series of experiences, each one of
> which makes us bigger, even though sometimes
> it is hard to realize this."
> —*Henry Ford (Peter, 1977, p. 185)*

We probably have all known clients whose entire lives have been spent moving passively from one crisis to the next. Exploring those times in-between crises will initially feel awkward for them. They may need a change in perception, which can expand their views, making room for solutions. Some clients are so into excuses, problems, and blaming it's like they have blinders on, covering anything positive or useful in their lives. And, unfortunately, there are many whose pasts are so full of abuse, humiliation, and pain that it is no wonder the present is dysfunctional. Solution thinking can be just the change these clients need. Using the past as a resource instead of an excuse is a valuable endeavor. Just as the term *survivor* has replaced *victim*, *resource* can replace *excuse*.

Solution Application: Sexual Abuse

"Sooner or later I have to give up
my hope of a better past."

—Unknown

The past—even the abuse, the pain, and the horror—can be a resource if we allow it. There are no stronger people than those who have lived through extreme pain. In *Reach for the Rainbow,* Lynne Finney wrote, "if I could function this well given what I had been through, I must have a lot of strengths" (1992, 80). Learning to view the past as a strength-building event, an ability-producing occurrence, and a time of good and bad is a step toward overcoming it. "There had to have been some time in my life when I was happy. All of a sudden it occurred to me that if I could take my mind back to painful events, why couldn't I go back to happy times?" (Finney, 1992, p. 70). Searching the past for happy, normal, better times aids in perspective. As Dolan pointed out, "Even during times of intense trauma, there can be moments of comfort and peace" (1991, p. xv).

This is not to say that solutioning replaces recovering memories, releasing feelings, or other healing interventions. It simply supplements other interventions with a hopeful perspective. As Johnston noted, "Over the last decade, the dramatic increase in recognition of the incidence of sexual abuse has resulted in substantial efforts by the mental health profession to develop appropriate services for victimized children and adult survivors" (1997, p. 101). Our job is to help survivors find the abilities, strengths, and talents it took to get to where they are today, and then access and use those to make the future what they want it to be.

"People are strong because they've come to
strength through trials and obstacles."

—Willyn Webb

Regardless of the problem, a timeline is often useful in discovering positive times, which may be accessed for solution ideas.

Practice 3.3 illustrates the use of a timeline in conjunction with the questions for finding potential from the past.

"Happiness is the interval between
periods of unhappiness."
—Don Marquis (Peter, 1977, p. 237)

PRACTICE 3.3

Past Perspective, Future Possibilities

Adapt the timeline to fit the life of your client, with more detail in some areas than others. This tool will follow through to the present and pretend potential questions. Put your plan on it, and use it to monitor progress.

For example:

- Let's put the major events in your life, positive and negative, down on a timeline so we will see the areas to explore for solutions. What was the best time in your life? Let's add in how you want things to be from now on.

Birth	Childhood	Adolescence	College	Now	Future

- It sounds like you've had some ups and downs. Let's get them down where we can take a close look at the better times and talk about where you want to go.

School	Now	Where you want to be now	Where you want to go

- Show me all of the good times and where they fit in with the problems we have been talking about.

Good times	Problem	Good times	Good times	Problem	Now

Follow through with:

- When things were better, what were you doing, saying, or thinking that was different? What can you do again?

- What are you currently doing that is working? What can you do more of?

- How do you want things to be? What will you be doing differently when you are on track to your visualized future?

- Let's make a timeline for next week and include all the solution ideas you are going to use.

Tomorrow A.M.	noon	after work	P.M.

The next day A.M.	noon	after work	P.M.

The next day A.M.	noon	after work	P.M.

The next day A.M.	noon	after work	P.M.

Add your own here: _____

_____

_____

_____

_____

_____

_____

STRIKE WHILE THE IRON IS HOT:
PRESENT POTENTIAL

"Experience is not what happens to a man; it is
what a man does with what happens to him."
—*Aldous Huxley, (Webster, 1992, p. 91)*

Finding and building on potentials for solutions that are *already happening in clients' lives* is probably the most motivating of all solution-finding methods. In fact, you may want to explore a client's present potentials before you do anything else. If a potential solution is something a client is already doing a little bit, he or she is likely to be able to do it again or do it more. Rather than bringing something back from the past, it is easier to do what is happening now even more. Most clients live in the moment, their reality is now, so using the potentials of the present to build solutions just makes sense. Especially with clients who blame or want to use their past for excuses, it is sometimes better to avoid it altogether, thus breaking a pattern of living in the past.

As you get to know other areas of clients' lives, additional potentials will surface. Many ideas come from places or situations where the problem doesn't intrude.

> [T]he therapist supports and builds on the client's current
> strengths, assets, and resources and is future-oriented, and
> assumes that the client's present situation contains within it
> the necessary resources to generate an effective solution.
> (Friedman & Fanger, 1991, pp. 44-45)

Practice 3.4 will serve as a starter sheet for searching the present for potential. As you begin thinking about solutions, potentials, and exceptions, the questions will flow. Remember to get as many details as possible, as these can lead to the formation of an achievable plan. The idea is to help your clients realize their own abilities for achieving success. You may want to practice these with a partner, because they are different from the counseling vocabulary used in most training programs.

PRACTICE 3.4

Present Potential

- How does your day go differently when (the exception happens/the problem doesn't)?

- When during the day is the problem better? What are you doing or thinking differently then?

- When are you already doing some of (your homework, being on time, walking away from fights, any goal or problem opposite)?

- When isn't this problem happening? What is different?

- What is going right in your life right now?

- When are you enjoying (school/work/family)?

- What do you like about each day?

- When are you least stressed, angry, scared, upset?

- What is your favorite time of day? Why?

USE YOUR IMAGINATION:
PRETEND POTENTIAL

This is my favorite area of exploration. Pretending a life without the problem, visualizing different behaviors, and imagining can ensure solutions. The pretend potential goes one step beyond setting treatment goals, to actually walking through a desired state of being, searching for behaviors, thoughts, and feelings that could be tried in the present. Pretending gives a vision, a needed future, and an escape from the problem, and eliminates the need for excuses—all of which motivates and empowers clients in realizing solutions.

Athletes have used visualization for years to make their desired performance a reality. Why not use it with clients to help make their desired solution a reality? Its positive direction is not only motivating but also inspiring for clients.

> By deliberately asking a long series of questions about the future, the therapist can trigger family members to create more of a future for themselves. (Tomm, 1987, p. 173)

Leading clients to a mental state in which they live *with* a future is a worthwhile intervention, regardless of the problem. By simply asking the questions you may instigate a solution-focused thinking process—a process clients might continue with after session and after therapy.

Additionally, by pretending a solution, clients get to remove themselves from the constraints of the problem for a moment and experience how it feels to be problem-free. This feeling itself can motivate them to begin taking steps toward a solution. By describing what life looks like and what they are doing differently when the problem is solved, they may begin to see what is necessary to achieve a solution. As Walter and Peller noted:

> [I]t enables clients to free themselves from the confines of how they have defined the problem. The confines of the problem definition very often allow for only a limited number of options for solutions ... Introducing a conversation around a life without the problem allows people to enter the realm of possibility. (Walter & Peller, 1992, pp. 76 &77)

By discussing the desired, positive future, you make obsolete the blaming, excuses, and causes. When you are talking about a pretend situation and what can be done to achieve it, the past has no room in the conversation. With one small question, forward motion begins: "How do you want it to be?"

The way you introduce pretend potentials is critical to the success of the process. *You must emphasize the positive, the personal, and the process involved,* or the discussion quickly becomes just another brainstorming session. The difficulty with brainstorming solutions is that most clients already are doing the best they can and have tried their ideas before—without success. But imagining a time without the problem—describing in detail what they are doing, thinking, and feeling *differently*—is within all clients' capabilities. By pretending, you give your clients permission to dream a little. And within this freedom, clues to real solutions can be found.

The pioneers in SFBT at the Brief Family Therapy Center in Milwaukee used the "miracle question" to help in this pretending:

> Suppose that one night, while you were asleep, there was a miracle and this problem was solved. How would you know? What would be different? How will your husband know without your saying a word to him about it? (de Shazer, 1988, p. 5)

In order for this to be effective—and not seem silly or embarrassing—*the question must fit with the client.* A simplified version of the miracle question that is especially effective with adolescents (who know *everything* and want *total* control, after all) is this:

- How do you want things to be?

Followed by:

- What does it look like? Tell me what you are doing and thinking differently when you go to school (wake up, etc.) tomorrow and this is happening (you get along, feel happy, etc.).

Describing what it looks like is the hard part for most clients, but it is the part that gives them the keys to solutions, things they can begin trying immediately. Sometimes it is helpful to feed a client a little on the "what does it look like?" response, especially if it seems there is a picture in mind, but it cannot be described behaviorally. In this case, you might ask about details:

- First thing tomorrow, when you walk in the door, what will you be doing differently than today? Will you say "hi" to her? How did you make that happen? Will you discuss the kids?

Or, in another scenario:

- Do you have your lunch? What are you doing with it? What does your boss say? What do you do next?

By asking for the details of the process, you get answers like, "I'll just smile at her when I walk in." Or, " I'll eat my lunch slowly and keep it down." These are small-step behaviors that clients can try tomorrow and be on the solution road. Most often these are skills they already have, but are not using. If you can get clients to describe behaviors, the likelihood that they will use them increases tremendously.

Walter and Peller (1992) discussed the importance of getting a process-oriented answer, not just the conclusion (solution). Many clients will tell you they want to graduate from high school, have a wonderful marriage, be happy, and so on, but they don't have a clue about how to get there. If you word your questions in ways that emphasize the "How are you going to get there?" aspects, your clients will have to consider ways to reach the desired state. This is an excellent place to use the strategies of teamwork. Sharing a pretend vision, then finding ways to get there together can be a real bonding experience. Walter and Peller suggested a version of the miracle question that stressed the process:

> If a miracle happened tonight and you woke up with the problem solved, or you were reasonably confident you were on track to solving it, what would you be doing differently? (Walter & Peller, 1992, p. 78)

This question allows the individual to pretend *doing the solution*, which is very different than pretending *not doing the problem*. It gives the client something to try. Using words like *miracle*, *pretend*, or *imagine* reduces the risk for clients, who often feel pressured during the typical brainstorming session to come up with the *right* answer (i.e., the one the therapist wants to hear). Taking away the constraints of reality may allow some useful ideas to emerge. With young children, you might try using a magic wand, a laser beam, or a remote control to take away the problem, and then ask them to describe what is different. By using words like *on track*, *on the road to*, *on your way*, or *in the groove*, you encourage an answer that will describe at least some of the *solution process*. Use whatever words fit the client and encourage a process. By using *doing* verbs, actions, thoughts, behaviors, and "the meanings they will be making" are included (Walter & Peller, 1992, p. 78).

Practice 3.5 describes a language to get clients involved in visualizing solutions. Some phrases are adapted from the work of SFBT therapists; others have been adapted to meet the needs of various clients. Pick a current client who seems stuck—one who is not making a lot of progress and is out of ideas—and propel him or her into the future by pretending.

PRACTICE 3.5

Pretend Potential

- How do you want things to be?

- Describe your vision of the solution.

- Tell me the first thing you do on a day without the problem.

- Pretend everything is the way you want it. Now describe what you are doing, thinking, feeling, and saying.

- Imagine yourself doing the solution. Describe what you are doing.

- When you are on the road to fixing the problem, what are you doing?

- So, let's say tomorrow you wake up, and you have not yet finished your homework, but you are thinking you are on track to getting it done, what are you doing differently? (adapted from Walter & Peller, 1992)

- "When the problem is fixed, if I were a fly on the wall and watching you, what would I see you doing differently? What would I see that would tell me you are feeling differently? How would *someone* in your family *know*?" (Walter & Peller, 1992, p. 79)

- If we had a magic wand and it made (boredom, anger, confusion, not caring) disappear, what would you be doing differently?

- Let's pretend the problem is fixed and you are (getting along with your husband, paying your bills on time, understanding depression, etc.). What are you doing? What does that look like?

- I want to visualize the solution with you. Can you describe what you are doing and how so I can see it in my mind?

- What would you like to see happen this week? What could you do to work toward that? How could you make it happen?

USING IT FOR ALL IT'S WORTH

After you have introduced the pretend process, you can discuss is on a feeling level, give it a reality check, and connect it to the present. This makes it more plausible for clients, helps decrease their fears, and motivates them toward the desired state. By asking clients about how each step of their pretend solution feels, you can walk them through the next day or week, experiencing potential roadblocks, considering difficult or scary spots, and finding the wonderful feeling of accomplishment at the end. In this sharing you can *be there* with them, understanding how difficult or wonderful the solution may be. Also, the mental rehearsal increases the chances for success.

Don't let feelings serve your purpose. When clients share that they will be happy, for example, respond with: "Tell me about being happy like it is a movie. What are you doing in your happy movie?" or "What are you doing differently when you are happy?" These questions illustrate little keys of behaviors, thoughts, or actions clients can try as potential solutions.

Of course, reality must also be injected. Questions like, "Which part of this could happen this week? Which parts may take a while? Which parts may never happen?" help the client glean the useful aspects of the pretend solution and leave the others. The pretend solution is only useful when it is incorporated into daily life. When reality is addressed in a process manner, it does not take away the motivation of the imagination, but puts it in perspective and in a time frame. Few clients can begin acting out their movie tomorrow, but most can begin a part of it, a thought from it, or a small behavior immediately.

The most difficult part for clients to imagine is how others might react. Often clients will want to *change others first* as a condition of their desired solutions. In this case, you might remind them, "We can't automatically control or change others, only ourselves." When they are describing the other kids not teasing them, their wives waking them up with breakfast in bed, their bosses admiring their work, you must stress the word *you* in your questioning. This is an intervention of empowerment. Gently forcing clients through questioning helps them create movies of their future in which *they control their fate.* During their movies, you sometimes have to pause them and re-ask the questions: "What are *you* doing? How can *you* make it that way? What would so and so say *you* could do to make it that way?"

A great connecting question to use with a well-pretended solution is, "When is this happening, even a little or some of the time, now?" Or, "What parts of this can you already do?" These questions allow you to build on skills clients already have in the current reality, putting part of the pretend potential in their hands before they leave your office. By connecting their pretend potential to their real potential, they gain confidence in their ability to achieve the imagined solution.

Practice 3.6 sums up the language used in pretend potential. Follow-through is as important as the movie that is created. When you begin using the pretend potential, you can use these practices as cheat sheets. Don't let any good ideas slip away because they seem too dreamy. Help clients put them in their current lives and make things better.

PRACTICE 3.6

Use It for All It's Worth

Feelings

- How does it feel when you imagine this solution? Which part is the most exciting? Which is the scariest? Which is most likely to happen tomorrow?

- When you finish telling me your movie of the solution, what feelings are you having?

- How do you feel about starting some of this tomorrow?

Actions

- What is happening in your happy movie? What are you doing, saying, or thinking?

- I'm not getting it. What are you doing first, second, next?

- What does successful look like, what are you *doing* differently?

- What would others say you are doing differently when you are (getting along, not depressed, etc.)?

Reality Check

- Which parts of this vision could happen this week? Which will take a while? Which are a bit unrealistic?

- Within reality, what can you use from this imagined solution to make things better for you now?

- Are some parts of this vision wishes? What could you do to start making your wishes come true?

You

- We can't automatically control or change others, only ourselves. What can *you* do to encourage this to happen?

- What are *you* doing when you are (getting along, not feeling mistreated, etc.)?

- How can *you* make it that way?

- What would so and so say *you* could do to make it that way?

- Rather than giving someone else all the power and control to make this successful solution happen, what could *you* do?

- Instead of changing others, what could *you* do as a solution?

Connecting

- When is this pretend solution happening, even a little bit, now?

- What parts of this can you already do or have you done in the past?

- What skills, talents, and abilities are you using in your pretend solution?

- Is there an idea from this you could try immediately?

The Dream Team

When a trusting, caring relationship exists between therapist and client and a solutioning process is ongoing, therapist input and sharing does not diminish the client's responsibilities. After clients have had full opportunity to share their pretend potentials, why not share your vision of what they are doing when the problem no longer exists? This is different from giving advice, lecturing, or teaching. It is in-the-moment sharing. You simply ask the clients if they would like to hear your pretend solution. The answer is almost always yes. Then you have the opportunity to feed the solution process, suggest, and enlighten a little, without incurring any additional responsibility.

The end of a successful solution may be the same, but the means make all the difference. It is a sharing, a dreaming together of how things could be—and from that process, you probably will find new ideas to try. Pretending within reality is an important skill you can model, as many clients seem a little confused with the difference between wishing and pretending.

I Wish . . . The Case of Hillari and Brian

Hillari and Brian, a young married couple, were talking about how they wanted their life to be, what kind of home they wanted to provide for their 1-year-old and baby on the way, and how they might get off welfare.

Hillari: I just wish it was easy and we didn't have to work.

Willyn: Let's dream, set goals, and visualize, not wish. Could I pretend a little about what a real future might look like? *(Hillari and Brian nodded eagerly.)*

I see Brian as a diesel mechanic and Hillari as a secretary. They are able to pay their bills and buy Christmas presents for the kids. If you were on your way toward making this movie happen, what would you be doing? Remember, we have to stay within reality.

Hillari: Oh, okay … well, maybe we could take some classes at the vo-tech while Brian is laid off this winter. I think we could get it paid for with a grant or something.

Setting up a winning dream team is a skill that can be perfected through practice. Having a relationship and a feel for your clients is your best assist.

Skill Highlight: Forming a Dream Team

Get a partner to play the role of a client. Practice setting up a dream team by giving your partner full opportunity to exhaust his pretend capabilities. Make sure he is pretending in reality rather than engaging in idle wishing. Ask permission to share your pretend movie of how the solution might go. Take the client through a successful, behavioral, motivating movie of a potential solution. When you are finished, ask which parts of the movie felt the best or seemed most likely to occur.

After the interaction, have your partner share the thoughts and feelings experienced while listening to your movie. Did your partner feel you were telling him or her what to do, giving advice, teaching, or sharing? Was your partner motivated?

Dream Team Checklist

____   Client has fully shared his or her pretend movie of the solution and is still in need of some solution ideas.

____   Client has accepted your invitation to share your pretend movie.

_____ The movie you are pretending has some elements that are within the client's current capabilities.

_____ You incorporate a debriefing of the movie that involves the client in ascertaining potential solution ideas.

BORROWING: PEOPLE POTENTIAL

"The essence of success is that it is never necessary to think of a new idea oneself. It is far better to wait until somebody else does it, and then to copy him in every detail, except his mistakes."
—*Abrey Menen (Peter, 1977, p. 455)*

Our final option to search for potential solutions is *people*. This is the last resort because we really want clients to find the abilities they need to solve their problems *within themselves*. However, clients are clients—people who need assistance. Some clients require more outside input. With solutioning, you can help these clients and still give them control and responsibility. The people potential is a two-fold process that will teach clients a skill for future use and help them find ideas for solutions in the present.

- First, you help the client explore how others have solved similar problems and borrow from their success.

- Second, you consider together how others might be used for support and encouragement as part of the solution being developed.

Many clients come from situations in which positive modeling and helpful human resources are scarce. Yet, how often do you hear about how well some ancestor, friend, or coworker handles problems? How many children would like to be just like the most popular, cutest, smartest, coolest kid at school? Have you ever listened as a client talked about how his father managed even worse circumstances in the old days? How about a client who wished she could take care of things like the woman on the sitcom she watched the night before? Why not use these references and desires to help your clients draw on positive potential behaviors or ideas that might lead to solutions?

What Would She Do? The Case of Nancy

Nancy was a high school senior who was struggling with family issues. Her mother had died of breast cancer when Nancy was 2 and her father was in prison; her aunt and uncle had adopted her at age 4. Her biological brother and sister, both older, were not adopted.

Nancy struggled continually with her adopted mother. She was always considering who was family and who was not. When she was mad at someone, that person was no longer part of her family, so people were constantly in and out of her "family." During fights, she often said things about who was her *real* mom. None of the other members of Nancy's family were open to coming to therapy. Nancy was experiencing a lot of hurt and confusion.

One person Nancy always spoke of positively and with respect was her grandmother. During a session in which Nancy was working on ways to cope with her situation without becoming depressed or homicidal, I decided to try some *people potential*.

Willyn: You always talk about your grandmother with so much respect.

Nancy: Yeah, she is really a strong woman.

Willyn: She is the one person who always remains constant, even when everyone else in your family seems in turmoil, and it's her house that people seem to come back to.

Nancy: She holds everything together.

Willyn: How would Grandma handle your situation?

Nancy: *(thinking for a moment)* She would accept things the way they are and not feel sorry for herself because her mother died or her dad was in prison. She would make the best of things with the mother she was with now.

Willyn: That sounds impressive. How would she "make the best of things?"

Nancy: *(thinking longer)* I suppose she would follow the rules and help around the house. Then there wouldn't be so much fighting.

This sounded like a solution that Nancy could use to take some of the constant turmoil and daily arguments out of her life. I hoped it would bring her enough emotional relief to work on grieving for her mother, contacting her father, or doing whatever other healing she required.

Willyn: Grandma really does sound like a strong women who is not afraid to get along, but would be willing to do her part. You sound like her in many ways. You are caring, like you said she is. Family is important to you, like it is to her. I'm thinking you are probably as strong as she is, too. What do you think?

Nancy: *(nodding and smiling)* I could try to handle the situation like she would. It would make me feel better if there wasn't so much fighting.

We made a specific plan of how to "make the best of things" on a daily basis, then added some additional goals around her biological parents. Nancy's fights with her adoptive parents decreased significantly; without all the hostility, they were finally able to communicate about her needs for both sets of parents. Nancy's self-esteem grew with each Grandma-like action.

By stepping outside of herself and into the actions of someone she admired, Nancy was able to experiment with some new behaviors. Trying a little bit of what works for others is often a first step toward realizing one's own capabilities. Finding and using role models, peers, or even celebrities as resources for solution ideas can begin as soon as the intake. Notice the intake in Practice 3.9 and the questions designed to establish some people potential:

- What relative do you admire most and why?

- What friend do you admire most and why?

- Who is your hero?

- What qualities does your hero have that you admire?

The hero question is important because it allows clients to look outside their life situations and beyond the bounds of reality, opening up additional avenues. The qualities are what are important and lead to solution ideas. A discussion of what makes a hero may be helpful. Heroes do not have to be alive, real, or even human. When clients are having difficulty naming heroes, you may want to use a little pretend and allow them to create heroes, name them, and consider what ideas could be used from the descriptions for problem resolution.

Including positive people in the intake or initial interactions creates a valuable resource base. But these positive people are only as helpful as their application to the life and purpose of the client. An idle conversation about the positive attributes of someone is probably not productive. Using the language of solutioning lets you and your clients draw from others solution ideas and how they could be used, while giving the clients empowerment and responsibility. This is very different from taking the advice of others, dodging personal responsibility, or imitating.

Practice 3.7 summarizes some of the questions that will help clients access helpful models, consider their solutions, and determine what may be useful. This is an intervention in itself and can be used in conjunction with various theoretical models.

PRACTICE 3.7

People Potential

- How would (your friend, grandmother, etc.) solve this problem or handle this situation?

- What would your parents do?

- What would your positive person/hero do in this situation?

- How do others your age deal with this?

- What have you seen that works for the other students, couples, workers?

- Tell me how _____ keeps this from happening.

- Describe how _____ (does her work, overcomes depression, stays out of fights, etc.).

- What would I (or your minister, your teacher, your brother, etc.) say you could do or try to solve this problem?

- What would (your boss, your best friend, your hero, your positive person) suggest trying?

- When you see others having the life you want, what do you see them doing that is different from what you do? What of that could you try?

- What behaviors of a successful person could you borrow?

- What solutions do you see others using that seem to work? Could you try any of them?

- Are there any solution ideas you can get from watching others handle this problem?

The Assist: Using Resources and Support

No matter what you call it—finding and using resources, networking, getting help, seeking assistance, or support systems—using people potential is a crucial skill for school, career, and life success. Sometimes taking responsibility means asking for help. We must never forget, no matter how much we empower, that clients come to therapy for help.

The therapist may make up the bulk of a client's support system. If that is the case, you may need to help the client do some recruiting and team building. As Huber and Backlund pointed out, "it's more important to be out in the world than to be in counseling' (1996, p. 60). Likewise, a real world team or resources and support are important for solutions. The idea that it is okay and sometimes necessary to get help underlies this discussion. Knowing when and how to seek help will benefit most clients, especially in learning how to be proactive in preventing problems in the future.

You may have discussed helpful people, resources, and supports while you were exploring past, present, or pretend potentials. Expanding them here may ensure successful solutions. The questions of solutioning will empower your clients to take responsibility and to use assistance in achieving solutions. A word of caution, however: People resources have to be just that—*resources*. Sometimes you will have to remind clients of the difference between getting support from others, changing others, and depending on others. We do not want to set up a situation for blame later on. The assistance they want cannot be "mother getting nicer," "my husband returning," or a diet pill. People resources are like tutors—someone to share the plan with, a support group, hotline numbers, and so on.

Using resources has to be up to the clients. They must take the initiative to ask for help. Your job is to help them know when they need help, how to find it, and how to ask for support. Many of the details will be solidified in the plan, but the possibilities begin here. Read through Practice 3.8; the questions speak for themselves.

PRACTICE 3.8

The Assist

- What would _____ say works for him or her? Could you ask him or her?

- What advice do you need? Where could you get it?

- What do (the school rules, company policy, marriage ceremony) say you could do?

- How might I help you with this?

- Who or what can help you?

- Who knows what you need to know?

- Where can you find the information you need?

- Who could support you in working toward your solution?

- Who or what has helped you in the past?

- Who or what helps you now?

- How might you find someone to help?

- Could you find a resource that can help your solution happen?

- Walk me through a visualization of you finding and using support.

Solution Application: Suicide Assessment

You may have noticed that the potential questions, especially the pretend and people ones, are similar to those used in assessing threats of suicide. The pretend questions will give you a feel for whether clients see themselves as being present in the future, and the people questions will show you available sources of support. Not seeing oneself in the near future and not having resources and support are two indicators of suicide potential. These questions are not meant to replace formal lethality assessments, but they can give you clues in detecting possible suicidal thoughts or feelings in your clients.

Skill Highlight: Keeping Score

A written record of discovered potential is not only helpful for case notes, for the memory, and for perspective, it also is a great self-esteem builder. As a skill, a talent, an exception, or a potential solution is shared, you can accentuate it by saying something like, "This is great. Let's get this down." Then grab the nearest piece of paper and jot down a two- or three-word summary of the potential. This may be something the client is sharing without realizing its full potential.

A word of caution here: Use a blank sheet of paper and be spontaneous. If you simply fill out a standard form, it's likely blank spaces will remain—and these may make clients feel less than adequate. You also do not want to put clients on the spot or make them feel as if they are taking a test—which do not fit solutioning at all. If you must use a form, put only a few lines on it and use the back as much as possible. This sends the message that the client is *overflowing* with potential solutions, which makes the client feel *exceptional.*

The discussion does not have to end here. As the interaction naturally flows you may end up with a list. As clients review their lists of exceptions and options, they gain confidence, feel more hopeful, and are motivated to overcome problems, which don't seem so huge anymore.

There is another advantage to a visual display of abilities and possibilities: Faced with such a list, clients have a harder time coming up with excuses or resistance. We've all had clients who seem to put more effort into *having* problems than *solving* them. These may require additional methods or interventions. Once the potentials are out in the open, the problem cannot be used as an excuse.

For clients with very low self-esteem, the reaction can be overwhelming. Seeing is believing, after all, and it's hard to argue with a written record of skills, abilities, exceptions, and potentials. So grab your paper as soon as an exception, skill, or talent is shared— the potential is so great you can't let it go by … you just have to write it down. You might say, "Wait a minute. This is good stuff! We'd better get it down so we don't forget." This enhances the reality of the skill and the likelihood that it will be repeated.

Solution Application: Grief

The case study that follows shows how exploring potentials can be especially useful in grief counseling. The reminiscent quality of past potentials facilitates sharing positive memories of the deceased, and a look at the future instills a sense of hope that life goes on.

Life Goes On: The Case of Margaret

Margaret and Ed had been married for 50 years and had three grown daughters. After Ed's fatal heart attack, Margaret couldn't seem to get back into life. When Margaret came to therapy she was barely meeting her own physical needs. Her hygiene was not good and she was depressed.

But Margaret became lively and talkative as we explored past potential. We started off talking about happy memories of Ed and ended with personal strengths, abilities, and coping skills Margaret had used during hard times in the past. These led to a new awakening of her individualism and self- (not couple) esteem.

As Margaret began using some of her previous strengths to get herself together physically, we began (in session 2) to explore pretend potentials. At first, Margaret had a difficult time imagining life without Ed, but as we continued she added in more and more activities she could do without him. Returning to her bridge club, going to visit her sister in California, getting the new oven he never thought she needed, and more. Some of these tied in to the past potentials and current positives she had also been discovering. This was our last session. At the end, after some great, detailed visualizations of a strong woman living life on her own, Margaret said, "Life goes on."

Skill Highlight: Listening for Potentials

> "Material for solutions lies with the client, and will become apparent to us when we listen and observe carefully for clues regarding client skills, strengths, and interests."
> —*Linda K. Tuyn (1992, p. 84)*

By getting in the habit of noting for clients when you hear them share a skill, a success, or a positive—even those unrelated to the problem—you form a knowledge base for solutions. Just as symptoms of the *DSM* categories may jump out at you as you interact with clients, with practice, so will solution potentials. And just like symptoms, when clients allude to potentials and exceptions, you will want to investigate further, questioning for intensity, duration, and frequency. Investigating for details highlights the potentials that can be used for solutions in the present. Once you've formed the habit of looking for strengths in the lives of your clients, you may be surprised at how many you find.

It is amazing how many clients are unaware when they share something that could be used as a solution. They do not realize what they have said, what it means, or that they really have the skill—until you point it out. Some clients are so encompassed by their problems, have been so abused, or have such low self-esteem they have a hard time acknowledging positive aspects about themselves or their lives. These clients typically become enthusiastic about therapy when the therapist catches and accentuates a positive.

Through modeling, you can empower clients to realize positives for themselves. After hearing potentials, ask questions that involve clients and allow them to realize it for themselves. This goes beyond a typical compliment. Act a little surprised and use the client's name: "John, do you realize what you just said?" Pause. "You said that you were really happy yesterday when you went for a walk after work. How did you think to do that?" Dissecting this interaction, you'll notice three distinct elements:

- First, you stop the client and give him the opportunity to accentuate the positive.

- Second, you restate—preferably in the client's words— the behavior, feeling, or thought that was positive or could be used as a potential solution.

- Third, you encourage the client to take ownership and responsibility for the positive by asking, "How did you do that?" This encourages him to realize that *he did it* and to process how.

Have a friend, spouse, or one of your children tell you about their day. Practice catching and accentuating the positives, giving responsibility, and building a knowledge base of potential solutions. You never know when you might need some. Use the following format to word your response.

1. "(Name), do you realize what you just said?" Pause.

2. "You said (specific positive behavior, thought, feeling, or success)."

3. "Wow! I'm impressed. How did you (accomplish, manage, think of, do that)?"

I Can Cope: The Case of Sabrina

Sabrina, a 17-year-old rape victim, was always saying that she had no coping skills except for drugs. One day she started explaining how she would go for a walk when she got really angry.

Willyn: Wait a minute, Sabrina. Do you realize what you just shared?

She looked at me with a puzzled expression.

Willyn: You just shared a great coping skill for anger—going for walks. How did you come up with that?

Sabrina: *(smiling)* Yeah, I guess I did. That does work. Cool.

We went on to discuss the details of going for a walk at the first signs of anger and formed a great plan.

Another day Sabrina told me that, when she got really sad, she wrote it all down and that made her feel better. Again I acted shocked.

Willyn: I think I just heard another coping skill, and it wasn't drugs. Did you?

Sabrina: *(thinking for a moment, then nodding slowly)* You mean writing it down and getting it all out when I'm sad? That's a coping skill? Hmmm, well ... it does help, now that I think about it.

Pretty soon Sabrina had so many alternative coping skills she no longer had an excuse to take drugs. A few sessions later she made a list of alternative coping choices for each time she felt tempted to use drugs.

As a practice exercise have a partner tell you about a problem (purposely slipping in a couple of references to nonproblem times). See if you can catch the potential, draw out the details, give responsibility, and lead to a plan.

"There is something that is much more
scarce, something rarer than ability. It is
the ability to recognize ability."
                    —*Robert Half (Peter, 1977, p. 37)*

You can begin establishing a potentials resource base as early as the intake form. This will not diminish any needed diagnostic information, but will start a thinking process that is future-oriented and solution-focused. "By eliciting information regarding those things that the patient values and enjoys, the therapist learns about strengths that can later be utilized in treatment, and also builds rapport" (Budman & Gurman, 1988, p. 53). You may choose to adopt the solutioning intake in Practice 3.9, or you may see one or two items you want to add to your existing form.

PRACTICE 3.9

Intake—Solution Style

Part 1 (to be filled out by the client)

Name:_____ Date: _____

Purpose:_____

_____

Coping skills:_____

_____

_____

Applicable medical information:_____

_____

Chemical use:_____

_____

Family traits and attributes:_____

_____

Who do you admire most in your family, and why?_____

_____

_____

Strengths, abilities, and talents: _____

_____

_____

Hobbies and leisure activities:_____

_____

_____

Friends (types, qualities, and positive traits of the relationship):

_____

_____

What friend do you admire the most, and why?_____

_____

_____

Who is your hero?_____

What qualities does your hero have that you admire?_____

_____

_____

What do you like about yourself, your job, your relationships, your life?_____

_____

_____

Part 2 (to be filled out by the therapist)

Clinical Observations (Include positive and negative aspects of each category.)

Appearance:_____

_____

Behavior:_____

_____

Feeling:_____

_____

Perception:_____

_____

Thinking:_____

_____

Strengths, talents, and abilities:_____

_____

Potential Solutions (problem exceptions, follow the map)

_____

_____

Past: When have things been better? When has the problem not existed?_____

_____

_____

Present: When do you not have the problem? When are things different or better?_____

_____

_____

Pretend: How do you want it to be? What do you want to happen as a result of therapy?_____

_____

_____

_____

People: Who are your positive influences, resources, and support?

_____

_____

_____

Diagnostic Information (to be filled out by the therapist)

Axis 1 (clinical syndromes and V codes): _____

_____

Provisional diagnosis: *DSM-IV* code:

_____   _____

_____   _____

Rule out:_____

_____

Axis II (Developmental and Personality Disorders):_____

_____

_____

Provisional Diagnosis: *DSM-IV* code:

_____   _____

_____   _____

Additional diagnostic information (Axis III-V):_____

_____

_____

GAF:_____

_____

_____

_____

POTENTIALS: IN SUMMARY

Practice 3.10 summarizes exploring potentials in a form you can use with clients or as a cheat sheet. As you become familiar with solutioning, you will find what works for you. Remember, even though the potentials are the heart of solutioning, this step may consist of only one or two questions. As solutions become obvious, you should head toward the plan to get the client out into the world and *doing* the solution. Many interventions are incorporated in this exploration. Pick and choose those that feel best to you and go from there. Most of all, have fun with the potential questions. If a client seems discouraged by a lack of ideas, switch gears until she is ready. Timing is everything.

PRACTICE 3.10

Combined Potentials

Past

- When has the problem not happened? What were you doing differently?

- When in the past has the problem lessened? What was different?

- When have you been successful in the past? How did you do that?

Present

- When is the problem not happening now? What are you doing differently?

- What times are you successful now? How do you do that?

- When is the problem less or the solution some?

Pretend

- Pretend your problem is solved. What are you doing?

- Visualize your solution. Tell me all the details of what you are doing, saying, feeling, and thinking?

- Imagine things are how you want them to be. What are you doing?

People

- What ideas for solutions can you get from others? What do they do?

- Who has had this problem before and solved it? How did they do it?

- How would (others your age, your positive person, your parents, etc.) solve this?

Chapter 4

Just Do It!
The Third P—Plan

The plan happens as the answers to the potential questions point the way to solutions. The obvious solution, the thing to do, an idea to try may already be clear. With this step you firm up the actions, thoughts, and behaviors clients will begin using immediately and increase the chances for a positive outcome through rehearsal.

The plan of solutioning varies from the goal, task, or homework discussed in other therapies. The plan is cocreated, according to the *starting five criteria* (see Practice 4.3). While I use the word *plan*, you will want to use words that fit your individual clients. Your clients may respond better to *goal, experiment, direction, new trend, preference, desire, recipe for success, formula for action, task, homework*, or something else completely. The main idea is that, after the therapist-client team has described a problem, established a purpose, and explored potentials, it is time to create plans to take some steps toward solving the problem. The plan is the solution or part of the solution that clients begin trying immediately, regardless of what you call it.

Once again, teaming is important and the language is specific. You cannot leave clients to form their own plans; you must collaborate with them. No matter how obvious the solution may seem to you, no matter how apparent the client's skills and potentials are, the client still may feel lost about what to do tomorrow or next week. Cocreating a plan and walking through it together will give the client not only direction but also hope, confidence, and motivation. This is different from more traditional stances in which the therapist *gives* the client a task or assignment. By waiting until after the potentials to form plans, you ensure they are concrete because you've already discussed the solution.

Sometimes you will have to do some more searching. Other times, the solution may seem fairly clear to you, but the client is not ready to do it. Situations like these are neatly covered by the flexible nature of solutioning. Through teaming, you can cocreate a plan that fits each individual client. To facilitate this process, solutioning provides three different types of plans, which are shown in Table 4.1.

TABLE 4.1
Picking the Perfect Plan

Positive	Pretend	Perform
1. "Observe for positives" (Walter & Peller, 1992). Notice what works (Metcalf, 1995). Watch for when things are better.	1. Don't do anything yet, just imagine yourself doing the solution. Visualize doing a plan.	1. Do past potentials again, in a new context. 2. Do present potentials more, or in another context. 3. Do a part of the pretend potentials. 4. Borrow some of the people potentials to do.

Regardless of the type, *the plan comes directly from the potentials clients share.* Clients have the lead in creating plans, not the therapist. The therapist, as team leader, uses the questions of solutioning to facilitate forming an achievable plan. Look back at the solutioning map in Figure 3.1 and see how the plan is directly under the potential it fits.

Solutioning adds the positive and pretend steps to plan options as baby steps, allowing clients to work up to performing. By giving clients authority to decide which type of plan to use, you give them choice, which leads to control and ultimately to responsibility. The language is the key. You *can* help create interventions for change and still empower clients with choice, self-control, and responsibility.

Skill Highlight: Picking the Perfect Plan

Picking the perfect plan involves questioning clients about their readiness. After discussing the potentials you will usually have a feel for what needs to happen next. Clients will pick their own plans. Use the following questions to transition from exploring potential solutions to firming up a plan. This step may not be necessary if the client is ready to use the solution discovered. But when a client seems hesitant, you can try these. Notice the assumptive language and the presupposition that a solution will happen.

- Of the ideas we have been discussing, which are you going to practice, think about, or do?

- Which ideas sound the best to you?

- Can you visualize yourself doing any of your potential solution ideas?

- Pick the idea that is going to be your solution.

- Have you found your solution, or do you need to look some more?

- Are you ready to begin doing some of the solution immediately, tomorrow, next week?

- Would you like to practice your solution in your mind first?

These questions do not go in-depth. The idea is to understand how clients are feeling about solutions. In answering these questions, clients can weigh the consequences of either trying the solution or not. Whether you have explored each potential avenue or found an obvious solution the client is anxious to try, a "What now?" question will put you on the same page, ready to begin making achievable plans.

Solutions are a process and they take time. As you read about the three types of plans, you will probably think of additional questions to use here. Again, your feel for things is your best guide. The majority of plans will be performing, but it is nice to have backup when the client is not ready for action. Clients make more progress with a developmentally appropriate plan than with a wonderful performing plan that fails or is never tried. Once you have chosen a type of plan, you are ready to firm it up, promote motivation, and give responsibility—together as a team.

DETECTING: THE POSITIVE PLAN

"Every good thought you think is contributing its share to the ultimate result of your life."
—*Grenville Klieser (Peter, 1977, p. 467)*

The *positive plan* option is one I use with all my clients at some point in the therapy process. You can use this exclusively as an intervention in itself, as a stepping stone, or in conjunction with the other plans. The positive plan teaches clients the valuable skills of broadening their perspectives, and noticing not only the problems, but also the positives. Noticing positives, small successes, and skills is helpful even when the therapy emphasis is on personality reconstruction, insight, behavioral modification, or any other treatment. This solutioning intervention is especially quick and easy to use, fits with any mode of therapy, and works at any point during the therapeutic process. In fact, this plan can be used during the initial phone conversation.

Skill Highlight: Making Appointments with a Plus

After you obtain preliminary information and set up the appointment, you can say something like this:

> "Okay, so we will be meeting on _____ at ___ . From now until then I would like you to notice what is good about your life, what works, what is positive. Okay? See you on Thursday. I'll be anxious to hear what you find."

If the client describes the problem during the initial call, you may refer to it in the "look for positives" directive. For example, if a client is having trouble with her husband, you might say, "From now until we meet, notice what is good about your marriage, and what is different about the times when you get along. Okay? That will give us a great starting point. See you soon."

This conversation makes a first step toward establishing a team because it allows clients to prepare for the session and gives them a chance to begin finding solutions. The potential questions are more easily answered when the client has already been looking for them. This saves time and allows the client more opportunity to share. Depending on your clientele, you may want to do some screening, however. You don't want to send a severely depressed or suicidal person looking for something positive that will not be found.

Below is a list of phrases you might use in the initial phone call. They are fairly generic and can be used regardless of the presenting problem or situation. After some practice you can tailor one to fit the client, the problem, or the situation.

- Between now and the session, try to notice everything positive about your life.

- Until your session, begin noting when the problem doesn't happen and things are better.

- While you are waiting for your appointment, watch for things you like about your life.

When the client arrives for the first session and shares positives instead of problems, you can begin using the progress questions (see chapter 5) and be well on your way to constructing solutions.

The positive plan is a helpful initial intervention when a client is not clear about the problem. Sometimes being able to define the problem is not as important as knowing what would be better. Instead of spending a lot of time finding out why clients are depressed, anxious, or angry, why not spend your time and energy on when they are less depressed, more relaxed, or happy? Sometimes solutions happen and clients get better, without ever knowing the problem's cause. If the client or therapist feels it is important to know the cause, of course you can work on that. But you will do so with more balance as the nonproblem times are discovered conjunctively. Asking clients to look for times when the problem is absent or better helps them direct their time and energy in a productive way and gives them the skills they need to find solutions. In some cases, the change in focus is the solution itself, as the following case study illustrates.

An Empty Nest: The Case of Lisa and Tony

Lisa and Tony had been married for 28 years, and both agreed those 28 years had been satisfactory. They had experienced their fair share of fights, but they were generally happy. They had three children, who had been the focus of their lives. The last child had moved out 18 months ago.

Tony and Lisa came to counseling because they couldn't seem to get along. Their fights had become so frequent they were considering separation. During the initial phone call I asked them to, "notice when you get along." When they came to their first session, they were full of times when they were happy, most of which involved time with the children and their families.

My developmental background was diagnosing *empty nest* and I was planning to invite the children to the next session when Tony suddenly shared, "We came to this session because we didn't want to cancel at the last minute. But we've decided we don't really need counseling. This last week, as we noticed times when we get along, we found quite a few and remembered some things we used to do together that were fun. We went hiking on Saturday, just like when we were dating. It was nice. We aren't fighting as much now. I think we're going to be fine."

Without ever knowing why they had been fighting so much, this couple rediscovered how to get along and enjoy each other again. The positive plan was their solution.

Researchers at the Brief Family Therapy Center have studied this phenomenon of change prior to or in anticipation of counseling. They asked 30 clients the following questions:

1. Many times people notice, in between the time they make the appointment for therapy and the first session, that things already seem different. What have you noticed about your situation?

2. *(If yes to #1)* Do these changes relate to the reason you came for therapy?

3. *(If yes to #1)* Are these the kinds of changes you would like to continue to have happen? (Weiner-Davis, de Shazer, & Gingerich, 1987, p. 360)

The researchers made no effort during the initial contact to encourage change, yet they reported:

> Of the 30 patients who were asked these questions, 20 reported having observed presession changes. All 20 answered "yes" to questions 2 and 3, indicating that the changes they observed were in or related to the problematic area. At least in part, they had already achieved what they wanted to achieve by coming to therapy. (Weiner-Davis et al., 1987, pp. 360–361)

With results like these, you can imagine the results of using the positive plan during initial contacts?

I'm Okay: The Case of Henry

Henry didn't call to make the appointment, his mother did. According to Mom, Henry was a depressed 8-year-old, who had made comments about wanting to die. Henry's mother was panicked. I set the appointment for two days later and asked her to notice when Henry was happy until we met. The two came in smiling. The first thing out of Henry's mouth was, "I feel better now."

Willyn: Great! How did you do that?

Henry: Mom isn't worried about me as much, and I can just act how I want.

Mom: When I was watching for happy times, I found them. And I realized that maybe he wasn't as depressed as I thought. I quit questioning how he was feeling and why and all that all the time, and we both relaxed.

For the remainder of the session we talked about how to keep the positive changes going and what to do in case of a backslide. Henry came for a few more sessions until both he and his mother felt things were okay and therapy was no longer necessary. The best part of the experience was that Mom and Henry both felt responsible for the changes. As Henry said, "I felt better before counseling."

Empowering clients by setting them up to find their own success is the best intervention of all.

Another time you will find the positive plan useful is when therapy has been ongoing without much progress. The positive plan can help clients move out from under the cloud of problems. Some clients are so encompassed by problems they have a difficult time coming up with ideas when exploring potentials; they may be unable to find exceptions or they may be playing the blame game.

If You Insist: The Case of Alisa

Alisa had two small children. She was full of guilt because she did not know the father of either, had failed at many jobs, and often lost her temper with her son. Alisa began counseling in a complaining, "woe is me" mode, near depression. As part of therapy, she worked on her parenting skills, took steps toward finding a new job, and learned some self-nurturing behaviors. Despite these efforts, her demeanor did not improve. I began ending each session with, "Notice what is good about your life," and beginning the next with, "What was good?" A couple of sessions later, Alisa came in smiling.

Willyn: What was good?

Alisa: I have a huge list of positives!

Previously, she had said nothing about positives and had complained about everything.

Willyn: *(shocked)* How did you do that?

Alisa: After I left the last session I realized that you were going to keep asking, so I might as well try it. So I did. Things were not perfect, but I realized maybe they weren't that bad either. I

think I was nicer to my kids when I was seeing them as cute and sometimes good, rather
than pains in the butt.

With this change in focus, Alisa made rapid progress,
her demeanor became conducive to change, and her self-
esteem rose.

The positive plan often has the effect of helping clients feel
better and gain more hopeful outlooks, which facilitates other work
or can be a treatment goal in itself. Many problem-filled clients
have to build up to being ready to take action. With it's small time
frame for follow-up, the positive plan is a perfect intervention to
facilitate their readiness, confidence, and life focus toward solutions. A word of caution, however: Pushing the positive plan on a
client who doesn't really have any positives will have a negative
effect. There is not a lot that's more depressing than trying to find
something that works in life and coming up empty-handed.

A final use of the positive plan is in conjunction with a pretend
or performing plan. For full inspiring and motivating effect, you
might say to clients as they get up to leave, "Watch for positives,"
"Stop and take note when something goes right," or "I'll be anxious to hear about what works." This gives them a solution focus.

Whether or not the problem is completely solved, clients usually will be able to identify some efforts that are successful. It is
the positive change, the small improvements, and the growth you
want to stand out in their minds. Even when performing plans are
not completely successful, clients often come back and say, "Hey,
I noticed that we don't fight when I get time to relax after work
first," or "I found out that reading before bed helps me sleep better." This is a great skill to give your clients.

In Practice 4.1 you will find some phrases for helping your
clients see the positives in their lives. While they are technically
directives, they do not come across as such when used within a
teaming relationship. Remember, you want to give clients the lead
in determining how much action to take.

PRACTICE 4.1

Detecting: The Positive Plan

- Look for what is good about your life.

- Watch for when things are better.

- See if you can find any times when the solution is happening.

- Watch for when the problem is not happening or is not as intense.

- Remember what happens that you want to continue happening between now and when we meet again so you can tell me about it.

- Watch for things you want to continue.

- Notice what works (Metcalf, 1995).

- Discover what is positive about school, work, family, whatever.

- When things seem to be working, stop and notice what you are doing.

- Try to find out what you are doing differently when things are better.

- Between today and tomorrow, focus on what happens that you like, that you feel good about.

- "Between now and next time we meet, we would like you to observe, so that you can describe to us next time, what happens in your family that you want continue" (de Shazer, 1985, p. 137).

Solution Application: Adult Survivors

Dolan (1991) described using an intervention similar to the positive plan in her highly effective work with adult survivors of sexual abuse:

> Having the client—and her partner too, if he or she is involved in treatment—look for any small and gradual signs of healing as therapy progresses can provide a much-needed positive orientation; this balances the effects of dealing with feelings related to victimization. (p. 33)

Dolan shared the feedback she received from a client: "Noticing how I'm healing even in little ways feels so much better than just thinking about all the bad stuff that happened to me" (1991, p. 33). Blending in solutioning, even in small, subtle ways, can have a powerful affect.

REHEARSING: THE PRETEND PLAN

"I have learned this at least by my experiment:
that if one advances confidently in the direction
of his dreams, and endeavors to live the life
which he has imagined, he will meet with success
unexpected in common hours."
—*Henry David Thoreau (Peter, 1977, p. 168)*

The pretend plan involves the thinking and feeling that precedes the action. It is the preparation—the rehearsal. Encouraging clients to think about, visualize, pretend, or imagine themselves doing their solution is private, safe, and personal. Often this rehearsal leads to star performances. The pretend plan plants the seeds of solution. With some nurturing and time, the reality blooms.

Like the positive plan, the pretend plan may be used alone, in conjunction with other plans, or as a step toward using the solution. The pretend plan is the mental practice that allows the client to take the solution into life without risk and to build up the confidence needed to enact it. We all like to test the waters. By freeing clients from the bounds of circumstances and reality, you allow them to take their potentials to the point of a plan. This allows something different to happen, even if only in the mind. It is a start. Epstein's definition of imagery supports the value of the pretend plan:

> I saw that the task of therapy—the task of being human— was to help realize freedom, to go beyond the given, to the newness that we all are capable of, and to our capacity to renew and recreate. This is what imagery, I have come to learn, makes possible. (1990, p. 11)

Further plans are needed only rarely. The client either no longer needs the plan or has already done it. Sometimes the change in thinking makes all the difference. When clients go ahead and do the solution—even though the plan was just to think about it—it's usually because they feel ready and anxious as a result of the mental practice. Epstein defined mental imagery as "the mind thinking in pictures." We are a visual, TV generation. When the mind is playing the right pictures, solutions happen. As swimming coach Alan Goldberg pointed out, "The power of mental rehearsal and internal images is based on the fact that images from the brain serve as blueprints for actions and behaviors" (1995, p. 24).

"The spirit is the master, imagination the tool, and the body the plastic material. ... The power of the imagination is a great factor in medicine. It may produce diseases ... and it may cure them"
—*Paracelsus (*Encyclopedia Britanica, *1911, p. 749)*

The use of pretend is hardly new. Freud himself "once successfully used imagery to treat a 14-year-old boy suffering from a physical tic—and he did it in only one session" (Epstein, 1990, p. 52). Western medicine is only beginning to understand the value of imagery in conjunction with physical treatments. As Norris (1990) noted, "the imagery a person holds of the disease process or of the healing process can affect the outcome of the illness to *any* extent" (p. 10).

The value is obvious, yet few of us use imagery because we lack the training or techniques. The pretend plan is a way to incorporate the value of images without having to jump in with both feet. For those trained in more intensive methods (biofeedback, hypnosis, waking dream therapy), the pretend will be easily blended and even extended with these complimentary interventions.

"Hi": The Case of Ashley

Fifth-grade Ashley's dream in life was to be popular like her sister, who was in high school. But Ashley was overweight and shy. She had been teased a lot and often used stubbornness as a defense when people tried to interact with her. These qualities made popularity seem like a distant goal.

But Ashley was quickly able to share potential solutions when I asked her, "Who has solved this problem that you could get ideas from?" She named her sister, who had not been popular in the early grades due to shyness, but who was now outgoing and had many friends. Ashley described many positive behaviors her sister modeled.

When I asked the plan question, "Which of these great ideas are you going to try first?" Ashley looked uncomfortable and thought for a moment. Finally, she volunteered that maybe she could start saying "Hi" to other kids when she saw them at school.

Because of her hesitation, I asked, "Are you ready, is it worth the risk?"

Ashley wasn't sure, so we used the pretend plan to find out. Ashley decided she would not do anything yet, just imagine herself smiling and saying "Hi" each time she passed a potential friend in the hall or during lunch. We decided she should use the mental rehearsal for a week and we'd see how she felt about it at the next session.

The next week, Ashley arrived thrilled because she had actually said "Hi" to two girls that very day. And each had said "Hi" back—they hadn't ignored her, laughed at her, or made fun of her at all. As we considered her progress Ashley said, "I knew I wasn't supposed to do anything yet, just practice in my mind, but I got so good at the practice, it just came out. I couldn't resist."

During the sharing and designing of a pretend plan, it is helpful to ask clients about their feelings as the mental movie is described. This gives you a feel for which parts are most difficult, which are most likely to happen, which are most unlikely, and what needs more work. Sometimes as clients take you through their pretend plans, fears, unplanned events, or negative images arise. This is a proactive, preventative activity. Through the intervention, clients can experience these fears, overcome them, solve them, and plan for them without the actual, real-life risk.

For many clients, visualizing is a new and unfamiliar activity. Some haven't really used their imaginations since childhood. Of course, awakening this skill takes practice for anyone. But for some problem-focused clients, using the imagination positively may be a completely new skill. For those who see the glass as half-empty it can be difficult to play out a pretend movie that is completely positive. I remember one client walking through his pretend plan to use more positive phrases with his wife and young son. He suddenly stopped and commented, "But it just wouldn't be *me* if I wasn't complaining." Making movies fit with the mindsets, personalities, and realities of clients is a worthwhile, if challenging, intervention.

You need to allow your clients many opportunities to practice controlling their pretend plans, making them come out right. Goldberg used the following instructions to help his swimmers gain control over their imagery exercises:

> Have them pretend that they are operating a VCR in their mind. When a negative image pops up, they need to hit the stop button, rewind, and then play the scene again. If it comes

up negative a second or third time, have them repeat it or
even put the movie in slow motion, until they play it right.
(1995, p. 25)

"If you don't know where you are going, you will
probably end up somewhere else."
—*Laurence J. Peter (Peter, 1977, p. 125)*

Solution Application: Eating Disorders

As the media in our culture continue to sell a nearly
unachievable body image, eating disorders have become the topic
of many studies in the past decade. As women confront body image and health issues, solutioning can provide a safe, nonjudgmental
way to explore differences, confront fears, and work out a change.
"Weight preoccupation and body image dissatisfaction are examples of thoughts and feelings that contribute to the development and continuation of engaging in eating disordered behaviors" (Scarano & Kalodner-Martin, 1994, p. 358).

The emphasis on images and thoughts makes the pretend plan
an intervention option that fits with many therapies for eating disorders. Solutioning's blendability makes it suitable as a component for programs that involve both education and the psychological context of the disorders. Additionally, solutioning has a built-
in goal of improved self-esteem as the teaming relationship focuses on the input of clients, the potentials of clients, and the
cocreated plan. Self-esteem, as facilitated through solutioning,
meets another treatment goal for eating disorders: "increase body-
esteem through self-acceptance" (Scarano & Kalodner-Martin,
1994, p. 360).

Thin Again: The Case of Melinda

Melinda was working on several family issues as well
as her problems with repeat dieting and occasional purging. She felt her life was out of control. As part of her
treatment, Melinda kept a purge diary, but with a
solutioning emphasis (Weiss, Katzman, & Wolchik,

1985). She kept track of the times she felt the need to purge, but resisted; the times she wanted to restrict her eating, but ate healthily instead. These pointed out times when Melinda used her coping skills to control her body and her life.

Melinda's diary started off with only one example, when she relaxed by laying down for 15 minutes with her eyes closed. Over a three-month period, in conjunction with a pretend plan to do nothing but *imagine* herself eating healthily, Melinda built to numerous examples and eventually stopped purging.

During this time, Melinda never made a perform plan. As she was able to do her pretend plan and write more examples in her purge diary, her self-esteem increased, which helped her make some important family decisions. These all worked together to help Melinda feel better emotionally; she also began to feel better physically because of her improved eating patterns and decreased purging. Blending in a small component of solutioning, the pretend plan made the difference in Melinda's ability to overcome her eating disorder and helped in her family treatment progress as well.

As clients play out desired movies in their minds, it gives them confidence in their ability to act in their lives. Like the little engine that could, if you tell yourself, "I think I can" often enough, you start to believe it, you start to control it, *you are empowered.* As Norris (1990, p. 50) noted, "Visualization is the consciously chosen, intentional instruction to the body" that helps clients take a giant leap toward self-discipline, self-control, and responsibility. If visualization can be used to decrease cancer cells, surely it can help our clients work toward their solutions.

> "If you think you can, you can. And if
> you think you can't, you're right."
> —*Mary Kay Ash (Webster, 1992, p. 3)*

PRACTICE 4.2

Rehearsing: The Pretend Plan

- Don't do anything yet, just imagine yourself doing the solution.

- Pretend your solution at least three times a day for the next week. Think about which parts you're going to do first.

- Each night before you go to sleep, play your solution movie.

- Practice your solution in your mind each time you see an opportunity when you might use it at some time in the future.

- Imagine yourself taking a deep breath each time you feel like swatting your baby.

- Pretend you eat a healthy meal and don't throw it up whenever you are hungry.

- Rehearse your pretend movie whenever you think of the problem this week.

Skill Highlight: An Added Twist

As the case studies of Ashley and Melinda illustrate, saying "Don't do anything yet" in conjunction with making plans to pretend, often has the paradoxical effect of actualizing the desired behaviors. As you form a pretend plan with a client, you should make it as specific as possible and have the client walk through it during the session. Then, as an experiment, at the end of the session say something like, "Remember, don't do it yet. Just think about it." Make sure you do not imply that the client is not ready or that it would not be a good idea to go further. Say it in a way that reinforces the *imagine, rehearse, think about, pretend, visualize* part. This is mostly a restatement of the plan, but with the added twist of *just this.*

Often clients come back *having done the plan.* In these cases, they will feel especially proud of their efforts, because *they chose to do the plan* and so took full responsibility for the results. Even if they do not take action, the plan—including the *don't do anything yet* part—is followed completely. This *do nothing* idea can also be used with the positive plan, as you say, "Don't do anything for three days. Just notice what is good about your life, when the problem isn't happening."

PERFORMING: THE PLAN

"The impossible is often the untried."
—*Willyn Webb*

Before reaching the perform stage of solutioning, your team may have found one great potential and moved directly down, or you may have explored many possible solution ideas, looked for positives, imagined doing the solution, and so on. No matter how the team arrives, there is a performance—*doing the solution.* It may seem like we have arrived here in a roundabout way. The therapist, with his or her expert knowledge, might have simply prescribed a solution long before this. This roundabout way of using well-formed questions, however, lets our clients tell us how *they* are going to solve the problem and exactly what *they* are going to begin doing differently tomorrow. This gives them control and responsibility, not to mention self-esteem, when the plan is achieved and the problem solved.

Notice on the solutioning map (Figure 3.1) that, when you find a potential solution, you can move directly down and have an automatic plan. It may be tempting to save time and say, "Okay, go for it," after the solution is found. However, taking the time to give your clients the opportunity to make a choice and tell you what they are going to do just works better.

As clients tell you their game plans, you can serve as team captain, helping them form perform plans that are doable. The starting five criteria for plans (see Practice 4.3) are great practice drills. As you read about each, you'll learn solutioning language to help make a plan that will happen. The starting five criteria were adapted from the suggestions of Walter and Peller (1992). They are worded personally, positively, in a process form, precisely, and in the present. These do not go in any particular order, and one or two questions will most likely do the job.

"Few things can help an individual more than to place responsibility upon him, and to let him know that you trust him."
—*Booker T. Washington (Peter, 1977, p. 430)*

Personalize

Plans to perform must be personal for clients—that is, they must be within their control. A plan for someone else to perform will not work as a solution, even if it is initially successful. Systemically speaking, individuals do have influence over others, and a change in one part of the system can affect the others involved or the entire system. However, that influence, that change, must start with the person making the plan. We cannot control others, and the plan must be *within the clients' control.* A plan will not work if it is contingent in any way upon circumstances over which the client has no control.

Many times clients have a difficult time seeing past their desires for others to behave differently or for their lives to get easier in some way. In this case, it may be helpful to ask about the likelihood of changing their friends, parents, children, coworkers, or lives. Repeating a phrase such as, "What can you do?" is usually effective. It also helps to use the clients' words when referring to the plan. This makes it more meaningful, personal, memorable, and doable.

When clients are having trouble personalizing the solution possibilities and forming a plan that involves their behaviors alone you may ask the following questions (adapted from the "key words" suggested by Walter and Peller):

- What will you/could *you* be doing differently?

- What would so and so say *you* could do?

- Which of the potentials we have discussed could *you* try?

- What could *you* do that might influence or encourage (so and so to change, work to get easier, or you to have more money, be skinny, or stop fighting)?

As clients begin to see their role in controlling their own fate, they may feel intimidated. Responsibility can be a scary thing, especially when you've never taken it before. Without the people to blame or the excuses, it is harder to try and risk messing up. However, as they take small steps toward responsibility and get a taste of control, clients will begin to feel empowered. This is one of the most valuable aspects of solutioning. So be persistent and re-ask the questions. Clients are experiencing a change of mindset as they take control of their lives and make them how they want them to be.

"I am the master of my fate;
I am the captain of my soul."
—*William E. Henley (Peter, 1977, p. 159)*

Positively

If you use words like *instead* and *differently,* the plan focuses on what the clients will be *doing* rather than what they will *not* be doing. This encourages a visualization, discussion, or rehearsal of the desired behavior and allows them to know exactly what to do. Most likely, if they knew how to not feel depressed, not be lonely, not fight, and so on, they would already be doing it. The plan of what to do *instead* of fighting, being depressed, and so on is the answer they need.

We do not want clients visualizing the problem each time they think of the plan or solution. Plans of *not doing something* (not lying, not stealing) or of not thinking a certain thought (not considering suicide, not feeling hate, etc.) are difficult to achieve. Some of the best-laid plans never get put into action because clients don't know *what to do instead*. You must cocreate a plan for what will be done. Set clients up for success with positively worded plans that create a mental picture of the desired behavior.

- What will you be doing *instead*?

- What will you be doing *differently*?

- What will you be *doing*?

Process

The next step is to make sure the plan is in a process form. This means *doing, thinking, practicing* the solution, rather than wishing or desiring. In order to get results and have success in the plan, *something must happen*. Using *how* and *-ing* verbs will make the plan doable (Walter & Peller, 1992).

- How will you be doing this?

- How will you be passing?

- How will you be getting along?

- How will you be controlling your anger?

- How do you plan on making money?

Precise

Answers to the questions listed above most likely will cover the remaining two criteria: having a plan that is *precise* enough to give clients clear direction and one that will happen in the *present*. Just because there are five criteria does not mean you have to ask five questions and get five answers. One answer usually covers them all. The variety of language is offered for clients who seem stuck in forming a plan that will be doable. When you think additional details and mental rehearsal would be helpful, the starting five questions can facilitate that process. By asking for more details, you make the plan more precise, more movie-like, more specific, and more achievable. Try these questions:

- How, exactly, will you be doing this?

- Now, specifically, what will you be doing first, second, and so on?

- Tell me about your plan as if it was a movie or a story.

- I want all the great details of your plan. What will you be doing when (you first wake up, when he comes home, when you are tempted to vomit)?

Notice the continued emphasis on you (personal) and the *doing* (positive and process), the *immediacy* (present), and the *details* (precise) all in one question. The difference in the achievability is amazing.

Present

> "There is no medicine like hope, no incentive
> so great, and no tonic so powerful as the
> expectation of something tomorrow."
> —*O. S. Marden (Peter, 1977, p. 251)*

Finally, you must make sure the clients' plans involve elements they can begin immediately. What good is a plan to graduate if the client is in 7th grade? What good is a plan to get a promotion if the client is on the verge of being fired? What good is a plan to get married when the client has no relationships? All of these are valid, long-term goals, but clients need a plan for what will be done *tomorrow* in working toward them.

Recently, I worked with a client who was struggling with issues over money matters. It was difficult for her to get past wishing for money and on to what she could be *doing* to get money. This is why using the word *plan* is more effective than using *goal*. For many, a goal is a far-off end state, and they have little direction for the process of getting there. A plan can serve that purpose. The following questions can help clients bring their plans into the present:

- "So if you were on track to making a decision now, what would you be doing or doing differently" (Walter & Peller, 1992, p. 55)?

- "As you leave this session and you are on a track to solving this, what will you be doing differently or saying to yourself differently" (Walter & Peller, 1992, p. 55)?

- So as you walk out of my office and back into your life, in the solution groove, what are you doing, thinking, saying, feeling, differently?

- So, starting tomorrow morning, when you are on your way toward making the honor roll, what will you be doing?

- When you're on the road to controlling your anger, what will be doing, feeling, and saying instead?

- This week when you're in the groove and communicating, how will you be doing it?

Notice how the other criteria are covered in these questions. In fact, a well-formed question tailored to meet the needs of the client may cover all five at once. Don't assume that the perform plan must be complicated. On the contrary, it is usually the most obvious, motivated, quick, and exciting step of solutioning. The starting five criteria can be used in conjunction with the pretend plan as well, in order to make visualizations achievable, doable, and successful. Practice 4.3 sums up the starting five criteria. Use it to help clients turn vague, unclear, or negative desires and goals into doable plans.

PRACTICE 4.3

The Starting Five Criteria

Through questioning, you can help clients create a plan that is observable and doable. This encourages the visualization of the desired outcome (solution), increasing the chances that it will happen.

1. **Personal**	"You"	"What will *you* (not your mom, boss, wife) be saying (doing, thinking)?"
	Use their words	"So when you *chill out* first you can ... "
2. **Positive**	"Instead"	"What will you be doing *instead* of shoplifting?"
	"Differently"	"What will you be doing *differently* when you are not drinking?"
3. **Process**	"How" and "ing"	"*How* will you be *doing* this?"
		"*How* will you be *talking* to your kids?"
4. **Precise**	"Specifically"	"How, *specifically*, will you ... ?"
	"Exactly"	"What, *exactly*, will you do next?"
		"What does it look like?
5. **Present**	"On track"	"When you go to work tomorrow and you are on track what will you be
	"In the groove"	doing differently or saying differently to yourself?"
	"Have the formula"	
	"On the right road"	

Source: Adapted from Walter and Peller (1992, p. 60).

SO LONG, SABOTAGE!

No matter how obvious the solution, how carefully worded the plan, the client may still have doubts, fears, or worries. Any successful team knows that the best defense is a good offense. As O'Hanlon advised, "Be sure to include or preempt any objections or barriers to carrying out the task assignment before finalizing it" (1996, p. 16).

In solutioning, the plan created through teaming is different than a task assignment given by a therapist. So you may already have covered this step. However, this is a worthwhile intervention anytime. This step can be referred to in many ways: dodging roadblocks, stopping setbacks, or "flagging the minefield" (Kral & Kowalski, 1989, p. 75). The idea is to ask clients to tell you of any challenges to their plan they can foresee. Then you *plan* how to avoid the challenges, cope with them, or decrease the chances of their happening, while teaching a skill for future use.

By discussing roadblocks *before they happen*, clients learn to handle them when they do. In other words, the team sets up possible sabotages and finds solutions for them in advance. The assumption that the plan *will happen* and *will be successful* is not diminished by asking, "Do you know of anything that could get in the way of or make the plan more difficult to achieve?" The answers provide the rest. Some clients are so confident and motivated by this point, they feel nothing can stop them. Others are a little nervous about actually going out and doing something differently.

Skill Highlight: Dodging Roadblocks

1. Be optimistic.

2. Be realistic.

3. Do not plant ideas of potential problems.

4. If clients do not foresee any possible setbacks or challenges, leave it.

5. Empower clients with confidence.

6. Compliment clients' abilities, coping skills, and foresight.

7. Build them up.

8. Remind them they can control only themselves.

9. Let them know you believe success will happen, but that failure is acceptable.

You might start by asking these questions:

- What could make carrying out your plan difficult for you?

- Is there anything that could get in your way?

- What is going to be the most challenging part of your plan?

- Describe for me the scariest or hardest part of your plan.

Just how much or how little time is needed here can only be assessed by knowing your clients and communicating with them about plans. A great way to do this is by adding in those invaluable, tell-all emotions.

Getting Emotional

Discussing with your clients their feelings about the plan highlights not only obstacles, worries, and insecurities, but also confidence, motivation, and hope. By going through the plan visually, mentally, and orally, you give them more time to rehearse, which decreases the unknowns and preempts surprises. By discussing their feelings, clients get more comfortable, more prepared, and ready to stop talking and start doing their plans. Talking about feelings gives the team a chance to relieve uneasiness and increase motivation. When clients are telling you their plan, stop them at a crucial point and ask, "How are you feeling right now as you tell me about doing this?" The answer to that question will provide a lot of insight into the likelihood of the plan's success.

Getting a feel for the plan also allows clients to make good choices about their own readiness, which parts they want to try, and how they can do their best. Some questions you can use when you are examining your clients' feelings are shown in Practice 4.5. Notice that the language assumes that the plan will happen. For clients who are already optimistic about their plans, your sharing of that optimism serves as a pep talk. For those who are a little unsure or nervous about their readiness, these questions allow you a chance to ease their fears through sincere expression, understanding, and empathy. By taking a moment to include clients' emotions, the plan is restated and rehearsed, and clients' thinking, feeling, and behaving parts are acknowledged and included in the solutioning.

Skill Highlight: Getting Emotional

- Revisit the feeling skills you already have, adding emphasis on the plan of solutioning.

- How do you feel when you are telling me about doing your plan?

- What feelings might come up when you go out to do your plan?

- What goes on inside of you when you imagine yourself (describe plan)?

- Are you excited, scared, nervous, or motivated about (describe the plan)?

- How are you feeling right now? How might you feel tomorrow?

- Which parts of the plan make you feel the most (excited, nervous, etc.)?

- What would help you feel more (motivated, etc.) and less (nervous, etc.)?

THE FINAL ELEMENT

"No man is an Island entire of itself; every
man is a piece of the continent."
—*John Donne,* (Devotions, *1624, #XVII)*

You can ease your clients' fears and increase their motivations, hopes, and chances of success by including people as supports. You can extend the mental movie and make it more real by including other players. As we discussed in chapter 1, solutioning acknowledges the systemic realities of our world. Clients' world views are not just the starting point, they are the ending point of solutioning. The plan must be incorporated into "the big picture." You might ask, "How might (your boss, friend, spouse, child) react when you (do your plan)?" Remember to stress to your clients that they cannot control how others will react. During this discussion it will become obvious who can support the plan. Asking clients with whom they might share their plan or whom they could ask for help is a first step in carrying it out.

PRACTICE 4.4

Adding People

- How might (peers, parents, etc.) react when you (describe the plan)?

- What will so and so do when you (describe the plan)?

- Who will notice when you (describe plan)?

- Who will be the first to know that you have solved your problem? What might they say or do?

- When so and so realizes you have solved your problem, what might they say, do, or feel?

- What if so and so reacts like (throw out possible reactions)?

- Who else do we need to include in this plan?

- Are you going to tell anyone else about your plan?

- Who will be your best ally against the problem?

- What will be your greatest source of support for completing this plan?

- Who or what can help you?

- Are you going to use any of the people you've used before?

- Are there people who are helping and supporting you now that you can continue with or use even more?

Add your own here: _____

_____

_____

_____

_____

_____

What If ... ?

Playing the "what if" game is like including people in the plan vision. You can facilitate a client's mental and emotional preparation for carrying out her plan by helping her consider a variety of outcomes. For example, "What if your boyfriend doesn't notice when you start getting in shape?" "What if your parents throw a party when your grades improve?" Or, "What might Lisa say when you tell her you want to get back together?" By considering potential reactions, both positive and negative, the client will be better equipped and feel more confident to handle whatever comes along. Obviously, we cannot brainstorm every possible result. The forward thinking process is valuable, as it puts the solution in the future.

SCALING OUT A PLAN

If you have been using a scale already, you've probably already seen its application in the planning stage. However, many people wait until the planning stage to use the scale. You can use scaling questions earlier in the process; they can serve both in the plan itself and as a helpful monitoring tool. In creating a plan around the use of a scale you:

1. determine where clients see themselves now;

2. determine where clients want to be;

3. discuss what the desired number would look like;

4. discuss what it would take to get to the desired number; and

5. firm up the plan for reaching the desired point on the scale.

As we review the scale and you try it out on some of your clients, you'll see it is a quick way to focus the conversation. It makes things visual, concrete, and clear right from the start. The scale works with many approaches. For example, you may be focused on healing from a painful past, but adding a scale during the last five minutes addresses daily life during the upcoming week. Practice 4.5 shows a form that uses scaling in a quick and easy format.

PRACTICE 4.5

Scaling Out a Plan

Name:_____ Date: _____

Purpose: _____

_____

Where are you on the scale right now?

_____

| 1 | 2 | 3 | 4 | 5 | 6 | 7 | 8 | 9 | 10 |

Worst   Best

Potentials: _____

_____

_____

Plan

Where do you want to be on the scale in ____ days?

How are you going to get there?

_____

_____

_____

Remember the starting five criteria:

Personal   Positive   Process

         Present   Precise

Get It Down

Once you have determined an achievable plan, it is helpful to get it in writing, for three reasons.

- First, giving clients a hard copy of the plan, in writing, makes it more important, serious, and real.

- Second, writing the plan down facilitates agreement and communication and helps in working out the fine details.

- Third, clients can take the written plan home, and you can file it and pull it out in subsequent sessions to check progress (chapter 5).

There are many ways to approach writing the plan. In this, as in many cases, your clients are your best guides. Having clients write the plan gives them ownership and responsibility. Or you and the client can both write the plan down simultaneously, as a final team effort, so that you each have a copy. Children can draw their plan or make a symbol or representation of it. Or you can write while a client dictates. Doing it together is more important than the final result.

The written plan does not have to be formal, detailed, or perfect. If you were jotting down potentials as they were discovered, the plan will fit nicely at the bottom of the page. If it makes sense for you, you can write the plan out neatly and have everyone involved sign it. Do whatever makes the most sense for you and your clients. Remember, however, that forms are somewhat restricting. The emptiness of a blank piece of paper allows the solutioning process to unfold as it happens with each individual client. When they use the plan while discussing their progress, clients' self-esteem soars as they look at the written plan and know "I did it," or "I did some of it." The written plan becomes an ongoing success story. By having a written account, clients are aware of exactly what they will try, then see what they did to solve the problem; they will have more than simply the feeling that things are better.

PRACTICE 4.6

Write It Down

Names of those involved in solutioning: _____

_____

_____

Purpose:_____

_____

Potentials:_____

_____

_____

_____

Plan:_____

_____

_____

_____

Progress:_____

_____

_____

_____

_____

Time It

Determining a time frame for monitoring and celebrating progress should be part of the plan. The time frame should be appropriate both situationally and developmentally. You must allow enough time for the client to make a true attempt, yet not so much that the initial feelings of success are gone. Clients usually have an idea of how long they need to give their plan time to work.

Solution success varies with each situation. A question such as, "When should we get back together and talk about the success of your plan?" or "How much time will the plan take?" will guide you. Breaking out of the traditional weekly counseling session may be beneficial to the plan's success. Too much or too little time in between sessions may inhibit progress. Set up sessions that fit the client's needs. But remember, too, that session times do not have to coincide with the time frame. Clients can try plans for two days or two weeks and monitor their own progress. Use the tools in the next chapter to get you and your clients into a permanent solution focus, continually noticing and monitoring the positives.

PLANS: IN SUMMARY

Solutioned plans flow from the potentials and typically require little effort. The momentum of the potentials carries on through the plan, and clients typically leave hopeful and motivated. The tools in this chapter are intended to facilitate doable plans. Try just a couple of the questions and see the differences. Practice 4.7 sums up plans, and Practice 4.8 includes a form that can be used for treatment planning. You can use this form in session with clients and as the treatment plan for your records, or simply blend the language into your own forms. When clients come up with their own plans as a result of solutioning, it eases the responsibility of writing plans for them.

The plan can be empowering. As you'll see in the next chapter, progress happens and clients take responsibility for it when they are involved in the creation of the plan.

PRACTICE 4.7

Solutioning Plans

Positive:

- Notice what works (Metcalf, 1995).

- "Observe for positives" (Walter & Peller, 1992, p. 126).

- Take note of the things you want to continue or do more of.

Pretending:

- When you imagine yourself doing your solution, what will you be doing?

- Don't *do* anything yet; just *pretend* yourself doing your plan.

- Practice doing your solution in your mind.

- Rehearse your plan in your mind each time you think about doing it.

Performing:

- What exceptions and potentials from the past can you try again?

- What current exceptions and potentials can you do more and in other areas?

- What aspects of your pretend potential can you begin doing now?

- What ideas from people can you begin trying?

PRACTICE 4.8

The Plan

Name:_____ Date:_____

The purpose of my plan is:_____

_____

The skills, abilities, and potentials I have to do this plan are:

_____

_____

_____

_____

_____

My plan is to:_____

_____

_____

_____

The following will help me do my plan:_____

_____

_____

_____

_____

I will share this plan with:_____

_____

_____

I will consider my progress on: _____

_____

I will discuss my progress on: _____

_____

Chapter 5

Forget Me Not:
The Final P—Progress

"Not to go back is to advance, and men must
walk, at least, before they dance."
—*Alexander Pope (Webster, 1992, p. 210)*

After initiating some portion of the 4-P process of solutioning—
whether in the form of a single question or by carefully following
each step with multiple purpose reconstructions, potential details,
and a complete plan—the final P of progress must not be forgotten. *Progress* is defined by Webster (1987, p. 940) as "2: a forward
or onward movement (as to an objective or goal): ADVANCE 3:
gradual betterment."

"Gradual betterment" sounds a lot like what happens in counseling. Regardless of the problem, the therapist's philosophy, the
treatment plan, or the methods, most clients improve as a result of
coming to therapy. In this chapter we will look at how solutioning
enables you to celebrate with clients the progress—or "forward
movement"—of their therapy. This is not your basic follow-up—
"maintenance of contact with or reexamination of a person (as a

165

patient), esp. following treatment"—or even follow-through—"to press on in an activity or process, esp. to a conclusion"—neither of which accentuates the advancing nature like progress (Webster, 1987, p. 940). The fourth P of solutioning is a simple, positive, motivating way, sure to improve your clients' self-esteem by giving them the tools and responsibility to monitor their own progress.

SEEING PROGRESS

SFBT therapists often spend the entire second and remaining sessions helping (or maybe even forcing) clients to consider all of the improvements, how they accomplished changes, how they will continue the changes, and whether it is time to end therapy. Other methods may focus only on what problems occurred in the last week. Somewhere in the middle, solutioning allows you to insert a progress question when and where it fits. At some point, asking questions like, "What was better?" allows clients to share, experience pride, and celebrate. Through this process changes are accentuated, responsibility given, and continuation discussed (depending on clients' reports, of course).

The time spent here varies with each client. Some clients want to spend the entire session discussing their progress; others have their own agenda they need to address, which is okay, too.

By discussing what clients did to improve, to make a positive difference, or to keep things from getting worse, you hold not only yourself but also the client accountable and add consistency to the therapeutic road. It takes only a couple of solutioning questions to help clients highlight changes and encourage continued efforts, increasing the likelihood of lasting change. As Friedman and Fanger noted, "In collaboration with the client, our job becomes one of facilitating and catalyzing a process of change that will become self-sustaining and maintainable in the client's everyday life" (1991, p. 6).

The emphasis of progress can be feelings, thoughts, behaviors, or perceptions, allowing minute elements of positive change, growth, or progress to be accentuated and attributed to clients. No matter what philosophy, method, or purpose underlies the therapy, empowerment, motivation, and self-esteem are always helpful elements. This chapter will give you a treasure chest of language to experiment with as you and your clients consider their progress.

Skill Highlight: The Whole Picture

Because of the therapeutic value of empathy and the intense relationships we form with clients, many come in and spill out all the pain, anger, and frustration they are experiencing, complete with details of events, behaviors, interactions, thoughts, and feelings. These are important aspects of client's lives, but they may not give the entire picture. Looking at progress sometime during the session is an effective intervention, providing clients with a broader perspective of themselves and the events in their lives.

This can be done without minimizing or cutting short anything else. In fact, clients will soon be adding their strengths, positive changes, and better times automatically. Sometimes progress is the starting point, sometimes it is the entire session, and sometimes it is not addressed until the client is about to walk out the door, when you might say, "Oh yeah, and what happened that was good during the week?" Progress elicits an attitude of "seek and you shall find," Indeed, psychiatric nurses Mason, Breen, and Whipple noted:

> increased frequency with which members of the nursing staff identify factors indicating improvements in patients' conditions. Patients, too, often point out progress they are making. Looking for improvements has resulted in the nursing staff commenting that it is now easier to provide positive feedback to patients and to give more credit to patients when desired outcomes are accomplished. (1994, p. 48)

Use solutioning to become a codiscoverer with your clients and to find out what worked, what was different, what was better. Then use that information for solutions. Nothing is more motivating than progress. Solutioning helps clients realize what they have begun; once they have that, often there is no stopping them.

> [T]here is no more powerful therapeutic factor than the per-
> formance of activities which were formerly ... impaired or
> inhibited. No insight, no emotional discharge, no recollec-
> tion, can be as reassuring as accomplishment in the actual
> life situation in which the individual failed. (Friedman &
> Fanger, 1991, p. 16)

Oh, Adolescence: The Case of Allison

I worked with Allison early in my experience with
SFBT ideas. Allison thought she had more than her fair
share of problems. From her perspective everything was
a problem: her pencil breaking in English, the boy on
the bus looking at her, her mother's constant nagging.
As I treated Allison for depression with traditional methods, I experimented with SFBT by asking her (usually
at the end of the session), "You've told me of a number
of problems you've experienced lately, but I'm curious
about what happened during the week that you liked?"

This is a watered down version of the SFBT questions and did not require her to share happy times, positive changes, or anything extreme. At first, Allison would
share things like the math teacher brought candy for the
whole class, or her sister made the volleyball team—in
other words, nothing directly to do with her. Then she
began sharing more personal things, like getting an A
on her English test or her mom buying her a new shirt
for cleaning the house. Eventually she was coming into
sessions sharing all of the fun, happy, exciting things
that were happening in her life.

We discussed what role she played in creating or
maintaining the changes, and how she would continue
them. She shared pride in herself, satisfaction with others, and an acceptance of the obstacles she encountered.

In one session Allison commented, "I'm starting to
sound like you. My friend Beth was crying because her
boyfriend dumped her, and I asked her what was good

about her life. My friend looked at me with a shocked look and we both started laughing. We realized that boys are not the end of the world and there are still good things. Our math teacher got mad because we were laughing so hard. It really helped my friend. The last time a boy broke up with her she cried all day. Now that I ask myself the questions like you ask, I feel better most of the time, too."

During the remainder of this session we decided therapy was no longer necessary because, as Allison put it, "I have the questions I need."

I thought to myself, "So do I," and began implementing more solutioning into my counseling.

The questions for checking the progress of solutions can be used at any point during therapy and with any approach. Practice 5.1 will give you some ideas to try with your current clients. Using it, you will find a wealth of information, client competencies, problem exceptions, and solution potentials. Clients may be making progress in areas you are not aware of, in ways that will facilitate their healing, or in ways that will improve their self-esteem and motivation to carry out their solutions and make life the way they want it to be.

"The deepest principle of Human Nature is the craving to be appreciated."
—*William James (Peter, 1977, p. 400)*

PRACTICE 5.1

Getting a Solutioned Response

After a Positive Plan

- What did you find in your life that you like, is positive, and works?

- What did your detective work unveil about the good in your life?

- Tell me about your observations of the positive.

- What did you discover you like about yourself, your relationships, or your life?

After a Pretend Plan

- How did your practice go?

- What benefits did you gain from visualizing your solution?

- Is your solution ready to go?

- Tell me about how your pretend plan happened.

- What parts of your visualization got easier?

After a Perform Plan

- What about your plan worked, helped, or went well?

- Tell me about the difference your plan made.

- Tell me about how your solution was successful.

- What parts of the plan helped the most or worked the best?

General

- What is good about your life right now?

- What did you like about your life this week?

- Which parts of your life are okay or better than the others?

- What areas of life did you enjoy lately?

- What day of the week is your best?

- What part of the day do you enjoy the most?

Feeling

- When did you feel better this week?

- What feelings did you have that you liked?

- Describe a happy time from the past week.

- When did you laugh lately?

- During what part of the day do you feel the best?

- What feelings do you have that you want to continue to have?

- Are there times when you would have expected to feel ... but you didn't?

Thinking

- What positive thoughts did you have this week?

- When this week were you thinking clearly?

- Did you make any good decisions this week?

- What thoughts did you have in mind when you (were feeling better, on track)?

- What messages did you give yourself about your solution?

- When you were enjoying the week, what thoughts were you having?

- What did you say to yourself that worked or helped?

Contextual

- When were things better? What was the situation?

- In what places are things better? What did you do to be in a better place?

- What situation was your favorite this week?

- When were you in a situation where you typically have a panic attack, but you didn't?

- In what situations did you use your solution?

Relational

- When did you get along with others this week?

- Who were you with when things were better?

- What people help you? Who are you with when you're feeling better?

- What relationships improved this week?

- What positive interactions did you have?

- Who else noticed when your solution was successful?

Borrowed

- "What happened that you want to continue to have happen" (de Shazer et al., 1986, p. 218)?

- So, which days were better?

- What are you doing that is good for you?

- "So, what was happening that you wanted to continue to have happen" (O'Hanlon & Weiner-Davis, 1989, p. 145)?

- What did you notice you were doing that gave you self-confidence?

- What good things have you been doing this week?"

- "How is this different from the problem which brought you in? Is this the kind of change you are looking for from therapy? ... As this course continues, will that be all right with you? Will you be satisfied" (Kral & Kowalski, 1989, p. 73)?

PRACTICING RESPONSIBLE SUCCESS

Once you know a client is making progress, the next step is attributing that progress appropriately. To make the most of progress, you need to go one step further and affect self-esteem, responsibility, and control; to do this, you need an additional question or two. Many clients are not in the habit of acknowledging, much less of taking credit for their accomplishments and growth. Some are victims who feel life happens to them and they have no control over it. Others are so encompassed in the blame game—so controlled by external forces—that even the positive seems out of reach. Progress questions will help them begin to take control and responsibility for their lives, starting with their successes.

You Did It! The Case of Haley

Haley came to counseling to save her marriage. She and her husband were barely 18, had been married less than a year, had a 10-month-old baby and another on the way. Her husband was working out of town, and on the weekends he was home, they fought so much they were considering divorce. Haley had been trying to get her husband to come to counseling for months, but he refused, so she finally came alone. Haley loved her husband, and felt he loved her, though he rarely said or showed it. While exploring potentials, Haley remembered the happy times when they were dating and when their son was first born. We developed the following solution potentials from what made those times different/better:

1. They did things together, just the two (and then three) of them, instead of always being at her father's house, where her husband would drink too much.

2. They enjoyed each other's company with fewer financial worries, chores, and responsibilities on their minds. They experienced loving greetings with kisses and hugs.

3. They both attempted to take care of the baby. (Lately he had not been helping at all).

Based on these potentials, Haley made a plan to make the upcoming weekend better. To cover #1, Haley planned a fishing outing for just the three of them. She prepared food and supplies so her husband would have no excuse not to go. For #2 Haley, asked her mother to watch her son so she could clean the house, prepare a nice dinner, go to counseling and de-stress, fix herself up, and greet her husband at the door with a kiss.

Managing #3 was tougher. Haley's frustration at being alone with a baby all week and then not getting any relief on the weekend had been coming out in violent outbursts at her husband. This resulted in a lot of yelling—which upset the baby so he would not quit crying and go to sleep. Haley said she couldn't even shower without taking the baby because her husband couldn't handle him.

We remembered back to the earlier times when he had helped. I asked for details, and she remembered teaching him how to care for the baby. Suddenly, it was as if a light bulb went off in her head. Haley said she might need to tell her husband what she had found that worked *now*. She realized that as the baby grew while her husband was away from home, he might be unsure of what to do. Maybe teaching him (the way she had before) would make a difference. Haley left, excited about their weekend together. The following week, she came in glowing.

Willyn: What was good about your weekend with your husband?

Haley: We didn't fight once during the entire weekend. My husband has really changed. My mom couldn't watch Derek, but it was okay. We all had a great dinner together. Bud was actually nice.

Willyn: Did you meet him at the door with a kiss instead of complaining, like you planned?

Haley: *(nodding)* But he was really different. He seemed happy to see me for once. We went to the lake on Saturday and it was really fun. He went without complaining or making up excuses. We even rented movies and watched them that evening. Part of Sunday we spent at my dad's. It was okay, though, because Bud left when I asked him.

Willyn: Did you have everything ready for fishing, so he didn't have any excuses, like you planned?

Haley: Yeah, I guess, but he was so different. He said the picnic looked great. I didn't have to yell that we never do anything together. He helped me with Derek. He even said I should go take a nap and he would watch him. I can't believe how different my husband was.

Willyn: That's wonderful. Did you teach him about what you've found that works with the baby?

Haley: Yeah, but Bud changed so much.

Willyn: How does this weekend compare to the ones from your past?

Haley: It was the best since I got pregnant the first time. We even talked about how we need to talk before our frustration builds up and we blow up and fight. It was really great. Bud was really great.

Willyn: What did you do to make the weekend great?

Haley: Bud was so different. He was really nice.

Willyn: What did *you* do to make the weekend great?

Haley: Well, I'm not really sure. I think Bud just thought about how awful the fighting was and decided to change.

She was not going to acknowledge any of her efforts or give herself any credit for the improvements.

Willyn: Wait a minute, Haley. I can name a number of things you did: You greeted Bud with a kiss, prepared a picnic, taught him about the baby. Do you think those things made a difference in how he reacted to you?

Haley: I did do all those things, didn't I? I even had him sit down and talk about how we might keep from fighting so much. I couldn't believe I did that. So the things I did may have helped things go so well? Maybe I caused some of the changes he showed? *(contemplating)* I probably did have some affect.

Willyn: Definitely! Sum up for me all the things you've done to make a difference.

The list she compiled was long, from coming to counseling by herself, to cleaning the house, to having him talk with her about their fighting. At the end of her list she said, "It wasn't all him, was it? He didn't just miraculously change. Some of it was because of the plan *I* had and what *I* did."

Willyn: How do you feel about all the great things you've just told me you've done to make a difference in your marriage?

Haley: Well, when I look at it like that, I am pretty proud of myself. It's a cool feeling to know I can make a difference in my marriage. We might just make it if we can have more good weekends. I can keep doing things like I did this weekend, and we can keep talking about how not to fight.

The rest of the session we spent discussing the fact that there would be fighting again sometimes, but that it, too, could be different. We discussed possible setbacks and which potentials could help make the next problem into a discussion instead of a fight.

The next session, Haley brought her husband with her. He had so enjoyed the changes that he had changed his mind about counseling and was willing to give it a try. I used some of the progress questions with both of them at the beginning of that session so they would not attribute the changes to counseling, but to themselves. They took control of their marriage and, after five more sessions (which focused on communication and parenting skills), they decided they no longer needed counseling.

I always remember Haley because she was so happy about the good weekend, yet without the progress questions, she would not have realized she had anything to do with it. The new pattern would have had little chance of continuing if she continued believing her husband had miraculously changed. The next week, when she had opened the door, upset about bills and the baby, they would have returned to the old pattern of arguing. Haley would have been left wondering why her husband had changed again.

The empowerment she felt from seeing her role in the marriage differently and from acknowledging some influence motivated Haley so much that the new pattern continued. She and Bud were able to work out ways to deal with the inevitable stresses of marriage without fighting uncontrollably or divorcing. Before, Haley had let life control her; now she was controlling her life.

It is important to make the most of it when clients take steps, even small ones, in the right direction. Many clients see their successes as chance events, give the counselor or someone else credit for them, or overlook them altogether.

Solution Application: Self-Esteem

Any counselor using any method would hate to let progress slip by unnoticed, be wrongly credited for a client's efforts, or miss a chance to empower and improve self-esteem. Of course, self-esteem is not something we can *give* to clients. Through solutioning, however, we can set them up to *earn* self-esteem. As

Hwang noted, "Self-esteem cannot be manufactured externally; it must develop from within" (1995, p. 488).

By following any progress, growth, or accomplishment with one little question—"How did you do that?"—solutioning enables clients to earn self-esteem. By sharing how they improved, they realize *for themselves* that they have the skills, abilities, and talents to make a difference—and that feels good. Note that this is different from showers of praise and compliments (deserved or not). Hwang also pointed out, "Too often, self-esteem programs send completely counterproductive messages ... by directing youngsters' attention toward their own basest inner gratification— no matter what you do, it's fine, because you are always wonderful and special" (1995, p. 488).

Having unconditional positive regard for clients and setting them up to earn self-esteem are complimentary attributes of the teaming relationship. In fact, the question, "How did you do that?" shows regard *and* encourages self-recognition. If you want your clients to gain self-esteem, you must allow them to earn it. Practice 5.2 gives some questions to help your clients own their successes. Practice 5.3 lets them take charge and write down their progress—discovering it, owning it, and projecting it into the future.

"When you dare to dream, dare to follow
that dream, dare to suffer through the pain,
sacrifice, self-doubts, and friction from the
world—when you show such courage and
tenacity—you will genuinely impress yourself.
Self-esteem is always forged from your efforts"
—*Dr. Laura Schlessinger (1994, p. 10)*

PRACTICE 5.2

Making the Most Out of Progress

My Favorite

- How did you do that?

General

- What part did you play in the good things you've just shared?

- Of the things you liked, which do you have control over?

- What did you do that made (this morning, Saturday, etc.) good for you?

- What exactly did you do, say, or think that made a difference?

Feeling

- How did you get to feeling better?

- What were you doing during the times you felt better?

- How did you manage to feel so great on Thursday?

- How did you not let your anger get the best of you?

- How did it feel when you took control and made things better?

Thinking

- How did you get yourself to think positively?

- What did you do to think clearly?

- How did you make that good decision?

- What thoughts were in mind when you (were feeling better, on track, etc.)?

- What messages did you give yourself about your solution?

- When you were enjoying the week, what thoughts were you having?

- What did you say to yourself that worked or helped?

Contextual

- How did you create a situation where things were better, or your solution was successful?

- What did you do to be in a better place?

Relational

- What role did you play in getting along with ... ?

- What did you do that made a positive difference with ... ?

- How did you get ... to help you?

- What effect did you have on the improvement of your relationship?

- What influence did you have in getting together with ... or having a good talk with ... ?

Feedback

- You really made that happen.

- That seems different than the way you handled it in the past.

- It sounds like you made a change in the right direction.

- You did (positive change) and (positive result) happened.

- When you (thought, felt, behaved) that way, it really made a difference.

- Sounds to me like you did a lot of changing.

- Sounds to me like you made some great things happen in your life.

- Wow! You really took control.

- It seems like things are better because of what you've done.

- It seems like things are better because of the changes you've made.

- Your (action) must have really made a difference with (you mother, friend, husband, etc.).

- What did you do new or differently that made a change, a difference, or helped? Which part of your plan worked?

PRACTICE 5.3

Making Progress

Things I did (solutions):_____

_____

_____

Things (solutions) I can do again, more, a lot:_____

_____

_____

New plan: _____

_____

_____

_____

_____

Solution Application: Domestic Violence

"Out of suffering have emerged the strongest souls; the most massive characters are seared with scars."

—*E. H. Chapin (Peter, 1977, p. 456)*

When you model, practice, and teach your clients to focus on solutions, strengths, positives, and personal abilities, you help them make a first step toward breaking the cycle of violence. Solutioning's emphasis on progress—owning it, taking responsibility for it, and building on it—is tremendously empowering. Empowerment and self-esteem help clients break free from the confines of learned helplessness as they acknowledge their strengths, abilities, and hope. Every step of the 4-P process is helpful, but the continued emphasis on progress draws out the hope in any situation.

Learned Hopefulness: The Case of Sheryl

Sheryl called me in the middle of the night from the emergency room. When I got there she was physically okay, but emotionally humiliated. She couldn't get over her embarrassment at having wet her pants when her husband hit her. Sheryl swore this was the last time, that she was never going back. I drove her to a safe house and we stayed up late, working out the details of her new life.

The next day when I went to pick her up (according to the plan), she was gone. The housekeeper said Sheryl had gotten up, called her husband, and had him pick her up. I couldn't believe it.

Sheryl called me a couple months later. She had been focusing on the positives in her life and was ready to talk. As she noticed things that worked, she realized she had more abilities than she gave herself credit for, that she wasn't stupid, and that maybe she could do better. She had also realized that the most important, most positive parts of her life were her children, and that they deserved better.

Over the next three months, noting small gains in progress, taking responsibility for them, and building self-esteem, Sheryl *chose* to leave her situation and make a better life for herself and her children. This decision took a lot of courage—and Sheryl had to build up a store of self-esteem, control, and hope *before* she could make such a big move. The building up happened because of solutioning's emphasis on progress.

Before, when her husband hit her, Sheryl believed she didn't have the strength to leave, that she couldn't make it on her own, that she had caused the abuse. The progress questions we worked on showed her a series of small steps she could take responsibility for—and that gave her *hope*. Sheryl did make it on her own. A year later, she wrote me a note saying that her children had given her a thank-you card on the anniversary of the day they had left.

TAKE IT AND RUN

> "It is never to late to be what you
> might have been."
> —*George Elliot (Webster, 1992, p. 12)*

Once you have a clear, detailed description of progress and the client is accepting ownership of his/her part, it is important to take steps—now, in the heat of pride, when motivation is at its best—to increase the probability of the changes continuing. The rehearsal visualized in the plan is now an instant replay of the progress. You want details, ownership, and responsibility for the changes. The team might make a new plan on how to continue and possibly expand or increase the changes.

Most clients will want a little more practice with their progress before terminating counseling. The progress questions serve as a quick and useful barometer for the need for therapy and encourage clients to project their progress into their future. This is where ownership, control, and responsibility are internalized. Clients cannot be dependent on other people, other circumstances, or other events for changes to continue. Positive change will go only as far as *they* can take it. Now it's time to use the starting five criteria questions again. If a client reports that he did not fight, did not feel depressed, whatever, ask what he did instead. Pursuing any progress will result in a precise description of what changes have begun and what needs to continue.

PRACTICE 5.4

Blast Off: Projecting Progress into the Future

- How will you keep these positive changes going?

- How are you going to continue this happening?

- What can you do so that this happens even more?

- How can you encourage the change to continue, increase, and last?

- Who can help you keep this positive progress happening?

- Name all the things you did that you can continue so the changes last.

- What will ensure that the difference you are seeing now will continue?

- What can you do tomorrow to help things stay on track?

- Tell me the main thing you did last week that you need to remember to keep it going strong.

- What parts of the plan are you going to keep doing?

Feedback

- Now that you know what works, you can do it again.

- I am so impressed that you've figured out something that makes things better (it's better to be specific), so you can look forward to life from now on.

- It sounds to me like you have what you need to continue feeling, thinking, or acting so great.

- You seem to feel proud of the changes you have made and are ready to keep it up.

MIXING IN REALITY

"True success is overcoming the fear
of being unsuccessful."
—*Paul Sweeney (Peter, 1977, p. 360)*

Of course, client progress rarely continues uninterrupted. Discussing potential roadblocks during the progress portion of the session will not take away from solutions that have begun, but will help prepare the client for possible setbacks while motivation, self-esteem, and empowerment are high. Using the suggestions and language you learned in chapter 4 will help you and your client prepare.

Even when progress is substantial and clients feel capable and want to continue the changes, "Many clients comment that it helps to have a plan when difficulties arise" (O'Hanlon & Weiner-Davis, 1989, p. 147). Problems that are serious enough to bring someone into counseling rarely go away, never to rear their ugly heads again. Problem reoccurrence may be a normal part of progress and solution development. It is not a black-or-white, win-or-lose situation—it is life, with ups and downs. Help your clients explore the future of their progress and prepare them for setbacks while you are celebrating the good things that are happening now.

Skill Highlight: Mixing

Being able to celebrate and acknowledging reality at the same time may take some careful wording. Here are some suggestions:

- "Is there anything that might happen in the next week or two which might present a challenge to keeping these good things going? What would that challenge be? How might you handle it differently this time? Is there anything else that might pop up which might be challenging?" (O'Hanlon & Weiner-Davis, 1989, p. 147).

- How are you going to overcome future obstacles or challenges to your solution?

- What about when things don't go perfectly? How will you adjust your solution and keep on going?

AND THE SURVEY SAYS ...

Can't you just hear the host of the old game show drawing out the suspense—"And the Survey says ... "—the audience and contestants anxiously anticipating the results? Is that the way you feel as you enter a session with a client, especially one who made a detailed plan in the previous session? Waiting for the results of clients' efforts can be suspenseful indeed. Both Walter and Peller (1992) and O'Hanlon and Weiner-Davis (1989) discussed typical client responses seen during subsequent sessions. Walter and Peller typically asked a question like, "How convinced are you that your changing will continue?" after getting a report of some positive change (1992, p. 142). This led them to draw one of the following conclusions:

1. The client is convinced she or he is on track and, therefore, therapy is completed.

2. The client thinks she or he is on track and thinks that more practice of the solution is needed.

3. The client thinks she or he is on track and will be convinced by success over time.

4. The client appears to be struggling and further solution development is needed. (Walter & Peller, 1992, p. 142)

O'Hanlon & Weiner-Davis categorized clients using the following group distinctions:

> There are those who return reporting a miraculous week—a "one session cure." Everything was perfect, far beyond their wildest dreams. This we call "the miracle group." The second category is the "so-so group." They had a better week than weeks previous, but there was still evidence that the problem was not completely resolved yet. The third group reports no changes or perhaps regression. This group we call "same or worse." (1989, p. 146)

The similarities in the client responses are obvious and perhaps oversimplified. Realistically, what choices are there other than getting better a little, a lot, or not at all? Of course, these happen on a continuum, with an infinite number of variations. Individual clients and their individual needs must be the main consideration in adapting a treatment plan and choosing further methods. A client may be feeling better but not thinking clearly, or acting better but not feeling better. Perhaps he is doing better at work but not at home, or a couple is improving as parents but still experiencing marital problems. The various categories of client responses listed earlier were based on a specific goal used in the solution-focused method and do not take into account the multifaceted nature of clients and their purposes for therapy. The better way, of course, is to look at individual progress and what actually happens in therapy (no matter which methods are used). Adapting the language of progress will allow you to meet the needs of all your clients.

However, some grouping is helpful for illustrating the different types of language solutioning provided for different client progress responses. The following categories of client progress may be helpful when you are experimenting with solutioning language. After gaining some familiarity with the questions, individual clients will replace the categories and your question choices will be automatic.

Adrenalines

Clients in this group are very excited about their week. Their emotions are high. They say they are happy, smile a lot, and are energetic, motivated, and hopeful. Their thoughts are encompassed by the wonderful events, feelings, or interactions of the week. Everything just seemed to click, life is perfect, and nothing can change that. They are on top of the world.

With this group, you need to ask exactly what they did to contribute to their success, what they can control and continue, and what happened that was wonderful but completely random. This will enable you to celebrate and reinforce accurately, based on what *they did* to make things better. Is the boss nice all of a sudden? Did a long-lost friend call out of the blue? Did a new outfit make the client happy? Remember, clues to solutions can be found only within the clients' actions. Solutioning will help clients realize what role they played (or not) in the changes and what they can continue. Maybe moving the desk away from the window and being more productive made for a nice week with the boss. Maybe persistence in maintaining contact with the friend for years, despite his rejection, finally paid off. Maybe feeling good is partially due to appearance. We have to help clients see progress for what it really is. Perhaps it is a step in the solution direction. The employee who moves the desk may be on track to improving productivity. The friend may be ready to start working on new friendships. The new outfit may be a baby step toward self-esteem.

We must also help Adrenalines consider challenges that might arise. You can use the questions from Practice 5.4 to consider roadblocks. How you view the Adrenaline-charged progress might depend on your orientation. SFBT therapists may feel therapy is no longer needed, behaviorists may consider the reinforcements that were in place during the week, family therapists may look at the interactions that took place, an astrologer would say the planets were in the right alignment. Practice 5.5 gives solutioning language and ideas for Adrenaline-charged clients that can be blended into any orientation.

Roller Coasters

Roller Coasters initially exhibit many of the same characteristics as Adrenalines. They are high and everything is wonderful. This can be a fun session, except that many times the same client will return the next week with a burst bubble. She has learned there are distractions at the new desk location, the long-lost friend only wanted to borrow money, or the new outfit has lost its appeal.

Roller Coasters may be in a life pattern of extreme ups and downs: Some are in cycles of violence, some exhibit black-and-white thinking, and some have very challenging circumstances that make lasting change difficult. You need to help them consider the role they played in making everything wonderful and, within that role, what they can continue doing. Roller Coasters also need to consider what happened that was completely out of their control and what may not last. Scaling is a valuable tool with Roller Coasters. Putting numbers on the ups and downs and making a plan to move up only one or two notches at a time helps them level off from their previous practice of shooting for the moon, temporarily finding it, then crashing back to Earth.

Yes, Buts …

Yes, Buts … have had a good week and made substantial progress, but they spend the session purposefully trying to discount the changes. This may be because they are more comfortable in a victim stance, because they are skeptical, because they want someone else to blame if the changes don't last, or because success is unfamiliar and scares them. Often these clients will tell you about times in the past when they felt this great … but it didn't last, and the disappointment was horrible.

The thoughts and the feelings of these clients rarely match. They want to protect themselves from feeling any disappointment by denying the positive current feelings and undoing their success. As O'Hanlon and Weiner-Davis noted, "The fear is 'easy come, easy go'" (1989, p. 147).

Some people know how to operate only in crisis. Solutioning is most difficult for clients with this problem mindset. They have a hard time envisioning a better future during the planning stage and an even harder time acknowledging progress when it happens. Mason, Breen, and Whipple identified "patients invested in maintaining the sick role" as characteristic of a decreased response to solution-focused therapy (1994, p. 48). Blending solutioning with other methods may be the best choice with these clients. Continued use of scales and the progress questions also may help them gain some sense of hope.

Time, Oh Give Me Times

This group resembles the discussion of Walter and Peller: "The client thinks she or he is on track and will be convinced by success over time" (1992, p. 144). Understandably, clients who have been problem-encompassed need to experience their solution over time before they are ready to discontinue counseling. As Walter and Peller noted, "the client still feels she or he needs to practice the solution for a longer period of time" (1992, p. 143).

Continued support, reinforcement, and practice will ensure their success. For some clients confidence comes when the practice is complete and they are sure of their solution. For others, during the practice of a successful solution, another issue will arise. Often the initial success enables the client to work on some other, perhaps more difficult area of life. The preliminary solution may be what some critics of SFBT have called the "band aid"—an initial improvement with deeper problems still requiring therapy (Todd, 1992, p. 172). Symptom relief may give clients time not only to practice that solution but to work on other issues as well.

Mary, Mary Quite Contrary:
The Case of Mary and Her Mother

Mary, a high school freshman, came to counseling with her mother to work on their fighting. They reported fighting every evening about almost everything. The fights included yelling, name-calling, and slamming doors. Each of them was exhausted. They were so angry with each other that a referee almost seemed a more appropriate choice for help.

During one session Mary shared that she and her mother used to say goodbye to each other every morning before school, but lately they were not speaking to each other much. Mary said her days were starting off negatively and continued that way. Mother added that she was experiencing a lot of negativity in her days, too.

I complimented Mary on her insight and ability to see a potential solution from the past (saying goodbye). After some more discussion, the two made a plan to say goodbye to each other each morning. We then worked out the details of Mary getting up in time on her own and Mother purposely pausing before leaving. They were to say goodbye no matter what had happened the night before. They even shared that, not long ago, a kiss goodbye had been the standard. I cautioned them not to move too fast, that they should just say goodbye the first week.

The plan had little to do with the topics of their fights, their communication problems, or why they had come to counseling. However, the two came back the following week much more open and hopeful. Mary had gotten herself up each morning and Mother had paused. They had parted with a pleasant goodbye each day, and the last two they had even shared a quick kiss.

Mary and her mother both said their days went better as a result of the more positive start. Most importantly, the morning pattern seemed to remind them that they did love each other. This opened the door for us to begin working on their communication style, the issues behind their fights, and so on.

Solutioning not only sped up but opened up the way for work that might not have happened otherwise. Within two months, Mary and her mother had established rules and consequences within the home, instated family meetings, decreased the intensity and frequency of their fights, and were making it through Mary's growing need for independence without further incident or need for counseling. Although solutioning was only a small part of their therapy, it was crucial to changing their attitudes toward each other, their hope, and their willingness for change.

Prove Its!

Some clients hold on to a belief that the differences and changes they are experiencing are mere chance. Both Walter and Peller and O'Hanlon and Weiner-Davis discuss this type of reaction. Walter and Peller include it in their third possibility: "the client's evidence for success is several successes or some marker the client has selected" (1992, p. 144). For O'Hanlon and Weiner-Davis, it falls within the miracle group:

> Even in the miracle group there are skeptics, and rightfully so. The method here is to add on only a small period of time to the longest time in the past that things went well and ask if that would be a difference that makes a difference. (1989, p. 147)

Some counseling methods may call this *resistance*, others *dependence*, others *learned helplessness*, and so on. From a solutioning perspective, a client's need for proof is understandable. During the time clients take to gain faith in themselves and their solutions, they also are learning and practicing the solutioning process.

But Will It Last? The Case of Joan

Joan kept repeating, "If we can make it from September through Christmas, our marriage will survive." The improvements she had seen during therapy were great, but she and her husband had a long history of domestic violence and alcoholism. She knew well their 10-year pattern of ups and downs, relapses and recoveries, and cycles of violence. Things had gone well before, but it never lasted.

Joan chose to continue counseling until the first of the year, so she could practice her solutions and see if the changes would last. As she continued to come in for support, praise, and practice, she also learned the 4-P process. Soon, she and her husband began doing together what Joan and I were doing in counseling: sitting down with an issue and going through the 4-Ps. This was in addition to the communication skills, insight, and understanding she had gained during our time together.

During our last session, when Joan had reached her benchmark, she said she had seen enough proof and gave the changes an 80% chance of lasting. And, she said, she was not concerned about the 20% chance of relapse because she had solutioning. She left hopeful, empowered, and in control of her life for the first time in years. She called a year later to let me know she and her husband were still sober and still married, and were now experts on the solutioning process!

Nothing, Nada, Zippos

Some clients are not able to attempt changes because of circumstances beyond their control. Others report doing the plan with no observable results. Even in these cases, however, clients often report changes in their thinking or feelings simply because they *have* a plan. It is empowering for them to feel they are taking control of their lives, even in small ways.

Sometimes clients must work first on the circumstances that prevented their plans. The client who returns without results probably is coming from a narrow world view. A solutioning intervention may bring a broader perspective. As O'Hanlon and Weiner-Davis noted, "When clients report that things have remained the same ... we do not accept this report at face value without further investigation" (1989, pp. 150-151). Asking additional progress questions usually turns up some difference as a result of the plan that hadn't been realized or acknowledged.

Often, you see the greatest boosts in self-esteem in this group, among clients who think nothing has made a difference and then realize something did. Sometimes small but significant change is hard to see when you are living and experiencing it. An objective party, a question, or a retelling may bring the difference to light. Solutioning progress questions are designed to do just that.

Rock Bottoms

This group resembles the "same or worse group" discussed by O'Hanlon and Weiner-Davis (1989, p. 150). Some clients fight getting better, and some have circumstances beyond their control that get worse. Others are using amazing coping skills just to maintain their current level of functioning. There is some truth in the idea that sometimes things have to get worse before they get better.

Solutioning can still be used with this group; but you must be careful not to discourage a client by repeatedly asking, "What is better?" when the answer is, "Nothing." SFBT purists would probably contend there is always some change to be found, but continuing the search at times can discount a client's true feelings. Empathy is sometimes a better choice. The progress questions can be used later, when the client can answer them with real positives—not just with something insignificant. De Shazer et al. (1986) used the following statement with clients who saw things as worse:

> It is our experience that if people don't do something right, things will get worse over time rather than remain the same. What are you doing? Have things hit bottom, and can you reasonably expect things to change soon? Or, have things yet to hit bottom and so things won't get better as quickly? (p. 218)

This statement blends in the ideas of solutioning while acknowledging the client's plight. Walter and Peller suggested "further solution development" when this occurs (1992, p. 145). O'Hanlon and Weiner-Davis suggested asking, "Whose problem is this, anyway?" (1989, pp. 150-151). This may be a perfect time for you to revisit interventions and methods that have worked for you in the past. You might have to remind yourself, "If it works, do it. *If not, do something different.*" No one method is suited for all clients at all times, and Rock Bottoms may be telling you they need something different. An intuitive therapist will listen to the client and know what to do.

Out of Controls

Out of Controls are masters of the blame game. They come into the session intent on changing their spouse, parents, boss, teacher, and so on. The notion that "You cannot control anyone but yourself" seems to go in one ear and out the other. "What will you be doing when things are better for you?" often is the million-dollar question, because they answer the first time with what *someone else will be doing first.*

Solutioning is perfect for these clients, because you don't buy into their victim stance, jump onto the blaming bandwagon through empathy, or encourage a holier-than-thou attitude that is beyond change. Persistence in asking and rephrasing all of the potential questions is the key. Often, Out of Controls must take a huge first step of accepting others, circumstances, and themselves before they can learn to use what control they do have. "For clients who prefer to use the session for identifying and amplifying the complaint, or who can only articulate changes that are needed to be made by other people, more time is required" (Webster, 1990, p. 20). That time is well spent when Out of Control clients gain control, take responsibility, and use their abilities to make a difference.

PRACTICE 5.5

Mix and Match

Adrenalines

- Of all the wonderful changes and events of your week, how many of them can you influence to last?

- Things really clicked for you this week! How many of those changes will continue?

- Of all the great changes, which one are you most proud of? How did you do that?

- How did you interact with or influence the people around you so that they made such positive changes toward you? Will it continue? Can you control it?

- "I am concerned that since all of your days were 'perfect,' when you have a day that is just 'normal,' you might incorrectly think that things are sliding back to square one" (O'Hanlon & Weiner-Davis, 1989, p. 149).

- Next week things might not be so awesome, just more regular. How are you going to focus on your positive changes then?

- Life rarely stays awesome, which is not to say that it couldn't still be really great, based on your efforts. What can you concentrate on that has worked for you during this awesome week that will help in the great, normal, or other types of weeks?

- What is the most important thing you have learned about yourself during this wonderful time in your life? How can you hold onto that or keep it going?

- What has been your greatest skill, resource, or thought this week? Can you continue with it?

Roller Coasters

- What role did you play in the positive changes? What can you continue?

- When have you felt this great before and kept it going? How might you keep these changes going?

- If you have a bad or not-so-good day, will you still be able to continue your changes?

- Nothing works 100% of the time. When these changes don't work, it is important not to abandon them, but to think of times and ways they do work.

- What can you learn from the up times to use during the down times?

Yes, Buts ...

- What is the best thing you did this week? Can you do it again next week?

- Is it okay to be proud of yourself? What are you most proud of right now?

- Who will notice you have made these positive changes in your life?

- What will they say you did?

- What will _____ say was the coolest thing you did to make a difference?

- You are telling me about a great week and some great changes you made, yet you are not enjoying it or seeming happy about it. What is going on?

- Your thoughts that you made a difference this week don't seem to match your feelings of worry. Could we talk about that?

- Who is proud of you? Is there anyone who doesn't want to see you do better?

- How are you feeling about the likelihood that the changes will continue?

Time, Oh Give Me Times

- How long must the changes last before you are convinced of their value?

- When might you feel confident in the solution?

- Do you feel continued practice will ensure that your solution will endure?

- Now that you have overcome(whatever), is there anything else you want to work on?

- It sometimes takes awhile to get used to being better. When you are comfortable with the changes, we can discuss ending.

Prove Its!

- Is there some benchmark that will signal you no longer need to come?

- Who will need to notice your changes first? How many people need to be aware of your changes before you are convinced they are for real?

- How long have changes lasted in the past? How long would they need to last now?

- Being leery of positive changes can protect you from disappointment, but sometimes it takes a little faith. There aren't many guarantees in life, and the proof you want may never happen. Do you think you could enjoy the changes you have made for what they are now?

Nothing, Nada, Zippos

- Are there changes in your plan you thought of during the week, even though you didn't get to try them?

- What is the main thing that kept you from doing some of your plan?

- Did you think about your plan?

- Did you notice a change in your thinking or feeling, regardless of whether you did your plan?

- What exactly happened during your week? How did you handle … ?

- How do you feel about your week in general?

- Would anyone you interact with say there were any changes or differences in your week?

- Go back to when you left therapy last week. What happened the next day? The next?

Rock Bottoms

- Is the purpose/goal still the same?

- Have you noticed anything you like about any area of your life?

- How have you managed to keep things from getting worse?

- What coping skills have you used this week to survive?

- Wow! You made it through a really tough week. How did you do that?

- Considering everything you've been through this week, I am amazed at how well you are doing. How do you do it?

- Do you want to make things better?

- What other people are involved in your coming to therapy?

- What things in your life do you want to continue, stay the same, or amplify?

Out of Controls

- What will *you* be doing when things are the way you want them?

- What can *you* do to encourage (so and so) to (change desired)?

- How might *you* influence (so and so) to (changes desired)?

- You can't control or change anyone but yourself.

- What would (so and so) say *you* could do?

- Let's test (so and so). Do (the behavior that person would want) and see what (he or she) does.

- Try an experiment. Since you can't get (so and so) to change, why don't *you* change and see what reaction you get?

WHAT'S NEXT?

Increasing the odds for making positive change last is a worthwhile intervention. We've all had families who come and go in therapy as they face the inevitable ups and downs of life. Sometimes changes are easier for clients to make than to maintain. Solutioning interventions—blended with continued support and reinforcement—will help with maintenance, which is the hallmark of true healing. For clients who need an extra boost to keep things going, here are some additional interventions:

1. Gambling

2. Experimenting, contests, and games

3. "Positive blame"

4. Interactive cheerleading

5. Recipes, formulas, and prescriptions

6. Scaling, percentages, and ratings

7. Journaling and storying

Gambling

Gambling or "betting" is effective with children and adolescents, who often are willing to gamble with their abilities, love a challenge, and are naturally competitive. "This method requires that the client can both describe the new behaviors in concrete terms and express a notable degree of confidence that she/he intends to continue the new pattern" (Kral & Kowalski, 1989, p. 74). In other words, clients must be clear on what they are betting will continue. Make sure the gamble is a safe one and the desired outcome can be achieved, then express your confidence while still making it a challenge.

And the Odds Are ... The Case of Sam

Sam was a 5th-grader who was taking medication for ADD. Recently, his mother had divorced her second husband, who had been with them since Sam was 1 year old. After the divorce, Sam's younger sister still spent time with the father because he was her biological father. Sam did not get to spend time with him, because the man was not his "real" father, although he was the only father Sam had ever known.

Sam had been having violent outbursts and yelling matches with his mother; he punched holes in the walls and sometimes got so upset he passed out. He had been suspended from school twice for fighting.

After two sessions, Sam and I had the idea that maybe he could manage his anger at school by holding it between his index finger and thumb and then letting it out on a bike ride later. (Mom had bought Sam a bike since he started therapy, and it was doing more to reduce his outbursts than anything)

Sam came back the next week and reported there had been a couple times when he *almost* hit the kid in front of him, who was always bugging him when they were supposed to be working. But, Sam had put his anger in its place and held it there until after school. Sam had noticed that this bothered the kid in front of him a lot. He seemed frustrated at not being able to provoke Sam into a fight.

At the end of the session, I asked Sam if he liked to gamble. He said he and his stepfather had bet on football games before and he liked it. I asked him if he would bet on his ability to keep his anger in place and keep from getting in trouble for another week. He agreed. We talked about how the kid in front of him would probably come up with some new strategies to make Sam mad.

Sam knew this week would be harder, but he felt he could do it. I told Sam I knew he could do it, too—but, just to make the bet worthwhile and give Sam more incentive, we could bet a milkshake on it. Sam said he loved milkshakes and he knew he could do it now.

Sam came back the next week with a huge smile, singing, "Where's my milkshake? Where's my milkshake?" He sat down and immediately told me about all the mean things the kid in front of him had tried to get him mad, but none of them had worked. In fact, that kid had been the one who got in trouble this week, not Sam. Sam felt more empowered than he had when he fought with the kid. He wanted to bet on everything from then on, even controlling outbursts with his mom. Sam worked out his anger, began sharing his feelings openly, and controlled his outbursts—and I bought a lot of milkshakes, sundaes, and banana splits.

Experimenting, Contests, and Games

Experiments, contests, and games are valuable in encouraging the continuation of solutions. They may become part of the revised plan or they can be used as part of the initial plan. After a client has made some progress, you have something tangible with which to experiment, create a contest, or play a game. The idea is to set up challenges for your clients, especially those who seem to value and respond well to competition.

For example, if a client's treatment goal is to quit smoking and he has not had as many cigarettes during the past week, you might ask him to see just how few cigarettes he actually needs to survive, just for a week. Note the element of paradox in it, as well. Asking a couple who can observe the most positive actions in the other during the week may help them gain a new, more positive perspective of each other. Or you could ask a child how many nice things she can say to her brother in a five-minute period or for a day. Metcalf (1995, p. 236) told a story of a school counselor dealing with two boys who wanted to participate in activities they were currently missing because of fighting. She set them up in a competition, "framing it as a contest," using the following scale:

Freedom from fights

1	2	3	4	5		5	4	3	2	1

Jimmy   David

These are small, fun ways to encourage clients to keep up the good work of making positive changes in their lives.

"Positive Blame"

We've already determined that solutioning is effective at eliminating blaming, but we have all had clients who know nothing other than blame. If this is the case, why not use it positively? Find a way to blame the positive changes on the client. This gives responsibility—a quality used to end negative blaming. Kral described how positive blame can be used in schools: "Once an exception has been identified, the teacher or parent is 'blamed' for its occurrence" (1986, p. 58). And Kral and Kowalski explained how positive blame could be used with couples:

> [I]t is often helpful in couples therapy to attribute a change in one partner to the other. This serves to reinforce the interactional nature of the shift, thereby implying that one's behavior has the potential to impact the other partner in a positive manner. (1989, p. 74)

Parents can blame their children for good behaviors and actions. Therapists can blame their clients for creating more change than planned during the week.

You Did It! The Case of Beth

Beth had a plan to communicate with her husband without yelling and without addressing any of their "hot" issues for two days—which she did. She also sat him down and talked to him about how they might prevent fighting when they felt their frustration building. This was far beyond what she had felt capable of trying at the previous week's session. So I *blamed* her for taking such a bold step to make her marriage better. She accepted the blame gladly and chose to continue her new efforts.

Interactive Cheerleading

Many clients benefit from having you point out the great changes or differences they have overlooked. You might say, "Wait a minute! You did what?" Then let them restate the positive they were about to brush past. When they say it again and see you smiling or praising them, it raises their self-esteem meter a notch. Clients with low self-esteem, problem-encompassed clients, and some others tend to diminish their own abilities and accomplishments. Interactive cheerleading is pointing out and reflecting back what they have already done that is an improvement, labeling it, and praising it. Sometimes, the praise is unnecessary because simply identifying and labeling the accomplishment makes the client feel great.

The *interactive* part of the cheerleading is accomplished by ending with a question. Adding, "How did you do that?" puts the authority back on the client. When you merely say, "Wow! That was a great skill," *you* are the expert. You achieve more when you give the client the expert status: "How did you develop that skill?" By tacking on a potential searching question, the behavior, skill, or thought is more likely to become part of the client's repertoire. You can let clients share and praise themselves, by asking, "How do you feel about it? What are your thoughts about it?" Once in a while you get a client who will not agree. Most of the time, however, asking a comment question allows clients to bask in their glory a little longer.

One word of caution here: Some clients respond so well to cheerleading and praise, they may hesitate to share concerns. They don't want to disappoint themselves or you by sharing something not worthy of praise. Children are more susceptible to this than adults. After initial positive reactions to cheerleading, your intuition will tell you if the client is giving you a glossy version of life and leaving something out. If this is the case, honest sharing is your best bet.

Letting It Go? The Case of Jill

Jill shared with me how she had "just let it go" when negative things had come up in her life the previous week. I applauded her efforts and labeled "letting it go" as an effective coping skill. Jill had really enjoyed my praise the week before, and I was suspicious about her need to continue receiving positive strokes. Toward the end of the session I simply asked her, "How well does 'letting it go' really work for you? Is it all gone when you let it go?" Jill looked at me and burst into tears. It was all still there, just under the surface, causing her a lot of pain. We were able to take a more honest look at her new coping skill, which helped her get through tough situations and cope with her life but could not be used to deny its realities.

Cheerleading feels good to therapists and clients alike. We spend so much of our day empathizing with the pain in our clients' lives that it's refreshing to celebrate and reflect back the joys as well. Listening for something to cheer about is a skill that will become more refined with practice. If you listen hard enough, you will find something to praise within each session.

Recipes, Formulas, or Prescriptions

Sometimes clients are not completely aware of what they have done to make a difference or a positive change in their lives. Spelling it out for them clearly—as their recipe for success, formula for change, or prescription for a better future—helps ensure that it will happen again. If you spend some time reviewing and restating, it will pay off in creating lasting change. Clients will come closer to doing it again if they can tell you the recipe, formula, or prescription that was the solution.

In reflecting, you may say what you think made the difference—but sometimes it does not sink in until the client restates it. This is a nice way to sum up the session: "Now, we've talked about a lot of good things that have happened in your life. With all of these ingredients, what would you say is the recipe for (less stress, better job performance, beating depression)? Practice 5.6 has more examples of how to get clients to restate their successes in a reusable format.

Scaling, Percentages, and Ratings

Whether or not you used a scale as part of the planning process, you'll find it useful for measuring progress. When clients are unsure about changes or unclear about their significance, a scale can put things in perspective.

Moving Up: The Case of George

George said the week was wonderful, with many positive changes. I felt he was nearing the end of therapy, but when I asked him to put the last week on a scale alongside prior weeks, it became obvious that he felt there was a long way to go. With 1 as the worst things could go and 10 meaning he no longer needed therapy, George rated the wonderful week a 5 and the prior week a 4. According to his rating, the changes made only 1 notch of difference, and there were 5 more to go before things were where he wanted them to be.

George moved up steadily and, when he reached 10, we terminated his therapy. Using the scale helped me understand the extent of his progress so that I did not overestimate the changes, encouraging him to prematurely end therapy.

I Can Go Higher! The Case of Julie

At the other end of the continuum, Julie came to session and told me about some amazing changes she had made in her life. In my thinking, she had really made the difference that could make a difference. However, when she rated her changes, she did so very modestly.

I told her the week sounded so wonderful, I was surprised she had not rated it higher. She said it was a great week, but she had experienced better and wanted things to be even better before she moved the rating up. I hadn't realized what a goal-oriented, high-achieving, self-motivated person Julie was inside, despite all the horrid circumstances of her life. Without the scale, I might have unknowingly encouraged her to settle for less. The scale helped her communicate to me the high standards she was reaching for—and eventually achieved.

Scales, percentages, and ratings provide a measuring stick and a shared world view. For behaviorists, percentages are not new. However, asking clients *how much of the time* they are experiencing positive changes adds a different twist. Often we get so caught up in helping our clients with their problems that all intervention tools are directly related to the problem. Using the same tools in relation to the problem-free or low-problem times is solutioning. Taking an intervention you already like and using it with a new perspective or different emphasis gives it a solution slant.

For example, in determining frequency, intensity, and duration, we might ask what percentage of the time a client is depressed, or how many nights a week she has nightmares. Why not ask instead how many nights a week she sleeps well, or what percentage of the time she is not depressed? The information gained is essentially the same. The message given, however, is very different. By asking for percentages of better times or ratings of positive events, we are reminding clients that these times *do* exist, that they *are* capable, and that hope *is* a reality. The focus is more motivating. This works whether you are doing the initial assessment or looking at progress. Potentials and exceptions can emerge from *any* progress made, making the solution road rapid and smooth.

Walter and Peller suggested asking, "How convinced are you—in percentages—that you will continue to do what you did this week?" This allows the client to share his confidence and empowerment simultaneously with his need for continued practice and support. "They just feel a need to repeat the solution because it is seen as a new skill" (Walter & Peller, 1992, p. 142).

You can use various ratings, depending on the client's situation. Sometimes letter grades, thumbs up or sideways, colors, or sounds work better than numbers. The idea is that the client is focused on times that worked, the positive changes, the growth aspects of progress as a result of the rating.

Colorful: The Case of Alicia

Alicia was concerned by her mood changes. When she tried to describe her moods, she became frustrated with her inability to put words or numbers to them. Finally, we hit upon the idea of using colors. The self-mutilating, suicidal times of the past were described as the black moods that just overcame her. Fluorescent purple or green fit the manic episodes. The rating took the shape of a scale, with black at one end, white at the other, and many colors in between. Alicia could draw her week on the scale, and it resembled the heart monitor peaks and valleys on TV emergency room scenes. At one point she could only describe her week as "some pukey pattern from the '60s, not tie-dyed, but all blended."

As she progressed in therapy and nothing black or fluorescent happened, we could see her progress as a dimming of colors to the point where the ratings no longer fit. When this happened, she stopped therapy.

Journaling and Storying

Another favorite intervention that can be solutioned is *journaling*. Looking in an already existing journal for better times may yield exceptions and potentials from the past that the client can use for solution ideas. Encouraging clients to write in the future tense can develop potential. Have clients answer the question, "How do you want things to be?" or keep a list of observed positives. You can observe daily progress by having clients write each day what is better, what is different, what is working. This not only encourages solution ideas but also trains clients to focus on the better times, acknowledge the differences they are making in their lives, and notice positive change as it happens. This gives them a sense of control over their lives on a daily basis.

When progress is made, we must help clients incorporate it into their personal *story*. For the victim with the low self-esteem or the problem-saturated client, this may be difficult. By storying their progress, clients take ownership of their accomplishments and are more likely to use them again. You can help clients take their progress into their future by writing or telling the next week's story, including the progress already made.

PRACTICE 5.6

What's Next?

Gambling

- How much are you willing to bet that you can keep these positive changes going?

- Maybe you could bet (your mom, teacher, boss) a pop that you can continue (being on time, doing good work, etc.).

- Let's bet a pop on it. Do you think you can continue to (think the good thoughts, use times outs, control your temper, etc.) for another week?

Experimenting, Contests, and Games

- Let's experiment with this new skill and see if you can do it for another week.

- Let's see who can (say the most nice things, do the most around the house, turn in the most homework, etc.).

- How about making a game out of it? Each time you feel like bingeing, put on your favorite outfit first.

- Let's have a stress-free contest.

"Positive Blame"

- You did it! You (positive behavior).

- You've really done it now! You've (positive behavior).

- It's all your fault *(sarcastically)*; you've (positive behavior).

- Who made (positive change) happen?

- Because of whose efforts, skills, and abilities did (positive change) happen?

Interactive Cheerleading

- Wow! You did a great job. How did you do that?

- I am so impressed with your (positive change). You must be proud.

- That is really awesome. How do you feel about it?

- I have a feeling you can do it (more, again).

- You know, very few things surprise me, but you have shocked me. How did you do it?

Recipes, Formulas, and Prescriptions

- Based on all we've talked about, what would you say is your recipe for (desired behavior, success, solutions, etc.)?

- It seems to me that you now have the formula you have been searching for. Can you tell me exactly how the formula goes?

- You've made some amazing progress. Based on that, what is your prescription for the future?

- Now you have it, the formula that works for (purpose). Say it to me one more time.

- After the strides you've made, what would you say is a good prescription for change?

Scaling, Percentages, and Ratings

- Where would you rate your progress on a scale of 1 to 10—1 being the worst and 10 being the point where you no longer come in?

- How many notches have you moved up since last week? How did you do that? How many do you want to move up by next week? How might you do it?

- How would you rate this week compared to last week? Where do you want to be by the end of next week?

- What rating would you give your progress: A, B, or C?

- How do you rate the week in general, thumbs up or sideways?

- What percentage of the time were you (desired state)?

- Give me the percentage of better times. What percentage would you like to realistically achieve?

- "How convinced are you—in percentages—that you will continue to do what you did this week" (Walter & Peller, 1992, p. 142)?

Journaling and Storying

- Based on your (progress, changes, difference), write how you want your week to happen.

- Look in your journal of the past week and list all the positive things you thought, felt, or did.

- Each day write what was better, different, or enjoyable.

- Keep a "what's working" journal so you'll have it for reference whenever you need it.

- As you write the future you want to have happen, underline all the things you are already doing to achieve it.

- Write the next chapter in your life.

- If you were to write the story of the success of the past week, how would it go?

- Tell me your success story.

- What is the sequel to your story?

PROGRESS NOTES

Notes can be used to restate, emphasize, summarize, plant ideas, and praise outside of the session during the week. You can send a note after the first session or any time thereafter, restating and reinforcing a client's strengths, coping skills, purposes, or plans. Just think how much perspective you gain when you sit down to write your case notes after a session. The little details are deleted, the relevant information summarized, the plan for the future envisioned—the value of the session becomes clearer. Why not allow your clients the same benefits of perspective and reflection? As White and Epston noted, "the [value and] utility of writing are as relevant to the reader as they are to the writer and as relevant to the therapist as they are to the person seeking therapy" (1990, p. 37). At the appropriate time, a short, handwritten note to a client may be the picture that is worth a thousand words. I knew notes were enjoyable and appreciated, but I never fully realized their value until one client told me.

Jumbled: The Case of Deanna

I got this note from Deanna:

> Dear Willyn,
>
> I tried to make some notes after our session to re-member everything we talked about, and it all seemed a little jumbled, so much had been going through my head. Then I got your note. It was only five sen-tences, but it helped me so much. The value of the session would have been wasted if it were not for that note. I reconnected with what we had done and put it to work in my life right then and there. Thanks so much.

This is what my original note had said:

> Dear Deanna,
>
> I was really impressed with your ability to let things go until you are at a time and a place to deal with them. This has been an effective coping skill for you, writing them down as you temporarily let them go. It has not turned into denial like when you were drink-ing and let them go, then tried to forget. You've got some amazing skills. I'll look forward to sharing the list of things you *temporarily* let go of this week with you next Friday.
>
> Great job!

Very few people are capable of walking out of a session re-membering everything of value. A little review is helpful. White and Epston noted this as a basis for their extensive use of written work: "[W]e could argue for the introduction of the written tradi-tion in therapy, in that it potentially provides for an expansion of the information that can be processed in our short-term memory at any one point in time" (1990, p. 36).

Each of my clients gets a note after the first or second session. It cements some important potentials and the purpose for therapy. Thereafter, I send notes after sessions with a lot of progress, sessions that need a little more perspective, during weeks that are to be especially difficult, or whenever else it seems useful. By writing solutioning-based notes to clients, you give them more for their money by extending the value of therapy. The time, effort, and expense are minimal compared to the results. Choose a couple of clients this week and write notes. They will be impressed that you were thinking about them outside of the session, they will feel valued, and they will take what the notes say to heart.

Skill Highlight: Write Away

I have listed some solutioning hints for client notes. Use these to write your own notes, and notice the positive results.

- Begin with something you are impressed with, a strength, a coping skill, a *potential*.

- Tie it to the previous session's progress or plan.

- End with a sentence that is hopeful, empowering, and motivating and will tie into the next session.

- Don't send too many or send them too often, or they may loose their value.

- Choose a note card with a design that is friendly, not clinical.

- Make the note personal and spontaneous, not formal and calculated.

- Use language that assumes positive change will happen, that the client will make a difference.

- Short and simple is usually most effective.

- Handwritten notes are more personal.

- Send congratulatory, sympathy, and get-well cards when appropriate.

Sample Notes

What follow are examples of notes I have sent at various times in therapy. Use them as guides, create your own notes, or see the work of White and Epston (1990) for more examples.

After the first two sessions:

> Dear Chris,
>
> I am so impressed with your strength in managing so many different obstacles at once. You are really an amazing person and an intricate part of your family. Taking care of you is one way to take good care of them. I am curious to hear about the ways you come up with to take care of you once in awhile, while still being strong for everyone else. See you in a few days.

After substantial progress:

> Dear Tabatha,
>
> Wow! I am so thrilled that you have figured out how to beat depression. Your new exercise program is really making a difference for you. I'll be anxious to hear how much better you continue to feel as you take such great care of yourself and your body. Good job!

Congratulations:

> Dear Charles,
>
> Congratulations on completing middle school. I am so proud of your determination to finish the job. As you embark on high school, remember that your skills of telling dad how you feel and asking teachers for help will get you through, just like they did in middle school. Great things are in store for you.

Sympathy:

> Dear Haley and Bud,
>
> I heard about your recent loss of Bud's grandfather. Times like these are difficult, but they can really bring a couple together. Take good care of each other. I'll see you next week and hear how you have loved and supported each other through this time of sorrow.

Get well:

> Dear Angela,
>
> Sorry to hear that the flu bug visited your house this week. As you continue to say nice things to yourself for another week, I'll have even more great differences in your life to hear about at our next session. Take care of yourself, and get well soon.

PROGRESS: IN SUMMARY

Listening for clients' progress is an important skill to develop. If you hear the improvements, changes, differences, efforts, and solutions in what clients tell you, you can acknowledge, praise, question, credit, and enhance them. It takes practice to illicit from clients what they did that was different, better, or hopeful, but it takes a trained ear to hear the subtle hints of progress that are intertwined with the discussion of the problem. Helping clients to do the same gives them a wonderful life skill.

You can begin by just listening and pointing out progress as clients share it. Later, you may find that questioning gets you there sooner. No matter which route you take, focusing on progress keeps therapy forward moving and motivating for both you and your clients.

Chapter 6

Solutioning Reality

As you have read about the 4-P process of solutioning, you probably have found interventions that will blend with your methods and those that will not. You also may have some questions, such as these:

- How does this fit in with managed care?

- What about diagnosis?

- Is there a way to solution record keeping?

- How about assessments, where do they fit in with solutioning?

Solutioning the realities of the constantly changing world of mental health will happen for you as you slowly alter your focus in the direction of solutioning. The material in this chapter is not intended to give you a lot of additional work, but to provide you with a sense of balance, perspective, and hope. Preventing burnout by expanding your perspective will be worth any extra effort.

MANAGING REALITY

According to the Center for Mental Health Services, "It is often observed that working in the managed behavioral healthcare industry is 'a dog's life,' because one year in the managed behavioral healthcare industry is like seven years in any other profession" (Freeman & Trabin, 1994, p. 44). Whether or not you feel this strongly, solutioning will help you meet the time constraints of managed care by providing interventions that facilitate rapid change.

One central theme in the literature on managed care's influence on the world of mental health is *flexibility*, which is an attribute of solutioning. As Bistline, Sheridan, and Winegar (1991, p. 151) stated, "It is our hope that mental health counselors will be proactive and will 'catch the wave' of managed care, instead of being left behind."

Regarding the time constraints required by managed care, Budman and Gurman noted, "If therapy is to be maximally effective in a brief period, therapeutic flexibility is essential" (1988, p. 20).

With even more conviction, Kochunas issued a "call for the resurrection of the imagination in the profession of counseling" (1997, p. 20).

To be effective in *any* amount of time and meet the needs of diverse individuals, couples, and families, therapists must be flexible, using a variety of interventions for each client at various points in therapy. Solutioning, as a whole or in parts, is one such option. In fact, solutioning may help you "catch the wave" of managed care.

Few successful therapists are ready to do a 180-degree turnaround—completely changing their approach, methods, or philosophy—simply to meet the needs of an HMO, PPO, or other such organization. However, some have voiced a concern that just such a change is what it takes to make it. According to Bistline et al.,

"The response of mental health counselors to the changing environment of the health care market has often been one of anxiety, confusion, and wariness" (1991, p. 147).

If this is the case, then solutioning is the answer. You do not have to become a brief therapy expert and throw out all your current, effective methods in order to serve your clients in fewer sessions. You just need the blendability of solutioning. For example, you might use a scale at the end of each session to facilitate improvement in current functioning while maintaining a focus on long-term issues. The result is improvement in daily life that enhances other therapeutic processes and speeds up healing, recovery, and change.

As Kochunas observed, "behavioral and cognitive approaches to counseling have demonstrated effectiveness for use in managed care settings. Counselors who find these approaches valid, but morally or aesthetically unsatisfying, face a conundrum for surviving in the managed care arena" (1997, p. 14). Adopting a totally new approach is not necessary. By incorporating a few questions, phrases, or interventions from solutioning, you will not be deserting your philosophy or methods, you'll just be more flexible.

What it all boils down to is meeting the needs of clients. After all, mental health is referred to as a *helping profession*. "Even under the pressures of managed care, no patient can proceed faster than they are able to" (Bromfield, 1995, p. 441). Meeting clients where they are, using methods that serve their needs, and doing so in a cost-effective way is what solutioning is all about. Nothing more is required to survive in managed care.

Solutioning isn't *the answer*—nor is brief therapy or any other single method. The answer is doing the best with what you have, where you are, according to what you believe. Fitting your treatment to clients rather than fitting clients into a theoretical model happens with solutioning. "This may be advantageous as it allows for more diversity, flexibility, and novelty in practice" (Kochunas, 1997, p. 17).

Skill Highlight: Flexibility

What does it take to be more flexible and still hold true to your basic philosophy of counseling? Kochunas cited this managed care coping skill: "All counselors would do well to diversify, to gain education about alternative paradigms" (1997, p. 19). Along the same lines, Bistline et al. outlined a critical skill for managed care as an "orientation to brief targeted psychotherapy" (1991, p. 151).

Neither of these suggests switching completely to brief philosophies, abandoning traditional methods, or shortchanging clients. Solutioning incorporates bits and pieces of brief, forward-moving interventions where and when they fit. Being flexible doesn't mean you have to jump into something with both feet. If you are trying to catch the wave of managed care, or even if you are just trying to keep your head above water, solutioning methods can help.

DIAGNOSING REALITY

You may be wondering how the reality of diagnosis fits with solutioning's focus on strengths, abilities, and solutions. As Furman and Ahola noted, "Most terms, even those meant to be purely descriptive and etiology-free, such as words in the psychiatric classification system *DSM-III-R* (APA, 1987), are often loaded with presuppositions about causality and treatment" (1992, p. 58). Using solutioning with clients to come up with workable, solvable-sounding descriptions does not mean that, as a professional, you cannot also use the terms of the *DSM-IV* in your diagnosis, notes, and reports.

However, you don't have to use the terms of the *DMS-IV* with your clients. For the most part, the general intake form and initial interviews will provide the information you need to make the diagnosis required by insurance companies and health maintenance organizations. With clients, you can use the descriptions discussed in chapter 2. Furman and Ahola gave this suggestion: "So-called psychotic symptoms can be worded as 'peculiar thoughts,' 'day-dreaming,' 'having ghosts,' 'being overly superstitious,' or 'being scared to death,' depending on the nature of the actual problem" (1992, p. 61).

Regardless of your counseling philosophy or approach, using negative, serious-sounding diagnostic terms with clients may not be the best idea, unless you are trying to convince them of your superior position, your knowledge, or their sickness. Why make problems seem bigger or worse than they are? We can be clear, honest, and serious about clients' reasons for therapy without over-doing it.

Remember solutioning reconstructions, which are designed to take the power away from the problem. Don't undermine this effort through your own, an agency's, or a reimbursement organization's need for a diagnosis.

One attribute of solutioning is its ability to broaden the horizons: "By using a language of options and possibilities that generate hope for change, rather than static diagnostic categories, we expand perspectives rather than constrict them" (Friedman & Fanger, 1991, p. 8). Solutioning facilitates being flexible about which words you and your clients use together and which words you use to meet the needs of reality, "replacing biological psychiatric labels with ordinary phrases drawn from everyday language can empower people in their search for solutions" (Furman & Ahola, 1992, p. 61).

Remember, the best replacement descriptions are those the therapist-client team designs together. Just for practice, let's look at some commonly used terms in the *DSM-IV* and see what strengths can be found within the disorders and what "ordinary phrases drawn from everyday language" we can come up with to replace the original terms. Practice 6.1 will get you started; you and your clients can take it from there. Friedman and Fanger put it this way, "What is called for here is avoidance of old generalizations [diagnoses] that dull your awareness to the individuality of each client" (1991, p. 73).

PRACTICE 6.1

DSM-IV-Revised Solutioning Style

Alcohol-Related Disorders	drinks too much, has difficulty controlling drinking
Anorexia Nervosa	dedicated, consistent, has a strong desire to be thin
Attention-Deficit/ Hyperactivity Disorder	energetic, has difficulty concentrating
Avoidant Personality Disorder	likes to be alone
Bereavement	grieving, sad about a loss
Bipolar Disorder	overly moody, has ups and downs
Depression Disorder	gets down, is sad a lot, feels low, has the blues
Dissociative Disorder	uses a left-over coping skill, checks out
Drug Related Disorders	uses or abuses drugs
Kleptomania	steals a lot
Oppositional Defiant Disorder	has a hard time getting along with others, is rebellious
Panic Disorder	gets really upset sometimes
Posttraumatic Stress Disorder	is a survivor in the healing process, has some left-over coping skills

Psychotic Disorders   has episodes, hears or sees
                               things

Schizophrenia   has an "in-the-corner lifestyle"
                               (White & Epston, 1990, p. 58)

TESTING REALITY

Diagnosis and assessment go hand in hand. We can't make a diagnosis without first assessing clients' problems, conditions, and symptoms. How does assessment fit with solutioning; or (for you psychologists), how does solutioning fit with assessment? The answer is obvious: Every time you do an assessment, you gain information about the individual—both pathological and positive, weaknesses and strengths, needs and abilities. It is a matter of seeing the proverbial glass as half-empty or half-full. Even the most positive thinkers can have a hard time balancing their focus, due to prior training or current habits. As Huber and Backlund noted, "Most counselors, trained to be enthusiastic psychopathologists, respond to the morsels of pathology that clients present and are misled into observing only the less competent parts of clients' functioning" (1996, p. 48).

The emphasis during use, interpretation, and delivery of assessment results is determined by the therapist. Accurate information, ethically and professionally given, can still focus on the positives. In fact, as Tuyn noted,

> [A]ny act of assessment is also an intervention, based on what we emphasize with our attention. Assessing with an emphasis on possibilities (what is going right in someone's life) is powerfully different from an emphasis on pathology (what is going wrong). (1992, pp. 85-86)

This is not to say that the pathology, the disorder, or the problems are ignored; they are simply balanced with positives and are put in perspective, "These dysfunctional components are viewed as merely segments of clients' full potential that are, at this point, most available to the clients' consciousness" (Huber & Backlund, 1996, p. 48). In fact, focusing on the positives, beginning with initial evaluations, will lead to interventions that build on preexisting strengths rather than causes of pathologies or details of problems.

Assessing strengths, skills, and positives—thus expanding the focus and balancing the "dysfunctional components"—happens during the exploration of potential solutions in step 2 of the 4-P process. In fact, the potentials step can be seen as an informal assessment itself. Potential questions facilitate the formation of new habits in assessing:

> We have noticed that not only are different results achieved with different models and approaches, but different data also emerge during the assessment process, leading to different definitions of the problem. In other words, problem definition in therapy is a function of the assessment process. (O'Hanlon & Weiner-Davis, 1989, p. 54)

Solutioning is designed not to replace traditional assessment but to broaden your perspective and those of your clients, blend in the positives, and emphasize qualities that will facilitate the formation of solutions.

Skill Highlight: Assessing Solutioning Style

Assessing solutioning style happens in two ways:

First, you balance results of currently used tests, including and possibly emphasizing the strengths.

Second, you explore potentials.

Go back through chapter 3 and review the solutioning questions there designed to help the team discover strengths, abilities, talents, exceptions, and coping skills. The sample intake in Practice 3.9 does much of the balancing act for you, without requiring a great deal of additional time on your part filling out paper work. This skill highlight does not give a new skill, but reinforces the solutioning language and interventions you've already been learning as you've read this book. In other words, solutioning has it covered. Blend in and adapt, meet your assessment and diagnostic needs, while still helping clients realize and use their strengths, talents, and abilities.

REALITY IN WRITING

The final realities that must be addressed are record keeping and accountability, which also go hand in hand. "Health care reform has created the need to minimize time spent in routine documentation and has forced a change in the format of follow-up notes from the subjective, objective assessment and planning (SOAP) style" (Klein, Bosworth, & Wiles, 1997, p. 1306). Although this statement is not directed specifically at mental health professionals, it rings true in our field.

Saving time in record keeping while still meeting the requirements of agencies, health maintenance organizations, and licensure may seem impossible. Remember the suggestions for listing potentials as they are discovered, writing down plans, and keeping records of progress *with* clients as enhancements to the solutioning intervention? Talk about killing two birds with one stone! Involving clients in the *process* of therapy, written or otherwise, is a component of the team concept *and* helps with record keeping. Using the forms in this book or changing your own documents will take care of many of your written requirements. You only need to add relevant observations and interventions, and your notes are complete.

Practice 6.2 can be filled out during or after sessions, with clients or alone, and includes a purpose (presenting problem details, symptoms, and diagnosis), potentials (assessment of strengths, abilities, and skills), a plan (interventions, treatment goals, time frame, duration), and progress (updates, growth, follow-up). If you add additional assessment information and a *DMS-IV* code, you have covered the requirements of treatment planning.

PRACTICE 6.2

Treatment Plan Solutioning Style

Name:_____ Date:_____ Type:_____

    Purpose (including emotional and behavioral symptoms):

    _____

    _____

    _____

    DSM-IV Diagnosis:

        Axis I _____ Axis II _____ Axis III _____

        Axis IV_____ Axis V _____ GAF _____

        Other _____

    Potentials (assessment of strengths, talents, skills, positives):

    _____

    _____

    _____

    _____

    Plan (date, treatment goals/interventions, duration):

    1._____

    _____

    2._____

    _____

3. _____

_____

4. _____

_____

Progress (updates, follow-up, growth): _____

_____

_____

_____

_____

Any additional information (use another sheet of paper):

Accountability is a final reality of an "increasingly explicit expectation that clients will achieve demonstrable improvement in their presenting problems as a result of counseling" (Kelly, 1996, p. 195). Of course, we are all accountable to our clients and strive to provide the best services possible. However, the world of managed care has placed additional emphasis on accountability, a "growing demand for mental health counselors to justify their treatment plans and techniques to managed care companies" (Kelly, 1996, p. 196). A solutioning plan that meets the starting five criteria, has a detailed focus on progress, and stresses a team relationship will take care of accountability. As Fairchild pointed out, "Although descriptive data provide important information regarding the breadth and depth of services, it does not provide information regarding effectiveness of services. The data most useful in providing efficacy information, process, and product (outcome) are collected less frequently" (1994, p. 28).

Process and outcome data are both built into solutioning. When accountability information is required, a quick perusal of client files—noting the purpose, plan, and progress—will illustrate the effectiveness of therapy. Some phone follow-ups for long-term feedback are the only additional information required.

For most of us, the most important accountability measures are those given through direct feedback from clients. When working together as teammates, we are more likely to communicate about the relationship, the process, and the effectiveness of therapy. During solutioning, most clients feel comfortable sharing whether counseling is meeting their needs or not. Clients' needs are always of utmost importance, and the emphasis on progress should bring their questions, concerns, satisfactions, and dissatisfactions to light.

When clients are valued as resources for solving their own problems, when their input provides the basis for solution construction, when their purposes and plans are cocreated, then clients themselves become more responsible and more accountable for their own progress. When you are not the all-knowing, diagnosing, prescription-giving therapist but a teammate, you share more responsibility and accountability, while practicing more effective therapy. As Gass and Gillis noted, "it is the authors' experience that solutions 'co-constructed' by therapists and clients (or clients alone) are generally more successful in generating lasting client change than those created solely by therapists" (1995, p. 68).

Therapists in no way abdicate their responsibility during this process. As team leaders they are still in charge, guiding the counseling process. The difference is the responsibility taken by clients.

Additionally, solutioning encourages choosing methods that serve the needs of clients, rather than rigidly adhering to a theory. As Budman and Gurman noted, "one cannot treat a theory. Thus, the therapist looking *only* for signs of Oedipal conflict, or *only* for cognitive distortions, can easily ignore major aspects of the patient's experience that are being communicated" (1988, p. 51).

Likewise, therapists who look *only* for positives, strengths, and solutions may ignore the feelings and details associated with the problem that need to be acknowledged, emphasized, and understood. Being accountable is being *with* clients, true to your beliefs, and effective in your methods. "Evaluation of a counseling program is an ongoing process rather than an event. The information collected is extremely important if counselors wish to improve the quality of their services to provide evidence to consumers" (Fairchild, 1994, p. 36). Each and every time the progress questions are asked, the counseling process is evaluated. The ongoing nature of progress, along with a detailed plan and a teaming relationship, should provide the information you need both to improve and to provide evidence of solutioning.

SOLUTIONING REALITY: IN SUMMARY

"Just because everything is different doesn't
mean anything has changed."
—*Irene Peter (Peter, 1977, p. 99)*

As we have considered solutioning the realities of managed care, we have talked of diagnosis, assessment, and accountability *attributes*, not *additions*. This is not to say that solutioning covers every aspect of mental health care. Solutioning, after all, is not a theory at all, but interventions that encourage growth, change, and flexibility in order to meet the needs of the growing, changing world in which we live.

Chapter 7

Adaptable, Usable, Doable

Solutioning with families, couples, children, and groups is natural. Once you are familiar and comfortable with the process and the language, you will make your own adaptations and create new interventions that have a solution focus. "[T]he possible clinical interventions are much more numerous when the therapeutic focus is on nonproblem behaviors" (Molnar & de Shazer, 1987, p. 356). But, as the saying goes, why reinvent the wheel? In this chapter you will find effective uses of solutioning specifically for families, couples, children, and groups.

FAMILIES

Solution-focused brief therapy has its roots in family therapy. And like SBFT, solutioning fits with families. Every part of the 4-P process can be used. The adaptation may be as simple as asking everyone in the room the solutioning questions. But, an especially useful practice with families, which will be highlighted in this chapter, is externalizing the problem and considering problem maintenance in order to establish a common purpose.

Andrews and Andrews (1995), early intervention speech-language pathologists who adapted SFBT ideas to fit their practice, noted the advantage of those ideas this way: "[They] enable family members to become full participants in identifying and implementing solutions to their problems" (p. 60). Family-centered therapy has always highlighted understanding and accepting many different views as valid. However, when the problem is not a family member, but an entity of itself, the family can team up *together* against it, reducing blame and increasing participation.

The first step in teaming up against a problem is agreeing on what the problem is. Many families spend considerable amounts of time in therapy determining their problems. Solutioning facilitates this process by externalizing. According to White and Epston:

> At times, when families or couples present for therapy, persons are in considerable dispute over the definition of the problem. These disputes make it difficult for them to work cooperatively in any attempt to challenge the effects of problems in their lives and relationships. In these circumstances, externalizing can establish a mutually acceptable definition of the problem and facilitates conditions under which persons can work effectively together. (1990, p. 54)

After a problem has been externalized, you can help families look at "problem maintenance"—each family member's role in, contribution to, or part in the problem. According to Metcalf, "This way of working lessens the chance of blame on one person in the family and encourages responsibility from everyone in solving the problem" (1995, p. 16).

A Person Is Not a Problem: The Case of The Hansons

Deanna, John, and Albert came to therapy at the request of Albert's school. Albert was a 4th-grader who had been diagnosed with ADD, was seen as gifted, but was reading at a 2nd-grade level because he refused to take chapter tests. He had been kicked off the school bus for his many fights. Albert, an only child, was being blamed for all the stress, hostility, and turmoil in the family. His parents had labeled him a brat, and he seemed to be living up to his title.

At the first session, Albert sat in his parents' laps, pinched their cheeks, and generally annoyed them while they told me their reasons for coming to therapy (blaming and complaining about Albert). As quickly as I could, I led them through externalizing the problem.

Willyn: I believe the problem is the problem, not a person. If you were to name or describe the problem we need to team up against, what would you say?

John: I'd say it is *yelling*. Deanna yells at Albert. I yell at them both. Then Deanna yells at me for yelling and we all just yell a lot. It's not a fun or relaxing atmosphere.

Deanna: I'll say! It's hard to tell the problem without naming anyone. I guess it's stress. I'm always stressed out because I'm afraid the teachers are going to call or he's into something, or nagging at me, and money, and it's just too much.

Willyn: Okay, so *yelling* and *stress* are problems that need to be worked on. Albert, what would you say is the problem we should work on?

Albert: I'm with Dad. Everybody is always yelling at me and I hate it. I yell back and then we fight and fight.

Willyn: It sounds like *yelling* controls and upsets everyone at times. *(They all nod.)* Let's team up against *yelling*.

Albert: *(who is really brightening, almost showing signs of relief that we are talking about* yelling *and not about him)* Yeah, let's kick its butt! *(An inappropriate comment perhaps, but it does illustrate the power of externalizing the problem.)*

Willyn: Deanna, how does *yelling* control you?

Deanna: Well, I guess when I am stressed out I just yell more. I yell about everything. The laundry, the chores, but mostly Albert. I probably yell the most. *(She's into the blame game—trying now to blame herself.)*

Willyn: So *yelling* controls you quite a bit of the time. John, how does *yelling* affect and control you?

John: When she yells at me, I defend myself, and sometimes when she yells at Albert, I defend him, too. I guess I yell when I am defending. It's just hard to be around so much yelling without yelling too.

Willyn: So you let defending cause you to yell. Albert, what do you do that makes *yelling* happen?

Albert: I don't do my chores and then there is yelling and stuff like that. *(Wow! Albert was sharing his faults, rather than trying to act so off-the-wall that his parents couldn't talk.)*

By the end of the session, each member of the family was ready to do his or her part to defeat *yelling*. Albert was going to do his chores. Deanna was going to count to five before saying anything when she was triggered by laundry, Albert, money, and other stresses. John was going to defend himself and Albert once a week at a family meeting where everyone could share equally without yelling. The plans were not 100% successful, and family therapy continued for 20 sessions; but once they could externalize the problem, they were on their way.

By looking at problem maintenance, the family teamed up, stopped blaming, and took individual responsibility for their parts in both problems and solutions. This way of thinking and operating continued as other, more difficult problems were tackled. Albert's behavior improved considerably; he even commented at a later session, "Now that I'm not the problem anymore, I don't have to be so mean." This was a very bright 8-year-old's way of sharing the relief he felt when the problem was externalized so everyone, not just him, played a part.

Considering problem maintenance does not require that everyone be in the room. One example came from a graduate student in a solutioning class I taught.

A Changed Perspective: The Case of Sandy

Sandy, a massage therapist who worked with clients suffering from severe pain, was interested in learning solution-focused interventions to help her clients. This she did quite successfully. However, she also discovered the value of solutioning with her own family. Although she did not have her family in therapy, she thought systemically and used solutioning to make a difference.

Initially Sandy tended to blame her daughter for their communication problems, saying, "she shows emotional apathy or outbursts." With solutioning, Sandy externalized the problem as a "cool manner" that was exhibited by everyone, not just her daughter. After this her focus changed completely. Externalizing the problem and looking at everyone's part in it—even if only one member of the family is looking—can change the focus so that solutions emerge within the new perspective. Following are some examples of how externalizing and looking at problem maintenance showed up in Sandy's journal:

> Linsey, your confident manner is admirable to me, but I am not understanding strong feelings because of your calm exterior.

From then on I was able to see more of her abilities and I even added my confidence in her ability from the past week's incident. Almost instantly she became more talkative and open to discuss more during our conversation.

After I realized that everyone played a part, I began to see Linsey differently. Introverted changed to self-confident and lazy changed to relaxed.

I myself began seeing that maybe there is really no problem at all. In fact, I have gained such an acceptance of her nature that I'm sure she feels it herself because I perceive that she is more open and honest with me. In kind of a roundabout way ... by changing my perception of the problem and working on the goal from that point of view, the whole interaction changed. (Class journal, 1996)

As you can see, it does not take complicated interventions or even the entire family's participation to make a difference. *Once problems are externalized, families are free to solve them.* I have highlighted problem maintenance to illustrate solutioning's use with family therapy, but the language, thinking, and worksheets from the previous chapters are valid and useful as well. Pick the ones you like best and apply them to a stuck family, a blaming family, or a family ready to move from the past to the future.

PRACTICE 7.1

Families Teaming Against Problems

1. *Externalize*

Use circular questioning.

- What would you call the problem the family is dealing with?

  - So we're all clear on it, let's name the problem you all have been describing. What would each of you choose as a name for the problem?

- You've all shared feelings and facts about this family's struggle. You've also done some blaming. Now that you've gotten some of that out of the way, try not blame each other anymore—blame the problem. In fact, let's name the problem so we know where to blame and what to solve.

- I believe problems are problems, people are not. Without naming each other, what would each of you say is the problem this family is going to be solving?

2. *Look at Problem Maintenance*

Now that we know what the problem is, let's look at the role each of you has in contributing to it, maintaining it, and then in solving it.

- Tell me how each of you affects or is affected by (gossip, secrets, anger, chores, jealousy, etc.).

- "I've often learned that problems are what I refer to as *maintained*. You know, that possibly people keep problems around by their behaviors with each other. Can you each tell me how you might possibly keep this tension in your family" (Metcalf, 1995, p. 12)?

- I believe that no matter what the problem, everyone in the family plays a part. What part do each of you play in (anger, fighting, tension, etc.)?

- What influence does each of you have over (externalized problem)?

Solutioning Genograms

Timeline Genograms. Genograms are a familiar tool for many therapists and the mainstay of systemic family therapists. Recently we have seen some useful adaptations of the traditional genogram format. Friedman, Rohrbaugh, and Krakauer introduced a timeline genogram in an attempt to overcome shortcomings they found with the traditional format: "The standard format gives dates but does not show temporal patterns directly. Thus, coincidences of life events, relational repercussions of loss, and lifecycle 'fit' ... can be easily missed" (1988, p. 293). (We saw this idea used in chapter 3 to help problem-filled clients gain a broader perspective of their lives.)

Finding exceptional times along the horizontal plane of life is encouraging. Future desires, plans, and progress also are easily plotted. With families, however, the horizontal timeline gets too crowded, so Friedman et al. developed "a modified genogram format in which time is plotted on the vertical axis so that events can be shown as they actually occurred" (1988, pp. 293-294). In conjunction with their timeline format, exceptional times, successful events, positive repercussions, and useful relationships-along with future desires, goals, plans, and so on—can be added in and among the traditional categories.

McGoldrick and Gerson (1985) identified three categories of genogram information: basic family structure, information about individual family members, and family relationships. Within these broad categories, you can ask for and include positives, exceptions, skills, strengths and so on. At an appropriate time during therapy, solution information—answers to the potential questions—can be added as a new category. The questions and language you have learned will serve this purpose and should blend in well with questions designed for the timeline format.

"Referring to both dimensions allows one to answer the important question: 'What was happening within the family immediately preceding and following a critical event?'" (Friedman et al., 1988, p. 297). Asking, "When were things better? What was the best time of your life? When has this family been happy, relaxed, okay?" opens up areas for solution exploration. Following with, "What was happening that was different during these times?" will lead you to a plan for success.

Future plans are easily added to the timeline genogram with questions such as, "What would you like to have happen in the future? What does it look like?" Plans take on a more real quality and are more motivating when they are visually represented as part of the family map. When the time is right, leading families out of the past and into the future, over which they have more control, will empower them in solution construction. The greatest contribution of the timeline genogram, used in conjunction with solutioning, is the addition of the future. A sample solutioned timeline genogram is shown in Figure 7.1.

> "I don't know who my grandfather was;
> I am much more concerned to know what
> his grandson will be."
> —*Abraham Lincoln (Webster, 1992, p. 15)*

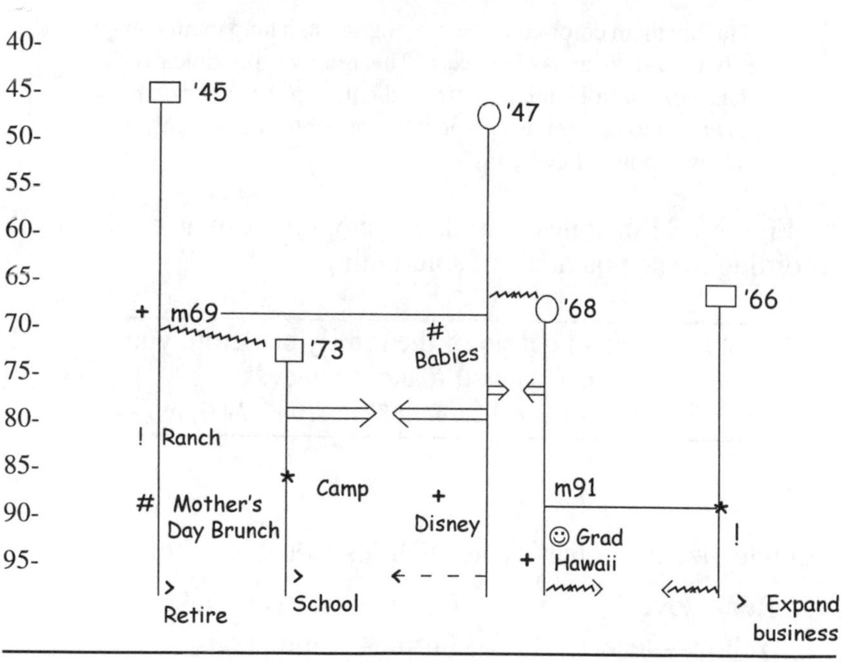

+ positive trip	* good experience	# happy time
☺ successful event	! exception to the problem	> future plans

Figure 7.1. A solutioned timeline genogram.

Color-Coding Genograms. For those overwhelmed by all the symbols, Lewis (1989) introduced color-coding to both traditional genograms and the timeline (1989). Solutioning genograms with color will broaden the focus of family therapy and bring new solution possibilities to light. When color-coding a genogram, you should include colors for positive characteristics, strengths, and differences as you get answers to the solutioning questions.

Lewis also suggested that, "as a diagnostic tool, the family does its own assessing" (1989, p. 172). During solutioning when the therapist involves the family and relinquishes some control of the genogram process, a team relationship is formed and responsibility is given to the family. It is an empowering process for families when they are able to color-code their own genograms with solution potentials.

> Having them color-code their genogram can help them identify their own areas of concern. This removes possible resistance or control battles and frees the therapist from trying to get them to talk about a particular topic or to see certain "obvious" points. (Lewis, 1989, p. 172)

Figure 7.2 illustrates a standard genogram format, color-coded according to the potentials of solutioning.

"If you can't get rid of the family skeleton, you
may as well make it dance."
—*George Bernard Shaw (Peter, 1977, p. 194)*

Individualize the potentials as qualities valuable to solutions.

Red—love	Green—creative thinker
Yellow—leader	Purple—courageous
Pink—caring	Blue—forward thinker
Orange—experienced	Brown—good communicator

Example:

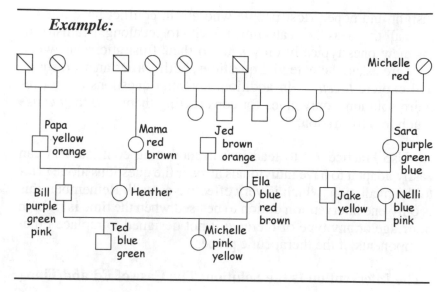

Figure 7.2. A colorful, solutioned genogram.

COUPLES

"The great secret of successful marriage is to
treat all disasters as incidents and none of the
incidents as disasters."
—*Harold Nicholson (Peter, 1977, p. 320)*

An exceptionally useful practice with couples is *solutioning
mediation*. Through this process, you model an effective means of
communicating, resolving conflict, and solutioning. You don't have
to learn any new skills to do solution mediation, just put the ones
you have to use in another context. Actually, solutioning mediation works well will all conflicts, not just between marital part-
ners. But it works especially well in marital counseling because of
the conflictual nature of most couples seeking counseling.

One advantage of solutioning mediation over traditional mediation is how quickly you move to externalize the problem and
end blaming, defending, and complaining. Additionally, structure
and guidance through the potentials give frustrated parties new

insight and hope. Most people who are in conflict have already tried all the ideas they can come up with to get along. Brainstorming new ones typically only adds to their frustration; but when they are asked the potential questions, both parties answer, share, and explore *together*. In addition, potential questions do not require solutions, only clues for constructing them—so they cause much less frustration.

Use Practice 7.2 to lead you in mediating conflict. You can easily adapt it to have individuals answer the questions alone prior to the mediation, which is very effective as well. Remember, this is only one intervention option to be used when the time is right in marriage or any type of therapy; it not designed to replace other components of the therapeutic process.

The Intervention Is the Solution: The Case of Ed and Tina

Ed and Tina, parents of a 2- and a 4-year-old, had been together for eight years, married for six. Their fighting revolved around money. They both had checking accounts and split the living expenses more like roommates than most married couples. What prompted them to come to therapy was an incident when Tina spent some of Ed's money she was supposed to deposit for him, causing him to bounce some checks. This had caused such a conflict they couldn't get passed it. Solutioning mediation seemed in order to bring some closure to the incident, so that other facets of their marriage could be addressed.

I began by asking each of them to state their "side of the story," needs, purposes, and feelings on the issue.

Ed: If I could trust her to do what she says and not spend so much money. I'm sick of hearing it. My friends are losers, I don't make enough, I don't help with the bills, and on and on.

Willyn: Tina, now it's your turn.

Tina: He doesn't realize how hard I'm working and that I need more money. I shouldn't have spent it without telling him, but it makes me mad when he has more spending money than I do and he wastes it on beer and his friends. It's all his fault.

Willyn: It sounds like the problem is *managing money*. Our purpose is to work out a way to manage money peacefully. Agreed? *(Both said yes.)*

Now let's look at each of your roles in managing money. Tina, what is your role?

Tina: I am supposed to deposit all the checks, pay the utilities, and pay half of the groceries.

Ed: I pay the house and car payments and most of the time all of the groceries because she has blown her money on clothes.

Willyn: So each has specific responsibilities for managing money. When does this system work?

Tina: It works when I can do my part and he doesn't spend too much drinking.

Willyn: Great. Could you clarify for me what you do when you do your part?

Tina: I have my share when I don't go shopping with friends over the weekend, which I don't do unless he has some big plans with his friends and I feel left out.

Willyn: So when you spend the weekend together, you are able to fulfill your responsibilities for managing money?

Ed: Yeah, she's got it right. If I don't go blowing money on beer, she doesn't go blowing it on clothes.

Willyn: What do you do differently when you don't go blowing money?

Ed: We play with the kids, clean the house, do yard work, stuff like that.

Tina: Yeah, we usually go out to eat as a family and that is nice.

Willyn: So, how do you want things to be?

Tina: I want to manage our money so we don't fight so much. I don't want a divorce. It would be too hard on the kids.

Ed: Yeah, when I put family first, money isn't that big of a problem.

Willyn: Based on what you have just shared, do you think you could do more of what works, staying home and managing money? *(Both nod.)*

For the next two weeks, try staying home on the weekend and doing things as a family, which will help you both meet your responsibilities for managing money.

Tina, stay home to keep from blowing money on clothes and have your part for groceries.

Ed, spend time with the family on the weekends by not making plans with friends and have money to take your family out to dinner.

Do you both agree to this plan? Are there any details we need to add?

Ed and Tina: We can do it for two weeks.

The two-week plan worked and during that time Ed and Tina reconnected with some feelings they had for each other. The friends, the jealousy, the outings became less of an issue and they started to rebuild their trust. This mediation was intended as an intervention to get past a painful incident and address the issues behind it. What happened instead was that the intervention worked so well, the other issues subsided.

"Almost all married people fight, although many are ashamed to admit it. Actually a marriage in which no quarreling at all takes place may well be one that is dead or dying from emotional undernourishment. If you care, you probably fight."

—*Flora Davis (Peter, 1977, p. 321)*

PRACTICE 7.2

Solution Mediation

Steps for Resolving Conflict

1. Establish a Purpose

Each individual needs an opportunity to tell his or her side of the story. This does not have to be extensive, and the sooner they are ready to go on, the better. Blaming, defending, and complaining do not lead to solutions. Some rules for good communication—such as "Use 'I' messages" and "Listen, then restate"—might be helpful. *The mediator must ask each individual each question.*

- **Externalize the problem.** Typically, the individuals see one another as the problem. However, with careful listening during the storytelling, you will be able to determine a common problem to externalize. *It is the mediator's responsibility to identify and name a problem the individuals can agree to solve.*

It sounds like the problem is … . Do you both agree to solve the problem named … ?

If yes, continue. If not, consider alternative problems to externalize.

- **Look at problem maintenance.** This is especially helpful in highly complicated situations, when neither will share responsibility or ownership of the problem, and when individuals are having difficulty getting past blaming.

What do you do to contribute to … ?

What is your role in … ?

A word of caution: These questions can lead to more blaming. Typically, however, they encourage responsibility.

- **Consider the possible results and consequences of continuing with or solving the problem.**

What might happen if you continue this conflict?

What are some likely results for solving it?

What is your purpose for solution mediation?

- **Write it down.** It solidifies the purpose when you write it down. Then you can refer back to the written purpose if necessary later on.

2. **Explore Potential Solutions**

- **Record any potential solutions as they are shared.**

Ask the questions of both individuals and allow each to answer.

When have things been better? When are things better?

What is each of you doing differently then?

- **Use the questions from chapter 3 to access past and present potential.** As soon as you can, move on to:

How do you want it to be? What does that look like?

This adds direction to the process. Do they want to be married, divorced, or separated, friends or enemies, have an intimate relationship or simply coexist? How would each of these be played out in real life? Get details. This usually becomes the solution.

3. **Make a Plan**

- **Summarize the potential ideas from the list.** Maybe even read through the list, so you don't give emphasis to any one idea.

- **Follow with a plan** that incorporates some, if not all, of the potentials. The plan must be agreed upon by all parties.

Based on all of the potential solution ideas, a plan for the ... (next two days, week, month, etc.) is to .... You will ... , and you will ... , so that things are better.

Do you both agree to this plan? Are there any details that need to be added? Is there any part you want to discuss further?

- **Finally, say to each individual, "Please tell me exactly what you will be doing."**

The beauty of creating a plan this way is that it comes directly from the potentials, the input of the clients. They are responsible for creating the plan, but did not have the nearly impossible task of phrasing it in either individual's own words while they were in conflict.

Using the starting five criteria from chapter 4 may be helpful in this process. Writing down the plan and having both individuals sign it will "set it in stone." This makes it seem official. Giving copies of the purpose, potentials, and plan also is a good idea, because they can be referred to during the week and pulled out for progress.

- **You may need to use a scaling question** to entice couples to meet in the middle:

Where are you now in relation to the purpose?

What would you be doing differently if you moved up one step?

How will you know when things are slightly better?

---

1   2   3   4   5   Purpose   5   4   3   2   1

Plan: Plan:

4. Check Progress

- **Ask questions to determine how well the couple is doing.**

What worked?

What will you continue?

What will you revise?

- **Follow the process again as needed.**

CHILDREN

"Children are our most valuable
natural resource."
—*Herbert Hoover (Peter, 1977, p. 105)*

Solutioning's applicability to adolescents is obvious. The control, responsibility, and language fit with the typical adolescent mindset of assertion and growing independence. Those of you who are brave enough to work with this challenging population may have seen how solutioning serves their needs. In fact, solutioning was initially developed, tried, and revised with adolescents.

If you work with younger children, who "lack the cognitive and emotional developmental growth to accurately communicate their inner thoughts and feelings" (Johnston, 1997, p. 102), however, you may be wondering how the language emphasis of solutioning can be adapted for your clientele. As Johnston noted, "To gain an accurate understanding of a child's world, adults are well advised to approach children from a developmental perspective" (1997, p. 102). Approaching children at their level fits with solutioning's emphasis on a shared world view, being with clients where they are, and working together or, with children, playing together.

Play Therapy

The primary method of working with young children is *play therapy*. Traditionally, there have been two play therapy methods, *nondirective* and *directive*. Recently, however, Rasmussen and Cunningham (1995) proposed that a cohesive, integrated approach to play therapy is most beneficial. It is within this blended approach that solutioning best fits. "A nondirective therapist focuses on developing a warm, friendly relationship with the child, facilitating free expression of feelings by establishing an air of permissiveness and acceptance, observing the child play and often affirming verbally what is seen," which is similar to teaming (Johnston, 1997, p. 104). This is a play team with the child as the leader.

After the relationship has been established and the child has had ample opportunity to play out his needs and grow, some more directive solutioning methods can be blended in. Rasmussen and Cunningham suggested that therapists "use nondirective principles to build therapeutic rapport, and then direct the therapy toward specified goals through focused intervention" (1995, p. 6). Creating exceptions through alternative play, telling new stories, and acting out a desired state are all solution-focused avenues for play therapy.

Sand Play.   Initially, for example, you might use sand play to allow "self-discovery by helping children formulate, in a concrete manner, pictures that depict personal experiences" and then for creating coping skills, as you become more directive in suggesting options (Johnston, 1997, p. 105). Sand play facilitates the reenactment of past experiences and allows the child to alter the outcome, which is an exception-building activity. Children can first "release their deepest wounds through the sand play process" and then create new, different, more normal, solution-focused pictures (Johnston, 1997, p. 106). These solution pictures can be developed through interactions with the therapist.

Cunningham and MacFarlane (1991) used a corrective and interactive technique rather than traditional (Jungian) interpretative and analytical methods (1991). Likewise, using the ideas and the questions of solutioning in conjunction with sand play, you can help cocreate a positive picture as the final stage of therapy.

Puppets.   Puppets are effective tools for play therapy; they allow children to share their feelings and then solution them by acting out alternatives. The solutioning question, "How do you want things to be?" may be adapted to "How could the frog treat the alligator?" "What is a nicer way for the monkey to act?" Or "Which feels better, when the monkey yells or when he talks quietly?" Using modeling in play therapy can teach children a solution focus. Children may not know appropriate ways of interacting, feeling, or behaving. Using puppets with a solution-focus can illustrate positive interactions, feelings, and behaviors, giving children coping skills, hope, and understanding.

Both of these mediums of nonverbal play therapy can be altered subtly with solutioning. The key to successfully incorporating solutioning into play therapy, once again, is *timing*. Becoming directive too soon may discount a child's feelings or hinder the healing process. On the other hand, leaving a child without exceptions and solutions for future use is a waste of opportunity. Connecting with children, doing what works for you, and thinking with a solution-focus may be the best adaptation of all.

Alone in a Crowd: The Case of Carol

Carol's mother brought her to counseling because she bit herself when she was mad or upset. The 5-year-old did not know who her father was, and neither did her mother (age 21). Mom had told Carol her father was in prison so Carol would quit asking to meet him. Carol's younger sister (age 4) "had been taken away from" Mom and was in full custody of Carol's first stepfather, whose brother had sexually molested Carol when she was 2. Carol now lived with her second stepfather and two new sisters (ages 3 and 2).

The best way to describe Carol is as a lost soul. It is amazing how alone a child can be even when surrounded by people. In therapy Carol spent a lot of time with puppets, playing out anger and frustration and receiving nurturing. After a few sessions, she became more outgoing and vocal, and her mother reported better interactions at home.

However, Carol's teacher called to let me know that Carol had been barking like a dog in class, and then claimed she did not realize it. In the next session, Carol and I played with her favorite puppets: a yellow bunny (comfort, nurturing) and a gray horse (Carol). Carol said, "Let's go to school." So we walked the puppets over to a corner of the room she had designated as school.

While at school the gray horse and the yellow bunny played out being great students and never getting in trouble. They did play work and handed it in to the teacher, a stuffed eagle that sat in the front of the pretend classroom. The yellow bunny modeled whispering, raising a hand to ask permission to go the bathroom, and asking the teacher for help on an assignment. After the yellow bunny modeled a behavior, the gray horse copied it.

The yellow bunny and the eagle (teacher) hugged and praised the gray horse for the quiet work time and the wonderful picture she drew. The bunny commented, "Wow! You are a really great student. You know just how to act at school."

My hope after the session was that Carol and I had played an exception-building activity and that she now had a plan for how to act at school. Sure enough, the next session Carol brought me a picture she had colored and shared that she liked school now. I checked with the teacher and her comment was, "Carol has been a model student this week. I hope it lasts."

"You can do anything with children,
if only you play with them."
—*Prince Otto von Bismarck (Peter, 1977, p. 103)*

Once Upon a Time ...

A final solutioning method that is useful not only with children but with all ages is *storying*. Children love stories, which bring meaning and learning to their lives. The solutioning process parallels the storying process and can be a powerful, empowering intervention. Approaching a solutioning conversation as a story creation is a good option with children.

White and Epston encouraged us to find and use the exceptions, potentials, and "unique outcomes" by inserting them into our life stories in place of the problems, thereby creating new possibilities in which we live and perceive our experiences (1990, p.

15). The past can be made more useful if we "restory" it with a solution slant. We also can put the present in perspective and prepare for the future through stories.

I have found storytelling useful with my own 2-year-old. Faced with taking her to a large party, I prepared her by telling her a story of how things might happen. "Once upon a time, a little girl went to a birthday party. There were lots of decorations and lots of children. The children were all playing with toys. They shared and took turns. It was so much fun." The story went on from there. The next day, when we walked into a noisy, crowded room full of new faces, my daughter was less intimidated because she had heard about it in her bedtime story the night before. This technique can be used in therapy as well.

The First Day: The Case of Charlie

Charlie started school this year. The first day was so exciting. He walked through the door and saw many new faces. Most of the kids were yelling and screaming. It was a little scary, but the other children seemed to be having fun. Charlie saw some blocks and decided to play with them first. He built a tower and then the teacher said it was time for class to start … .

This story helped an unsure 5-year-old prepare for the first day of school. The accuracy of the story is not as important as the feelings and ideas. It's okay to be nervous, it can be fun, and so on. These future stories are easy and fun to create. Ideally, the child will tell you the story. This is a miniature version of the pretend plan that builds schema and allows a visualized rehearsal of upcoming events. You can use stories in conjunction with plans or to ease children into a new situation. Most of all, stories can be a bonding experience between therapist and child. A shared story is a shared experience and a special moment.

Skill Highlight: Storying

You can create a new story of the past using the reconstruction questions, or a new story for the future using the potential and plan questions. Using solutioning as a story process—what White and Epston referred to as *re-authoring*—is an effective intervention. The solutioning questions can be used to create a new story. Just look at the similarities of the processes:

Story	Solutioning
1. Introduction	1. Open conversation
2. Problem	2. Purpose
3. Event sequence	3. Potentials exploration
4. Resolution (problem solution)	4. Plan (solution)
5. Conclusion (results)	5. Progress (results)

- We have discussed the importance of beginning solutioning, building a relationship, sharing the client's world view, and teaming. All of this is the *introduction of the characters* and setting of the story. As we listen to the problem, the situation, the interactions, we can help clients create new stories by looking at their problems differently.

- Using the reconstruction tools to *set a scene* of hope is the beginning of a success story. Through the reconstruction process the problem unfolds, just as in the opening of a story. However, with solutioning, the problem that unfolds is seen as temporal, solvable, and more hopeful.

- The next part of the standard story is a *sequence of events that leads to the resolution of the problem*. This mirrors our exploration of potentials as we travel in the present and the past and to our imagined future, and use our characters, which all combine and lead to the resolution of the problem. As we discuss this event sequence with clients, they see the positive side to the story and realize that there will be a happy ending.

- The episode of resolution in stories is referred to as the *climax*, and is usually dramatic. During solutioning, there often is a dramatic point when the client realizes that the problem is not permanent, that there is potential, that the solution has been found. This becomes the plan. The plan really is the climax—everything comes together and is summed up, cemented, rehearsed, and ready to go.

- Finally, the *conclusion* of most stories sends the main character off to live happily ever after. *Happily ever after* is a fairy tale, but *better* is a reality of the empowerment, perspective, and focus of solutioning. The result of creating a new story, looking at problems differently, and finding solutions within becomes a life-long coping/problem-solving skill, which may contribute to happily ever after.

- An additional element of many stories is the *moral*. Progress brings the effects of a morale to solutioning. When clients consider the results, take responsibility, and learn from plans, the value of the story continues.

- *Sequels* have become a common element of many stories (especially in the movies). Progress and the revised plan or ongoing efforts of solutioning can be viewed as the sequel, part 2 of a greater story. Some clients go on to make trilogies and epics as they take storying solution-style into their everyday lives by adding a solution focus.

Practice 7.3 gives you some language for creating stories with clients, whether they are children or adults. Remember to have fun as you follow the 4-P process as if it were a story.

PRACTICE 7.3

Create Your Own Future

- When you are chilling out more and things are going smoothly, what will you enjoy most?

- After you have raised your grade to a C average, what will be the first privilege you will ask your parents to give back? What next?

- Who will be most shocked when you begin getting along?

- "If I were a fly on the wall, what would I see you doing this afternoon in your first-grade classroom that would tell me things had changed for you" (Metcalf, 1995, p. 45)?

- Describe the video game (movie, story) of your life from now on. Tell me how you win over the problem, how other characters react, and all the successes you have.

- If I asked your best friend how she saw you acting differently during choir next week, so that you didn't get points taken off, what do you think she would say?

- When you turn in your homework this week, who do you want to know?

- Like a real scientist, report for me the results of your experiment with winning over (the problem).

- Pretend this is a game show and you are in a contest against depression. Be the game show host and tell me who wins and how. Don't forget the prizes (benefits).

- When you are no longer in trouble, what do you think you'll be able to do that you haven't been able to do for awhile?

- When you complete a week of all smiley faces and get to go to computers on Friday, what is the first computer game you are going to play?

- If I were your shadow tomorrow (or next week) when things are better, what behaviors would I see as different?

After you experience the value of new stories as a solution-focused intervention, you may want to have clients create their own. They can create new stories as part of their pretend plan or as a task assignment outside of the session. If you want to give your clients more structure for the process, or if you appreciate the use of a form yourself, Practice 7.4 will give you some ideas. Use this form or adapt it to fit the clientele you work with most often. Note that the story structure, not the 4-P process, is the basis of the form. Equipped with the questions and language of solutioning and this form, you and your clients will soon become authors, creating success stories.

PRACTICE 7.4

Once Upon a Time ...

> **Introduction** (Open the conversation, share world views, and listen for setting and characters.): _____

> _____

> _____

> _____

> _____

> **Problem** (Describe, normalize, and externalize the problem; establish a purpose.):_____

> _____

> _____

> _____

> _____

> _____

Event Sequence (Question about exceptions to the problem and potential solutions—past, present, pretend, people.):

_____

_____

_____

_____

_____

Resolution (Make a plan to try a potential and solve the problem.): _____

_____

_____

_____

_____

_____

Conclusion (Add in what worked—don't forget the happy ending!):_____

_____

_____

_____

_____

_____

Write more chapters, sequels, part II, and so on as you continue solutioning.

GROUPS

Solutioning and group counseling share many of the same characteristics. Corey and Corey (1992) defined a counseling group as one that "deals with conscious problems, is not aimed at major personality changes, is generally oriented toward the resolution of specific and short-term issues, and is not concerned with treatment of the more severe psychological and behavioral disorders" (pp. 10-11). This matches perfectly solutioning's emphasis on solvable problems and an achievable purpose. Solutioning and group counseling go hand-in-glove together.

Corey and Corey also noted, "The group is characterized by a growth orientation, with an emphasis on discovering inner resources of personal strength," which is almost a definition of the potentials (1992, p. 11).

Furthermore, these groups "translate their insights into concrete action plans" (Corey & Corey, 1992, p. 11), which is what happens in solutioning as the potentials are made into plans that meet the starting five criteria.

The opportunity for practicing solutions, ongoing support, and enthusiasm are additional group characteristics that are inherently solution-focused. The following guidelines will help you build on these preexisting conditions with solutioning.

Solution Application: Solutioning Groups

Use teaming. Make sure all members are valued and respected, and member input is the basis of solutions. Encourage team members to cheer each other on. As group leader, the therapist serves as the team captain, facilitating growth and improvement through time management and questioning.

Use circular questioning. When asking solutioning questions, make sure each team member has a chance to consider his or her own answers and the answers of the group.

Use people potential. When exploring potentials, emphasize the wealth of people potential available within the group.

Share plans. Coconstruct plans and have members rehearse them with each other, practicing for the real world. Firm up details through questioning.

Celebrate progress, support growth, and encourage responsibility. Share results of the plans with a focus on what worked as the basis for revision.

Juhnke and Osborn (1997) structured a group using solution-focused interventions for adults who had experienced some form of violence. Their *Solution-Focused Debriefing Group* used three sessions. The first followed a seven-stage sequence of "Critical Incident Stress Debriefing," and the remaining two were solution-focused.

Juhnke and Osborn used the language below to create the solution focus of the group:

> Many times those who participate in a debriefing experience indicate that they begin to notice some positive changes. What things have you noticed since our last meeting which suggest that healing has begun for you? How did you make yourself go out and start enjoying yourself again? How did you decide it was time to get back to your life? (1997, p. 72)

According to the authors, "These ... questions reinforce cognitive decisions and suggest internal rather than external dynamics, which foster recovery" (Juhnke & Osborn, 1997, p. 72).

Exploring potentials is the primary group focus. "Another important aspect of the SFD group is helping participants identify common elements that exist during symptom-free times" (Juhnke & Osborn, 1997, p. 72). As for past potentials, they said to participants, "Adults frequently have survived many difficult experiences and hardships. How many of you have survived the loss of a parent, child, or partner? What were some of the things that you found helpful in surviving that loss?" (Juhnke & Osborn, 1997, p. 73).

They also used the people potential: "I wonder what new coping behaviors the group might suggest or what behaviors they have found helpful for themselves?" (Juhnke & Osborn, 1997, p. 73).

Scaling questions also are not forgotten. Juhnke and Osborne noted that such questions "help participants identify the degree of improvement experienced since the previous session and can help participants determine beneficial behaviors."

Finally, "the participant is ... asked to make journal entries during symptom-free times" (Juhnke & Osborn, 1997, p. 74).

In fact, you can design a group based entirely on solutioning. I have used solutioning groups successfully with adolescents, but their applicability is universal. Mixed groups of 8 to 10 adolescents with *various presenting problems* work well, because they sidestep the issue of adolescents needing to *outdo* each other. Divorce groups, grief groups, and so on tend to be problem-focused. The kids want to compare whose divorce experience was the worst, who had more reason for grief, and so on. When various problems come together, the focus is on solutions.

For example, if one member is struggling with the divorce of her parents, there is usually someone else in the group who has lived through it and can help. If a member is dealing with a death, other members who have been through it can help. This seems to encourage the sharing of coping skills, positive modeling, and the borrowing of potential solution ideas. This is my favorite, but I encourage you to use this format with topic-focused groups as well.

SOLUTIONING GROUP PROGRAM

Group Guidelines

Optimum group size is six to eight members. You can adjust this according to the needs and developmental levels of your population. Group sessions usually last 60 to 90 minutes. What follows is a program for a solutioning group of six consecutive sessions and a two-week follow-up session. The questions facilitate the group discussion. The activities can be done during the session or as homework.

Invitation to Solution

There will be a solutioning group starting on _____ at _____ . You are invited to attend. I am sure you have all the skills and resources you need to live the life you want. This group is designed to help you find and use them for solutions. Be thinking of what would make your life better, what problem you would like to solve, or what change you would like to make.

If you plan to attend, between now and when the group meets, please notice all of the good and useful aspects of your life. See you soon!

The Program

Session 1: Purpose

"*Momentum*: Once your are moving in the direction of your goals ... nothing can stop you"
—*Successories poster*

Objectives

1. Members will get to know one another and one another's problem situations and reasons for coming to group.

2. Members will feel empathy, understanding, and support as they share difficulties.

3. Members will learn about confidentiality and the group process.

4. Members will begin building trust by sharing their stories.

5. Members will feel a sense of hope and empowerment by taking steps to work on their problems.

6. Members will experience a normalizing effect as they learn that others have problems similar to their own.

What do you want to work on? Set the solution stage by establishing cohesiveness within the group. Discuss confidentiality and logistics. Inform members that they will be acting as a team against problems, and that the first step is establishing a purpose for being in the group. The purpose is what they will be working on during the next six weeks. During the first session, allow them to share their purposes, describe their problems, without interruption or intervention. You might explain to them that this is their only chance to gripe, complain, and blame. Starting with the next group meeting, the focus will be on solutions.

Depending on the topic of the group, you may need to establish some ground rules for purpose. The problem must be one the group member has direct influence over. It can't be changing others, winning the lottery, or getting smarter or prettier. The problem must be one that can be affected during a six-week period. The problem must be something the member is truly invested in solving, not something trivial. After the ground rules have been established, the following language should facilitate the group interactions.

Focus Questions

* What is your reason for coming to the solution support group?

* What about your life would you like to make better?

Activity

Notice what happens in your life that works, that is positive, and that you want to continue for next time, and make a list.

Session 2: Problem Reconstruction

"A problem well-stated is a problem half-solved"
—*Charles F. Kettering (Peter, 1977, p. 408)*

Objectives

1. Members will realize *they* are not the problem—the problem is the problem.

2. Members will see their problems as more temporary and solvable.

3. Members will discover reasons for solving their problems.

4. Members will normalize problems.

5. Members will realize they have power over problems and that change is constantly happening.

6. Members will learn how to set a purpose for what they want to achieve in the next six weeks.

What was better or different? The remaining groups are all started with this question. Change and improvement happen continually throughout the six weeks. Helping members notice the changes is motivating. Externalize and reconstruct the problem, then form a positive purpose (solution) statement to be worked on for the remainder of the group. Depending on the topic of the group, you may need to establish some ground rules for purposes.

Focus Questions

- If you feel the problem is you or someone else, let's separate it and objectify it as something outside of you. For example, if I am going to work on my temper, I might name my problem *anger*. If I am going to work on getting along with my mother, I might name my problem *fighting*. What would you name your problem?

- As each member names his or her problem, share if you have had a similar problem before. That will help you realize that we are not alone and that problems are more normal than you think.

- Share the possible results of keeping the problem.

- Share the possible results of solving the problem.

Activity

Make a solution statement that reflects your purpose for coming to group, but not in the form of a problem. Make it a solution statement of *how you want things to be*, what you want to achieve.

- So, how do you want things to be?

Session 3: Present Potentials

> "For every rule, there is an exception"
> —*Unknown*

Objectives

1. Members will see that problems do not happen 100% of the time.

2. Members will experience and take responsibility for the positive changes that are happening.

3. Members will learn and practice the skill of looking for the positive, focusing on exceptional times, and finding their own solutions.

4. Members will receive validation for the good in their lives.

5. Members will gain self-esteem by finding and sharing their nonproblem behaviors (i.e., talents, skills, and abilities).

What was better or different? This is where the value of manipulating problems is illustrated. You will be amazed at the improvement! Don't forget to give members time to celebrate. Follow through with questions like, "How did you do that? Could you do it some more? You really made that happen, how?" Then explore more potentials. Start with the present. Notice that each question is followed by a clarifying, control-giving, responsibility-taking, and plan-building question.

Focus Questions

- When is the problem not happening now? What is different?

- What is good about your days? How do you do that?

- When are you least (angry, scared, stressed, etc.)? How do you control it?

Activity

This week, keep track of your observations of what works, what is positive, when things are okay, and what *you are doing* differently during those times. Jot them down for future use.

Session 4: People Potential

> "The essence of success is that it is never necessary to think of a new idea oneself. It is far better to wait until somebody else does it, and then to copy him in every detail, except his mistakes."
> —*Abrey Menen (Peter, 1977, p. 455)*

Objectives

1. Members will gain additional solution ideas from each other.

2. Members will build their self-esteem by helping each other.

3. Members will solidify their own abilities and coping skills by sharing.

4. Members will learn it is okay to ask for help.

5. Members will put together a list of resources for future use.

What was better or different this week? One value of this group is that a wealth of people potential is right there in the room. Group members most likely have already been sharing their ideas of what works, borrowing ideas from one another, and using each other as resources. The support is built-in. Now it is time to help members see the value of what they have been doing. By looking to the examples, ideas, and modeling of others, members will find great solution ideas. This is one of the life skills you want members to take from the group.

Focus Questions

• What ideas for solutions have you already gotten from the group? How did you do that?

• What examples, modeling, and ideas can you give each other now?

• Learning from others is part of finding your own solutions. What positive people, good role models, and resources do you have? Could you use them for solutions if you need to for a future problem?

Activity

Make a list this week of all the positive people in your life who will serve as solution resources now and in the future.

Session 5: Past/Pretend Potentials

"Allow for possibilities!"

—Bumper sticker

Objectives

1. Members will gain a new view of their pasts, not as full of problems, but as resources for solutions.

2. Members will learn how to look at their pasts and see the positives.

3. Members will learn how to apply past skills, abilities, and exceptions to current and future difficulties.

4. Members will learn how to visualize solutions.

5. Members will learn how to rehearse their solutions through imagery.

6. Members will validate their solution movies by sharing them with the group.

7. Members will have their solutions enhanced by adding in the details.

What was better or different this week? Now that you have a number of exceptions under your belt and members are trying exceptions and potentials, the answers to the opening question will take more of the group's time—which is great!

Focus Questions

*   When in the past have you not had the problem, overcome it, or solved it?

*   What were you doing differently then?

*   When have you done your purpose or goal before?

- Describe your vision of the solution. Tell it like a movie, with lots of details.

- Who is noticing that you are succeeding or doing the solution?

- How are you feeling as you do your solution?

Activity

Practice this movie during the next week.

Session 6: The Plan

"Just do it!"

—Nike advertising slogan

Objectives

1. Members will learn how to form achievable plans.

2. Members will share their plans with the group.

3. Members will rehearse their plans.

4. Members will gain motivation and support for doing their plans.

5. Members will gain self-confidence in their ability to carry out solutions.

"I have learned this at least by my experiment:
that if one advances confidently in the direction
of his dreams, and endeavors to live the life
which he has imagined, he will meet with success
unexpected in common hours."

—Henry David Thoreau
(Peter, 1977, p. 168)

What is better or different? How did the movie rehearsal go?
The positive and pretend plans have already been happening.
You probably also have seen a lot of performing, changing,
and doing things differently. Some members' problems are
already solved. That's great! Now it's time to form a plan to
continue what has been working, try what has been discovered, and make the desired solution a reality. Each person
will end the group with a plan statement that meets the starting five criteria. The questions below should help members
form achievable plans.

Focus Questions

• What will *you*, not anyone else, be doing?

• What will you *be doing*, not what won't you be doing?

• Starting this week, specifically, *how* will you be doing
this?

Activity

Tell the group you will meet in two weeks, and have each
person write down his or her plan.

Two-Week Follow-Up: Progress Check

> "Not to go back is to advance, and men
> must walk, at least, before they dance."
> —*Alexander Pope (Webster, 1992, p. 210)*

Objectives

1. Members will share what worked when they tried their
plans.

2. Members will gain support, praise, and encouragement
for their efforts.

3. Members will take responsibility for their thoughts, actions, and feelings during the two-week period in which they tried their plans.

4. Members will learn to take what works and do more of it while revising what did not.

5. Members will gain an idea of what they can continue to do after the group has ended, to continue their current solution when new problems arise.

How did your plan go? Note that this question assumes that the members tried their plans; it simply asks for progress reports. The members are already in the habit of sharing their positives by this time. If you just ask for what is better, you run the risk that you will get feedback that is positive, but not necessarily related to the plan. After each member has had an opportunity to update the group on the progress of his or her plan, these follow-up questions encourage them to take responsibility, look to the future, and continue their empowerment.

Focus Questions

• What are you going to continue doing?

• How do you want things to be from now on? How are you going to do that?

• What skills and questions from this group can you continue to use?

Activity

Ask the members to answer this question:

• Based on what was shared and learned, what will you do differently in the future when an obstacle gets in your way or you have a problem?

ADAPTABLE, USABLE, DOABLE: IN SUMMARY

This discussion of the possibilities of using solutioning with families, couples, children, and groups is just the tip of the iceberg. It would take another entire book to share the wealth of solutioning as it has been adapted and used by therapists in varying situations. Using solutioning in a way that fits your owns needs is what is important. As you adapt, use, and do solutioning, you will find what works for you and your clients. I would love to hear about how you blend solutioning into your own practice. Please address your success stories to:

Willyn Webb, MA, LPC, NCC
Solutioning Counseling and Consulting
220 1585 Road
Delta, CO 81416

Or call: (970)874-7390
FAX (970)874-7390

email: cwebbd@aol.com

Chapter 8

Sharing the Wealth

"Knowledge exists to be imparted."
—Ralph Waldo Emerson (Webster, 1987, p. 274)

After experiencing the value of solutioning, you will want your clients to learn solutioning as a skill for future use; to some degree, this will happen through your modeling. Your clients may adopt some of the language, use some of the thinking, or begin seeing things differently. According to Webster (1990, p. 21), "clients often report that they have learned how to solve their problems more effectively, and have been able to generalize to other situations."

Ensuring lasting change, however, may require more direct methods. Teaching the 4-P solutioning process directly to your clients is one option. What follows is a curriculum for purposely teaching solutioning, whether to a single client or to an organized group. The curriculum is flexible: You can use each lesson plan to teach a one-hour session, combine two for a two-hour session (or longer) with a short break between lessons, and adjust it to fit the developmental level of your participants.

HELPFUL HINTS AND ENHANCEMENTS

Remember as you approach the curriculum that it is a spring-board; it is not specifically written for any particular audience. You can adapt the role-plays using scenarios that are applicable and meaningful to your clientele. Do not spend a great deal of time preparing the anticipatory set or the closing activity. Just ask the suggested questions:

At the beginning of each class (after the first): "What was different or better?"

At the end of each class: "Do you have any questions to ask, comments to share, or praises to give?"

These questions take care of preparing for the learning and bringing everything together. Both will enhance motivation. The students will have a wealth of personal observations to share that directly support your teaching.

Another useful practice is to have a solution box; participants can anonymously fill out comment cards and put them in the box, which gives you ongoing feedback and evaluation. You can use standardized cards with the following questions:

- What is a useful part of this class?

- What would make the class better?

- What would you like to do more of?

- What has been helpful for your learning in the past, in other classes, etc.?

Decorating the walls with posters that use solutioning language also enhances the learning environment. A few examples might be:

Notice what works!

This is an exceptional class!

You are the director of your own life. How do you want it to
　be?

You also can use commercial motivational posters that support
the thinking of solutioning. It's a good idea to simply inundate
your students with positives, quotes, jokes, and so on. You also
can use questions or motivational quotes from this book to help
set a solution-focused stage.

I did not include getting acquainted activities because those
are so class-specific. I do recommend using them, however. Risk
taking, sharing, and learning will be enhanced if the class feels a
sense of trust, cohesiveness, and support. Start with something fun
and safe. For example, ask the person next to you the following
three questions and then introduce him or her to the group:

- What is your name?

- What is one positive thing about you?

- What would you like the class to know about you first?

With some classes, role-plays are a fun and effective way to
practice solutioning language. You can begin with scripts and gradu-
ally build up to spontaneous simulations. This is most effective
with skill-building classes (such as parents who will be using
solutioning with their children, couples who will be solutioning
together, etc.), rather than with individuals who are working on
personal problems.

You should give handouts to the students *as you use them,* rather
than in a booklet. This allows your students to grow, learn, and
discover together. When they get the handouts in advance, someone usually jumps ahead and tries everything without a full understanding or a chance to practice. This creates a chance to fail and
can make the other students feel behind.

Finally, always remember that your modeling of a solution focus
and your use of solutioning language are the best, most effective means
of communicating the process. Use the language, focus on the posi-

tive, help make solutions happen, and the learning will be substantial. Most of all, have fun and enjoy your participants!

THE 4-P PROCESS OF SOLUTIONING: CURRICULUM OUTLINE

Lesson 1. The 4-P Process of Solutioning

Objectives

1. Participants will learn the definition, use, and value of solutioning.

2. Participants will become familiar with the solutioning map as a guide in using the 4-P process.

Lesson 2. Purpose

Objectives

1. Participants will learn to establish a purpose for solutioning by looking at the results of either maintaining the problem or solving it.

2. Participants will learn how to externalize the problem.

Lesson 3. Reconstructing

Objectives

1. Participants will learn problem manipulation tools like *describing*, *temporizing*, *normalizing*, and *scaling*.

Lesson 4. Potentials

Objectives

1. Participants will consider problem-free, nonproblem, and low-problem times as potential solution ideas.

2. Participants will learn how to access past or present times when things were/are better or different in looking for solution alternatives.

3. Participants will learn how to visualize desired states as sources for clues to solutions.

4. Participants will learn how to borrow from others either as examples or as resources of potential solution ideas.

Lesson 5. Plan

Objectives

1. Participants will learn and practice the three types of plans: positive, perform, and pretend.

2. Participants will learn the starting five criteria for achievable plans and how to develop a plan that meets the criteria.

Lesson 6. Perfecting the Plan

Objectives

1. Participants will learn and practice skills for making plans more successful, dodging roadblocks, getting emotional, adding people, scaling, and recording.

Lesson 7. Progress

Objectives

1. Participants will learn to assess what was successful about the plan, to accept responsibility for the positive changes or differences, and to project into the future.

2. Participants will learn an ongoing thinking process to focus their attention on successes rather than failures and on taking ownership for these.

Lesson 8. Celebration (optional)

Objectives

1. Participants will have the opportunity to review and put it all together.

2. The group will celebrate the learning and growth that has taken place.

3. Participants will rehearse the language of solutioning.

4. You will bring closure to the class with an ending party, ceremony, or graduation.

Additional Lessons *(optional)*

Building Blocks: For adult or high-functioning participants, you may find it helpful to give an introductory lesson explaining some of the beliefs behind solutioning.

Teaming: You may want to give a lesson focusing on listening, reflecting, empathizing, and respect. Teaching basic communication, interaction, and relationship skills is especially useful for groups who will be using solutioning together, such as parents, families, and couples.

Purposeful Thinking: You might give a separate lesson emphasizing the results and consequences of solving or maintaining the problem for those participants who need additional motivation.

Potentials Practice: You can easily divide the potentials lesson (Lesson 4) into two separate lessons, either to provide more practice or to separate and emphasize those that best fit the needs of your participants. You also can spend an entire lesson discussing *people potentials* as resources and supports. Developing a community, family, or friend support system is a worthwhile adjunct to solutioning.

LESSON PLAN 1. THE 4-P PROCESS OF SOLUTIONING

Anticipatory Set: Think for a few minutes of the last time you solved a problem. How did you do it? What worked?

Purpose: Today we are going to learn a new problem-solving method that builds on and uses the skills and resources you already have. The philosophy behind this method is that people already have all they need to solve problems, they just need a way to access their skills and build solutions. This quick, practical method will help you ask yourself a few simple questions as a path toward solutions. Are you ready for responsibility and ability through solutioning?

Input: Go over Handouts 1 and 2, briefly overviewing each step–perhaps on an overhead projector.

Check for Understanding: Have the class name the 4 Ps together. Have each student turn to the person on his or her right and name the steps of the 4-P process. Then have each turn to the person behind him or her and define solutioning.

Modeling: Use Handout 3. Show a video of or role-play a character using solutioning to solve a problem. Use these processing questions for the role-play:

- What was different than you expected?

- What worked?

- What part did you like?

- Did the language sound different?

- Can you see yourself solving problems like this?

Guided Practice: Have the participants pair up, choose a pretend problem, and discuss it using the questions on the solutioning map. They should work on the answers together. Spend 5 to 10 minutes on this activity.

Closure: Have a whole-class discussion/debriefing of the practice activity. Use the following questions to facilitate discussion, bring closure to the lesson, and motivate participants for the next.

- Which parts were most like your style or language of problem solving?

- Which parts were different from your style of problem solving?

- What language did you like?

- What parts are you anxious to learn more about?

- During the practice and debriefing, participants will gain a feel for the language, get a glimpse of what is to come, and have their appetite whetted for more.

Independent Practice: Between now and the next meeting, notice the positive in your life. Observe what works, when you are successful, and exceptions to problems.

Handout 1. An Overview of the 4-P Solutioning Process

The 4-P solutioning process is a problem-solving method that uses questions to cripple excuses, encourage responsibility, and create solutions. Solutioning can happen as a whole or in parts, in order or at random.

The Purpose: The first step in finding solutions is creating a clear, detailed definition of the externalized problem. Use very specific language to reconstruct the problem, take care of negative labels, and create a motivating purpose.

The Potentials: To find and describe potentials, you must look at times without, before, or beyond the problem. The potentials offer keys to solutions. *Past exceptions* to the problem are times when things were better. *Present potentials* are current times when things are satisfactory. *Pretend* or visualized representations of the purpose are movie-like explanations that answer the question, "How do you want things to be?" Finally, there are *people potentials*: You can either find examples of how others have solved the problem or use people as resources and for support. Questions will help you realize all the potentials available as solutions to the problem. Finding potentials may take one or several questions.

The Plan: Three types of plans–*positive*, *pretend*, or *perform*–encourage working up to doing the solution. The first step of the solution itself is choosing from the potentials–selecting a thought or behavior to do again (from past potentials), to do more of (current potentials), or to try (pretend, people potentials). The plan is *precise*, in the *present*, *personal*, *process-oriented*, and worded *positively*. The next steps are rehearsing and visualizing the solution, adding emotions, incorporating people, and accounting for possible roadblocks or setbacks. A positive change will begin here.

The Progress: Monitoring the solution process with questions helps you determine what is going right, when the problem is better, or when things don't get worse. Paying careful attention to progress encourages responsibility, builds further potentials and self-esteem, and ensures continued success in solutioning.

1. Purpose

Externalize, reconstruct, describe, normalize, temporize the problem.
Question the results of keeping and of solving the problem.
Extablish a joint purpose.

2. Potentials

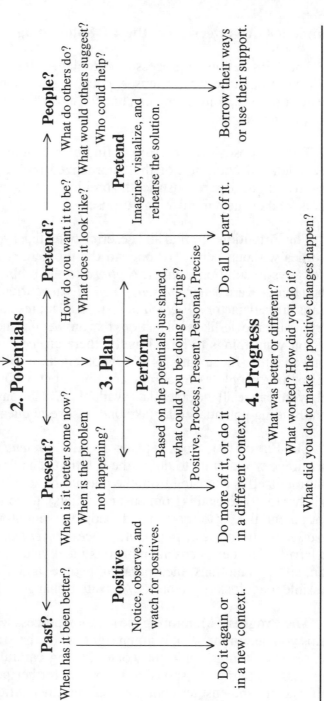

Past?
When has it been better?

Present?
When is it better some now?
When is the problem not happening?

Pretend?
How do you want it to be?
What does it look like?

People?
What do others do?
What would others suggest?
Who could help?

Positive
Notice, observe, and watch for positives.

Pretend
Imagine, visualize, and rehearse the solution.

3. Plan

Perform
Based on the potentials just shared, what could you be doing or trying?
Positive, Process, Present, Personal, Precise

Do it again or in a new context.

Do more of it, or do it in a different context.

Do all or part of it.

Borrow their ways or use their support.

4. Progress

What was better or different?
What worked? How did you do it?
What did you do to make the positive changes happen?

Handout 2. The Solutioning Map

Handout 3. "I Think I Can"

Setting: John (or Julie) is shown pacing the floor, obviously upset, and thinking out loud.

I can't believe it! I *can't* lose my job. It was so awful when he yelled at me. He's the meanest boss in the world. Why should he care if I take a nap once in a while? I'm tired, and I need it. Wait a minute, this isn't getting me anywhere. I need to solution this problem.

First I'll decide on a *purpose*. Let's see, I can't name my boss as the problem. People can't be problems. What would he say was the problem? Probably sleeping. That's what keeps getting me in trouble. Okay, I'm going to work on *sleeping*. What will happen if I continue sleeping at work? I'll get fired. What will happen if I control sleeping and only do it at home? I'll keep my job and my boss will be happy. I won't get yelled at so much. On a scale of 1 to 10, with 1 being no sleeping at work and 10 being sleeping all the time, I'm at 4. I don't sleep that much. What would I have to do to move to 2? That would make things better.

A look at the *potentials* should help. *Present:* What do I do differently when I don't sleep at work? I'm not as tired and I don't sit down by the window in the sunshine. I stay focused. *Past:* When in the past have I felt more rested at work? When my TV was broken and I didn't watch so many late movies, I didn't feel sleepy at work. *Pretend:* How do I want things to be? I want to feel rested and not tired at work ... but I really like watching movies. I need to visualize myself not being tired at work. What does it look like, like in a movie. *I wake up when the alarm goes off and get up instead of hitting the snooze button. I do some exercises with the TV and get ready for work. I feel fine—I'm even smiling some. At work I am focused and my eyes are not heavy. I do good work and the boss notices. I feel great. After work I stop and rent a video to celebrate. I only get one, because I don't want to stay up too late.* That's it! I need to watch just one movie a night. Then I won't be so tired. On weekends I can watch a bunch and stay up late, just not during the work week.

I'm ready to make a *plan*: I'll only watch one movie a night during the week and as many as I want on weekends. I won't sleep at work or get in trouble. I'll keep my job. Who will be the first to notice? My boss. How will I feel? Rested, better, not so worried about losing my job. I'd better write this down. I'll try it for one week and see how it goes.

LESSON PLAN 2. PURPOSE

Anticipatory Set: What was different or better? What is a purpose for solving problems? Don't answer, just think about it.

Purpose: Today we're going to start filling in the blanks on your solutioning map, giving you the language and skills to solve problems. The first step is forming a purpose. Remember, you don't have to go in this order; when you face a problem, you may not need all of the tools you are going to learn today. But, it makes sense to follow this order, because the majority of problems start here.

Input: Go over Handouts 4, 5, and 6 with participants. Do one at a time and then check for understanding, model, and practice before going on to the next. Each participant should have his or her own copies, and you might use the overhead projector.

Define Externalizing: Make the problem—not a person—its own entity. Think of it as something *out there* that can be controlled and solved.

Check for Understanding/Modeling: Choose a problem, maybe one from the anticipatory set, and externalize it on the overhead. Get input from participants when choosing a name, looking at characteristics, and so on. Do two or three problems until students get the idea. You can set up a family or couple scenario that lets you explain how a problem is seen as a person, and have the group externalize it.

Guided Practice: Using Handout 5, have the participants think of a problem they are dealing with or have dealt with in the past. Have them fill out "The Externalizer."

Input: Discuss reasons for solving the problems in the anticipatory set. What are some likely consequences of solving or maintaining the problem? The language of solutioning helps you get a picture of the future with and without the problem, which can be motivating and empowering.

Modeling: Have two participants read the role-play in Handout 6.

Check for Understanding: Did looking at the results of the externalized problem affect the solutioning process? Would Mark have been into controlling his anger without the motivation of results? What helped him establish a purpose for controlling his anger? Who came up with it? Did that make a difference? What allowed that to happen?

Guided Practice: Think of a problem you have. What is your purpose for solving it? Ask yourself questions from Handout 6, and write down your answers.

Closure: Are there any questions, comments, or positives? Remember, your view of a problem affects your chances of solving it. Have your views of problems changed during this class? Next week, we'll look at problem manipulation tools that are designed to take away the problem's permanency and the power.

Independent Practice: Take "The Externalizer" home and fill it out for any problems you encounter during the next week. Continue looking for positives.

Handout 4. Externalizing

Identify the Problem

- Sounds like the name of the problem is _____ .
- So, you are battling fear.
- So, it's not your mom you want to change, but fighting.
- Is there a symbol, color, or sign that fits the problem?
- At work, when fear comes to your desk, what do you do?
- Who else notices when depression comes to visit?
- What does fighting do to interfere with your relationship with your mom?
- What are some characteristics or traits of your problem?

Investigate Your Influence on the Problem

- Tell me about times when you have beat anger and kept your cool.
- How have you stood up to fear?
- What happens on days when you win over depression?
- Tell me what you did to keep fighting from interfering.
- What influence do you have over the problem?

Give Yourself the Power

- How did you keep your cool?
- How did you stand up to fear like that?
- What skills do you use to win over depression?
- Which qualities make it hard for fighting to interfere.
- What power do you have over the problem?

Have a Reason

- What will be better/different when the problem is solved?
- What will happen if you choose to maintain the problem?
- How will you feel after you solve the problem?
- What are the benefits of solving the problem?

Handout 5. The Externalizer

Name: Date:

What name would be appropriate for your problem? _____

_____

What characteristics does it have? _____

_____

_____

What influence do you have over the problem?_____

_____

_____

When do you beat it, control it, or manage it? _____

_____

_____

What skills, abilities, and talents do you have that help you win over your problem (even for a little while)?_____

_____

_____

What are some reasons for solving the problem? What is your purpose for solutioning?_____

_____

_____

Handout 6. Never Say Never

Steve: When have you resisted *anger* and not gotten in a fight after someone called you a name on the playground?

Mark: Never. If someone calls me a name, I beat them up.

Steve: There has never been a time you did not let anger have control? I bet there is someone you haven't beat up.

Mark: Well, Leroy called me a not-too-bad name one time. I was supposed to spend the night at his house that night, and I knew if I beat him up I probably wouldn't get to go. That time I let it slide. He was just teasing anyway.

Steve: Cool! So you *can* control anger when you think about what might happen if you don't? Like not getting to go to a friend's house or something.

Steve: Yeah, I guess so.

LESSON PLAN 3. RECONSTRUCTING

Anticipatory Set: What was different or better?

Play a modified version of the name game with the group for a few minutes. You will name a problem label that sounds pathological, serious, permanent, and difficult to solve (for example, *depression, addiction, attention deficit disorder*). The students will give it an action description that is in solvable, everyday language. Note the descriptions in Handout 7 and the *DSM-IV* descriptions in chapter 6.

Purpose: In order to make problems seem more solvable, we are going to learn some quick, practical, and easy language tools. You may or may not need these when you approach your specific problems, but it's a good idea to have them under your belt when you're facing a problem that seems huge, insurmountable, and neverending. The four tools are *describing, time traveling, normalizing*, and *scaling*.

Input: Go over each skill briefly as you give the students Handout 7.

Check for Understanding: Say a problem out loud, then reconstruct it using one of the tools and have the class say which tool was used. For example:

The problem is *depression*.	The reconstruction is, "You are sad sometimes."
The problem is a *dysfunctional family*.	The reconstruction is, "Your family fights sometimes."
The problem is *stealing*.	The reconstruction is, "You haven't always stolen things."

The problem is *overeating*.	The reconstruction is, "You are at a 6, and by cutting out candy, you could be at a 4 by next week."

Modeling: Ask a student to share a problem he or she is experiencing or has experienced in the past. Have other participants ask questions from the handouts, and see the difference it makes in the power of the problem.

Guided Practice: Review the handouts and choose a question from each you can ask yourself when you face a problem. Use the questions on a current problem. Make your own problem cheat sheet.

Closure: Taking away the power of problems is as simple as asking yourself a few questions. Your focus makes all the difference. Are there any questions, comments, or positives you want to share?

Independent Practice: Use your cheat sheet on a problem you come up against this week and notice the difference. Ask others (coworkers, friends, family members) who are dealing with problems the questions and see how the process affects their problem-solving efforts. Continue noticing what works.

Handout 7. Reconstructing

Describing

What solvable action description—in normal, everyday language—can you use to refer to the problem?

In what situations could you see the problem as useful, okay, more solvable?

For example:

depressed	=	is sad sometimes
victim	=	has overcome hardships
stressed out	=	is coping with a lot
oppositional	=	likes to debate

Time Traveling

Use the past tense when referring to the problem. Attach *sometimes* to problem descriptions. Talk about *when*, not if, you solve the problem.

Normalizing

Call the problem a *difficulty*, *obstacle*, *concern*, or some other less serious sounding word. Realize that others have the problem also. Remember similar problems you have had and overcome before. Remember, everybody has ups and downs in life.

Scaling

With 10 being the best things could be and 1 being the worst, where are they right now? Where do you want them to be? Next week? What will that look like?

1	2	3	4	5	6	7	8	9	10
Worst									Best

LESSON PLAN 4. POTENTIALS

Anticipatory Set: What was different or better? Think of a problem you have. Think about *but don't answer* these questions. Give a few seconds of silent think time after each.

- Does it happen all the time?

- Were there times before the problem?

- Can you imagine your future without it?

- Can you think of others who have successfully dealt with a similar problem?

- Could you borrow ideas from them?

Purpose: Today you will experience the heart of solutioning. The language you learn will help you begin training yourself and those around you to see exceptions instead of problems, successes instead of failures, abilities instead of deficits, and solutions instead of problems.

Input: Give participants Handout 8. The idea behind the questions is that problems do not happen 100% of the time, and finding those exceptional times will lead to solutions. Creating a vision of the solution or borrowing from others are additional avenues for exploration. Equipped with these questions, solutions will become apparent, will come from within, and will give you hope.

Check for Understanding: This is a quick way to check that the material is making sense. The logistics are up to you, but don't spend a lot of time on it. Define *past potentials* for your neighbor. (Answer: times in the past when the problem did not happen.) Have your neighbor define *present potentials*. (Answer: current exceptions to the problem.) Tell the person behind you what *pretend potentials* are. (Answer: an imagined future without the problem.) Tell the person in front of you what *people potentials* are. (Answer: successful solutions from others.)

Modeling: Have a volunteer come up and simulate going to a friend for help with a problem. You be the friend and model asking the potentials questions. This provides a good chance to review the purpose and problem tools of the previous lessons.

Guided Practice: Divide participants into groups of three. Have one person be a friend with a problem, one a friend who knows solutioning and who helps with the problem, and the third an observer who asks solutioning questions, asks the others to clarify points, reminds them to pause for understanding, and so on.

Closure: Brainstorm additional ways to question for and access potentials. Once you make this shift in thinking, you will never see problems the same way again. Are there any questions, comments, or positives?

Independent Practice: Take the worksheet for potentials home, use it with a problem, practice the language with someone who has a problem, or review the potentials so you are ready for the next problem that comes up. As you watch TV this week, see how many potential solutions you can come up with as a sitcom family faces a problem. Continue noticing what works.

Handout 8. Potentials Worksheet

Past

When has the problem not happened? What were you doing differently? _____

_____

When in the past has the problem been smaller? What was different? _____

_____

When have you been successful in the past? How did you do that?

_____

_____

Present

When is the problem not happening now? What are you doing differently? _____

_____

What times are you successful now? How do you do that? _____

_____

When is the problem less or the solution some? _____

_____

Pretend

Pretend your problem is solved. What are you doing? _____

_____

Visualize your solution. Tell the details of what you are doing, feeling, and thinking. _____

_____

People

What ideas for solutions can you get from others? How do they do it? _____

_____

Who has had this problem before and solved it? How did they do it? _____

_____

How would others your age, a positive person, or your parents solve this problem? _____

_____

Summary of Potential Solutions

_____

_____

_____

_____

Additional language you could use to explore potential solutions: _____

_____

_____

_____

LESSON PLAN 5. PLAN

Anticipatory Set: What was different or better? How has your search for positives been going? How has your focus changed? Write down a plan you have for next week.

Purpose: Today we'll learn how to use what we have done so far for solutions. Remember, in the future you will be doing all the steps together, culminating in an achievable plan, which is a step toward or maybe even the solution itself.

Input: There are three types of plans: *positive*, *pretend*, and *perform*. Which one you use depends on what you are ready for. You have already been doing the positive plan. The pretend plan and the perform plan are summarized in Handout 9. The perform plan should meet the starting five criteria shown in Handout 10.

Check for Understanding: How many types of plans are there? How many criteria are there for an achievable plan?

Modeling: Demonstrate making a plan that meets the criteria using a sample vague statement on the board or overhead projector. Ask the class the criteria questions.

Guided Practice: Redo your plan for the week that you wrote down earlier. Make a new plan that will meet the starting five criteria.

Closure: Can you pretend this new plan? Can you rehearse it in your mind? Do you feel more motivated to do it than before? Are there any questions, comments, or praises?

Independent Practice: Practice using the questions of the starting five criteria with all plans. Ask your family, friends, parents, or children what their plans are, then ask the questions from the worksheet until a plan that meets all the criteria is solidified. Notice the results. What works? Think about the plan you made today. Don't do anything yet, just imagine yourself doing the plan.

Handout 9. Positive and Pretend Plans

Picking the Perfect Plan

- Of the potential solutions you discovered, which are you ready to practice or do?

- Which ideas sound best to you?

- Pick the exception or potential that is going to be your solution.

- Have you found your solution, or do you need to look some more?

- Are you ready to start doing some of the solution tomorrow?

- Would you like to practice your solution in your mind first?

Three Types of Plans

Positive	Pretend	Perform
• Observe for positives (Walter & Peller, 1992). • Notice what works (Metcalf, 1995).	Don't do anything yet, just imagine yourself doing the solution.	• Do past potentials again, in a new context. • Do present potentials more or in another context. • Do a part of the pretend potentials. • Borrow some of the people potentials.

Positive

- Look for what is good about your life.

- Watch for when things are better.

- See if you can find any times when the solution is happening.

- Notice things you want to continue.

- Keep a diary of potential solutions.

- Try to find out what you are doing when things are going well.

Pretend

- Don't do anything yet, just imagine yourself doing the solution.

- Pretend your solution at least three times a day for the next week. Think about which parts you're going to do first.

- Rehearse your solution movie whenever you think of the problem.

- For the next few days, visualize yourself doing the solution each time the problem is trying to take over and control you.

- What things could you say to yourself in doing the positive or pretend solutions?

Handout 10. The Starting Five Criteria

1. **Personal**	"You"	"What will *you* (not your mom, boss, wife) be saying (doing, thinking)?"
	Use their words	"So when you chill out first you can..."
2. **Positive**	"Instead"	"What will you be doing instead of shoplifting?"
	"Differently"	"What will you be doing differently when you are not drinking?"
3. **Process**	"How" "-ing"	"How will you be doing this?"
		"How will you be talking to your kids?"
4. **Precise**	"Specifically"	"How, specifically, will you..?"
	"Exactly"	"What, exactly, will you do next?"
		"What does it look like?"
5. **Present**	"On track" "In the groove" "Have the formula" "On the right road"	"When you go to work tomorrow and you are on track, what will you be doing differently or saying differently to yourself?"

Source: Adapted from Walter and Peller (1992).

LESSON PLAN 6. PERFECTING THE PLAN

Anticipatory Set: What was different or better? Now, don't answer this, just think to yourself, "How did the plans go?" Would you like to learn some additional ways of making plans successful?

Purpose: Sometimes the greatest potentials lead to wonderful plans—but, for some reason or another, they just don't happen. Using the skills of dodging roadblocks, getting emotional, adding people, scaling, and recording you can perfect the plan, rehearse some more, and ensure your success.

Input: Go over the skills in Handout 11, explaining each briefly.

Check for Understanding/Modeling: Take the same plan used in the previous lesson's demonstration and consider the new elements, perfecting the plan. Have the group participate by adding the details as you ask the questions; or, you can have a student ask the questions while you observe.

Guided Practice: Take the plans from last week and expand, modify, and revise according to the results of your efforts and the new skills.

Closure: Sit and visualize your plan. Include all the details and run through it in your mind as if it was a movie.

Independent Practice: Tell someone your plan as if it was a movie, including all the steps, the people, the feelings, and the behaviors. Then, if you feel ready, do your plan. Notice what works.

Handout 11. Perfecting the Plan

Dodging Roadblocks

- What could make it difficult for you to carry out your plan?

- Is there anything that could get in your way?

- What if (describe) happens?

- What is going to be the most challenging part of doing your plan?

- Describe for me the scariest part of your plan.

Getting Emotional

- How do you feel when you tell me about doing the plan?

- What feelings might come up when you go out to do your plan?

- What goes on inside of you when you imagine yourself doing the plan?

- Are you excited, scared, nervous, or motivated about doing the solution?

- How are you feeling right now as you tell me about doing your plan?

Adding People

- How might (peers, parents, etc.) react when you do the plan?

- What will so and so probably do when you do the plan?

- Who will notice first when you do the plan?

- What reaction do you think you might get?

- What if so and so (throw out possible reactions to consider)?

For Support

- Are you going to tell anyone else about your plan? Who?

- Who will be your best ally against the problem?

- Who will be your greatest source of support for completing your plan?

- Who or what can help you?

- Are there any people who have helped before that you could use now?

Scaling

- Where do you want to be in _____ days? How?

_____

| 1 | 2 | 3 | 4 | 5 | 6 | 7 | 8 | 9 | 10 |
Worst   Best

Recording

- Get the details of your plan (your new success story) down in writing.

Timing

- Add in a time element. (For example, I'll do my plan for three days.) Then monitor your progress.

LESSON PLAN 7. PROGRESS

Anticipatory Set: What was different or better? Spend the first few minutes celebrating what was successful about participants' rehearsals or performance of their plans. Allow time for open sharing. Compliment, praise, and model new skills. Ask, "How did you do that?"

Purpose: If you don't look at the progress you are making toward a solution, you will miss many worthwhile skills, abilities, and exceptions. Continually evaluating what went right will ensure lasting success of potentials and an ongoing focus that will prevent or solve future problems, difficulties, and trying circumstances.

Input: Go over Handout 12.

Check for Understanding: Think about why it is important to monitor progress and take responsibility for your improvements, and about how you can continue them. Who would like to share with the class?

Modeling: Ask for two volunteers to come to the front of the class. Have one share the results of doing a plan and the other ask the progress questions. Have the class notice what works.

Guided Practice: Write down answers to the progress questions or form progress questions that would be appropriate for the situation.

Closure: Think about the solutioning process as you have learned and experienced it. What are your favorite questions? Which parts do you see yourself using in the future? What worked?

Independent Practice: Use solutioning with the next problem that comes up. Teach it to someone else. Practice having a solution focus.

Handout 12. Progress

Get a Solutioned Response

- What worked?

- What is good about your life right now?

- What did you like about this week?

- What positive thoughts, feelings, and interactions did you have this week?

- What happened that you want to continue?

- When were things better? What was the situation then? What were you doing, saying, thinking, or feeling differently?

Getting the Most Out of It

- How did you do that?

- What part did you play in the good things you've just shared?

- Of the things you liked, which do you have control over?

- What role did you play in getting along with so and so? How did you get so and so to help you?

- Who else noticed when your solution was successful?

- What did you do new or differently that helped?

Blast Off

- How will you keep these positive changes going?

- How can you encourage the changes to continue, increase, or last?

- Who can help you keep this positive progress happening?

- What will ensure that the positive difference, change, or solution you are experiencing now will continue?

- What can you do tomorrow to help things stay on track?

- What parts of you plan are you going to keep doing?

- Now that you have most of your solution, what's next?

- Now that you know what works, you can do it again.

Mixing in Reality

What could be challenging to continuing this progress? How are you going to overcome future obstacles to your solution?

What about when things don't work perfectly? Will you adjust your solution and keep right on going?

Revised Plan/Solution: _____

_____

_____

_____

_____

_____

_____

_____

LESSON PLAN 8. CELEBRATE! (OPTIONAL)

Three questions should guide your celebration:

1. What did you learn that you will continue to use?

2. What three solutioning questions are your favorites?

3. What did you learn about yourself from solutioning?

Allow participants the opportunity to think about their answers to the questions as they mingle, have refreshments, and share solutions.

Lead a whole-class discussion around the three questions (open sharing). Pass out individualized diplomas with an area of growth you have seen in each participant listed on the certificate. Read each out loud as it is received at the front of the room. Use the example in Handout 13, but personalize it so it works for your participants. Make the most out of this self-esteem-building opportunity. End with applause and send participants off full of confidence in their new solutioning skills.

Handout 13

GRADUATE OF
SOLUTIONING

THIS IS TO PROCLAIM THAT

_____

(Client's name)

HAS SUCCESSFULLY LEARNED
SOLUTIONING.

FROM THIS DAY_____ , 19XX,
FORWARD, PROBLEMS DO NOT
STAND A CHANCE!

_____

(Your signature)

IN CONCLUSION

As you continue down your own solution path, remember to be flexible. In learning new methods, it often is tempting to jump in with both feet after initial success. Solutioning is not intended to be a full method of treatment, but intervention options to blend and adapt. If you initially walk away with two or three new questions to use with clients, this book will have achieved its purpose. As those are effective and incorporated into your personal script, come back for more. An awareness of the messages, meanings, and change-producing effects of your language will do as much to enhance your therapeutic value as any new question or phrase.

Seeing clients through solutioning will broaden not only their treatment horizons, but your perspective toward change, counseling, and even life. Enjoy seeing the good, the positive, and the solutions. Enjoy working as a therapist, caring for clients, and teaming with them against problems, for this will bring solutions. As my grandmother always reminds me,

---

"Stop and smell the roses."

—Unknown

References

American Psychiatric Association. (1995). *Diagnostic and statistical manual of mental disorders* (4th ed.). Washington DC: Author.

Andrews, J., & Andrews, M. (1995). Solution-focused assumptions that support family-centered early interventions. *Infants and young children, 8*(1), 60–67.

Bandler, R., & Grinder, J. (1979). *Frogs into princes.* Moab, UT: Real People Press.

Bistline, J. L., Sheridan, S. M., & Winegar, N. (1991). Five critical skills for mental health counselors in managed health care. *Journal of Mental Health Counseling, 13*(1), 147–152.

Bonnington, S. B. (1993). Solution-focused brief therapy: Helpful interventions for school counselors. *The School Counselor, 41*(2), *126–127.*

Bromfield, R. (1995). The use of puppets in play therapy. *Child and Adolescent Social Work Journal, 12*(6), 435–444.

Budman, S., & Gurman, A. (1988). *Theory and practice of brief therapy.* New York: Guilford.

Buhler, P. M., & McCann, M. (1989). Building your management team. *Supervision, 50*(9), 14–15.

Carpenter, J. (1997). Editorial: Investigating brief solution-focused therapy. *Journal of Family Therapy, 19*(2), 117–120.

Corey, M. S., & Corey, G. (1992). *Groups process and practice (4th ed.)*. Pacific Grove, CA: Brooks/Cole.

Cunningham, C., & MacFarlane, K. (1991). *When children molest children: Group treatment for young sexual abusers*. Orwell, VT: Safer Society Press.

Czyzewski, K. M. (1996). Rapid EAP: Solution-focused therapy in employee assistance. *EAP Digest, 16*(2), 16–19.

de Shazer, S. (1985). *Keys to solutions in brief therapy*. New York: Norton.

de Shazer, S. (1988). *Clues: Investigating solutions in brief therapy*. New York: Norton.

de Shazer, S., Berg, I. K., Lipchik, E., Nunnally, E., Molnar, A., Gingerich, W., & Weiner-Davis, M. (1986). Brief therapy: Focused solution development. *Family Process, 25*(2), 207–222.

Dolan, Y. M. (1991). *Resolving sexual abuse: Solution-focused therapy and Ericksonian hypnosis*. New York: Norton.

Donne, John, (1624). *Devotions XVII.*

Downing, J., & Harrison, T. (1992). Solutions and school counseling. *The School Counselor, 39*, 327-331.

Duckworth, E. (1987). *"The having of wonderful ideas" and other essays on teaching and learning*. New York: Teachers College Press.

Encyclopedia Britanica (11th ed.). (1911). Volume 11. New York: Encyclopedia Britanica Company.

Epstein, G. (1990). The power of imagery. *New Realities, 10*(3), 11, 52–53.

Fairchild, T. N. (1994). Evaluation of counseling services: Accountability in a rural elementary school. *Elementary School Guidance & Counseling, 29*(1), 28–37.

Finney, L. D. (1992). *Reach for the rainbow: Advanced healing for survivors of sexual abuse.* New York: Putnam.

Flores, F. P. (1992). Team building and leadership. *Supervisory Management, 37*(4), 8.

Freeman, M. A., & Trabin, T. (1994). *Managed behavioral healthcare: History, models, key issues, and future course.* Washington, DC: Department of Health and Human Services, Center for Mental Health Services.

Friedman, H., Rohrbaugh, M., & Krakauer, S. (1988). The time-line genogram: Highlighting temporal aspects of family relationships. *Family Process, 27,* 293–303.

Friedman, S., & Fanger, M. T. (1991). *Expanding therapeutic possibilities.* Lexington, MA: Lexington Books.

Furman, B., & Ahola, T. (1992). *Solution talk: Hosting therapeutic conversations.* New York: Norton.

Gass, M., & Gillis, H. L. (1995). Focusing on the "solution" rather than the "problem": Empowering client change in adventure experiences. *Journal of Experiential Education, 18*(2), 63–69.

Goldberg, A. (1995). Mental rehearsal for peak performance. *Swimming Technique, 31*(4), 24–26.

Haley, J. (1973). *Uncommon therapy: The psychiatric techniques of Milton H. Erickson, M.D.* New York: Norton.

Horton, T. (1992). Delegation and team building: No solo acts please. *Management Review, 81*(9), 58–61.

Huber, C. H., & Backlund, B. A. (1996). *The twenty-minute counselor:* New York: Crossroad.

Hwang, Y. G. (1995). Student apathy, lack of self-responsibility, and false self-esteem are failing American schools. *Education, 115*(4), 484–489.

Johnston, S. M. (1997). The use of art and play therapy with victims of sexual abuse: A review of the literature. *Family Therapy, 24*(2), 101–113.

Juhnke, G., & Osborne, L. (1997). The solution-focused debriefing group: An integrated postviolence group intervention for adults. *Journal for Specialists in Group Work, 22*(1), 66–76.

Keeney, B. (1983). *Aesthetics of change.* New York: Guilford.

Kelly, K. R. (1996). Looking to the future: Professional identity, accountability, and change. *Journal of Mental Health Counseling, 18*(3),195–199.

Kiser, D. J., & Piercy, F. P. (1993). The integration of emotion in solution-focused therapy. *Journal of Marital and Family Therapy, 19*(3), 233–242.

Klar, H., & Coleman, W. L. (1995). Brief solution-focused strategies for behavioral pediatrics. *Family-Focused Pediatrics, 42* (1), 131–141.

Klein, C. J., Bosworth, J. B., & Wiles, C. E. (1997). Physicians prefer goal-oriented note format more than three to one over other outcome-focused documentation. *Journal of the American Dietetic Association, 97*(11), 1306–1310.

Kochunas, B. W. (1997). Preserving soul: Rescuing diversity in the managed care era. *Counseling and Values, 42*(1), 12–21.

Kral, R. (1986). Indirect therapy in schools. In S. de Shazer & R. Kral (Eds.) *The family therapy collection: Vol. 19. Indirect approaches in therapy* (pp. 56–63). Rockville, MD: Aspen.

Kral, R., & Kowalski, K. (1989). After the miracle: The second stage in solution-focused brief therapy. *Journal of Strategic and Systemic Therapies, 8*(2–3), 73–76.

Lewis, K. G. (1989). The use of color-coded genograms in family therapy. *Journal of Marital and Family Therapy, 15*(2), 169–176.

Lipchik, E., & de Shazer, S. (1988). Purposeful sequences for beginning the solution-focused interview. In E. Lipchik (Ed.), *Interviewing* (pp. 105–117). Rockville, MD: Aspen.

Mason, W. H., Breen, R. Y., & Whipple, W. R. (1994). Solution-focused therapy and inpatient psychiatric nursing. *Journal of Psychosocial Nursing, 32*(10), 46–49.

McGoldrick, M., & Gerson, R. (1985). *Genograms in family assessment.* New York: Norton.

Metcalf, L. (1995). *Counseling toward solutions: A practical, solution-focused program for working with students, teachers, and parents.* New York: Center for Applied Research in Education.

Metcalf, L. (1997). *Parenting toward solutions: How parents can use skills they already have to raise responsible, loving kids.* Englewood Cliffs, NJ: Prentice-Hall.

Molnar, A., & de Shazer, S. (1987). Solution-focused therapy: Toward the identification of therapeutic tasks. *Journal of Marital and Family Therapy, 13*(4), 349–358.

Murphy, J. J. (1994). Working with what works: A solution-focused approach to school behavior problems. *The School Counselor, 42*(1), 59–65.

Norris, P. (1990). Visualization and imagery in healing. *New Realities, 10*(3), 8–10, 50.

Nylund, D., & Corsiglia, V. (1994). Becoming solution-focused forced in brief therapy: Remembering something important we already knew. *Journal of Systemic Therapies, 13*(1), 5–12.

O'Hanlon, W. (1996). *The handout book.* Omaha, NE: Possibility Press.

O'Hanlon, W., & Weiner-Davis, M. (1989). *In search of solutions: A new direction in psychotherapy.* New York: Norton.

Oxford dictionary of quotations (3rd. ed.). (1979). Oxford: Oxford University Press.

Paull, R. C., & McGrevin, C. Z. (1996). Seven assumptions of a solution-focused conversational leader. *NASSP Bulletin, 80*, 79-86.

Peter, L. J. (1977). *Peter's quotations: Ideas for our time.* New York: Morrow.

Rasmussen, L. A., & Cunningham, C. (1995). Focused play therapy and nondirective play therapy: Can they be integrated? *Journal of Child Sexual Abuse, 4*(1), 1–20.

Reuss, N. (1997). The nightmare question: Problem talk in solution-focused brief therapy with alcoholics and their families. *Journal of Family Psychotherapy, 8*(4), 71–76.

Rhodes, J. (1993). The use of solution-focused brief therapy in schools. *Educational Psychology in Practice, 9*(1), 27–34.

Rogers, C. (1951). *Client-centered therapy.* Boston: Houghton-Mifflin.

Rosenhan, D. L. (1973). On being sane in insane places. *Science, 179*(4068), 250–258.

Scarano, G. M., & Kalodner-Martin, C. R. (1994). A description of the continuum of eating disorders: Implications for intervention and research. *Journal of Counseling and Development, 72*(4), 356–361.

Schlessinger, L. (1994). *Ten stupid things women do to mess up their lives.* New York: HarperCollins.

Shenkle, A. M. (1989) The making of a meta-teacher. *Learning, 18*(8), 31–33.

Shires, B., & Tappan, T. (1992). The clinical nurse specialist as brief psychotherapist. *Perspectives in Psychiatric Care, 28*(4), 15–18.

Stewart, S. (1996). The blame game: Why can't we accept responsibility? *Youth 16*(2), 3–4.

Todd, T. (1992). Brief family therapy. In R. L. Smith & P. Stevens-Smith (Eds.), *Family counseling and therapy* (pp. 162–175). Ann Arbor, MI: ERIC.

Tomm, K. (1987). Interventive interviewing: Part II. Reflexive questioning as a means to enable self-healing. *Family process, 26*(2), 167–183.

Tuyn, L. K. (1992). Solution-oriented therapy and Rogerian nursing science: An integrated approach. *Archives of Psychiatric Nursing, 6*(2), 83–89.

Walter, J. L., & Peller, J. E. (1992). *Becoming solution-focused in brief therapy.* Philadelphia: Brunner-Mazel.

Washburn, P. (1994). Advantages of brief solution-oriented focus in home-based family preservation services. *Journal of Systemic Therapies, 13*(2), 47–57.

Weakland, J. H., Fisch, R., Watzlawik, P., & Bodin, A. M., (1974). Brief therapy: Focused problem resolution. *Family Process, 13*(2), 141-168.

Webster, D. C. (1990). Solution-focused approaches in psychiatric/mental health nursing. *Perspectives in Psychiatric Care, 26*(4), 17–21.

Webster's 21ˢᵗ century book of quotations. (1992). Nashville: Thomas Nelson.

Webster's ninth new collegiate dictionary. (1987). Springfield, MA: Merriam-Webster.

Weiner-Davis, M. (1992). *Divorce busting: A step-by-step approach to making your marriage loving again.* New York: Simon & Schuster.

Weiner-Davis, M., de Shazer, S., & Gingerich, W. J. (1987). Building on pretreatment change to construct the therapeutic solution: An exploratory study. *Journal of Marital and Family Therapy, 13*(4), 359–369.

Weiss, L., Katzman, M., & Wolchik, S. (1985). *Treating bulimia: A psychoeducational approach.* New York: Pergamon.

White, M., & Epston, D. (1990). *Narrative means to therapeutic ends.* New York: Norton.

Index

About the Author

Willyn Webb, M.A., L.P.C., N.C.C., is a licensed counselor in private practice, operating Solutioning Counseling and Consulting, where she works with individuals, couples, and families. She is an adjunct professor for Adams State College and member of the American Counseling Association and American Play Therapy Association, among many others.

Dedicated to empowering all helping professionals with the power and language of solutioning, Willyn is also the author of the forthcoming book, *The Educator's Guide to Solutioning*. Throughout the United States, Willyn energetically provides solutioning workshops and trainings. She lives with her husband and two children in Colorado, where she enjoys ranching and running.

For more information on workshops, trainings, or lectures on solutioning, contact Willyn at:

Solutioning Counseling and Consulting
117 Meeker Street #7
Delta, CO 81416
(970) 874-7390
email: cwebbd@aol.com